TRAINING FOR THE CROSS-CULTURAL MIND

A Handbook for
Cross-Cultural Trainers and Consultants

by
Pierre Casse

SECOND EDITION

The Society for Intercultural Education, Training and Research
Washington, DC

Dedicated to Christiane
who knows that she knows

First Edition
April, 1980

Second Edition
February, 1981

Copyright © 1979, 1981 by
Pierre Casse

Library of Congress Catalog Card No. 80-50160
ISBN 0-933-934-06-8

Manufactured in the United States of America

0 9 8 7 6 5 4 3

Table of Contents

ACKNOWLEDGEMENTS

The author wishes to express his gratitude to the following for permission to use the materials indicated:

The Department of State, Foreign Service Institute, for excerpts from the article, "Culture Shock and the Problem of Adjustment to New Cultural Environments," based on a talk by Dr. Kalvero Oberg in 1958.

Situation Management Systems, Inc., for an adaptation of materials included in the Negotiation Skills Program and distributed by Situation Management Systems, Inc., of Boston, Massachusetts.

Messrs. Stephen Rhinesmith and David Hoopes, for various excerpts from "Reading Materials," Intercultural Communication Workshop, published by the Regional Council for International Education, University of Pittsburgh.

Dr. Edward C. Stewart, for portions of the contrast-American role play found on pages 107-111.

BNA Communications, Inc., for the chart entitled "Differences Between Logical and Creative Problem Solving." This chart is from M.O. Edwards, "Comparison of Logical and Creative Problem Solving," *Bulletin on Training*, January-February 1979 (Vol. 4, No. 1), BNA Communications, Inc., Rockville, Maryland. It is reproduced with permission of the publisher and copyright holder, BNA Communications.

John Wiley & Sons, Publishers, for the chart describing the double-loop learning process, from C. Argyris, *Increasing Leadership Effectiveness*, New York: John Wiley & Sons, 1976; also the accompanying "Learning How to Learn Matrix."

Gerald Duckworth and Company, Ltd., for *The Herman Grid* (page 58); *The Bird* (page 61); and *Indian or Eskimo?* (page 68).

Brooks/Cole Publishing Company, for "Measuring one's own ability to practice empathy: A self-assessment exercise" (page 140); from *Interpersonal Behavior*, by H.C. Triandis. Copyright © 1977 by Wadsworth, Inc. Reprinted by permission of the publisher, Brooks/Cole Publishing Company, Monterrey, California.

Scientific Methods, Inc., for "The three basic assumptions toward intergroup disagreements and their management," (page 172), which originally appeared as Figure 1 from *Managing Intergroup Conflict in Industry*, by Robert R. Blake, Herbert A. Shepard, and Jane S. Mouton. Houston: Gulf Publishing Company, 1964, page 13. Reproduced by permission.

The World Bank, for the photo "At the Door," (page 69). World Bank Photo by William Graham, 1973.

Basic Books, Inc., for exercises with the Knives and Glasses, from Edward deBono, *Five Day Course in Thinking,* copyright © 1967 by Edward deBono; published in the United States by Basic Books, Inc., Publishers, New York.

Hutchinson & Company, Ltd., for excerpts from *Anatomy of Judgement,* by J. Abercrombie (1967): "The Hidden Man," (page 28), and "The Three Triangles" (page 60).

Brislin, R.W. and Pedersen, P.B., for their proposal to the German Foundation for International Development for a cross-cultural communication trainer training program (page 242).

Anspacher, S.J., for the article "On Independent Consulting in Intercultural Communication," page 254. This article first appeared in SIETAR's *Handbook for Trainers,* prepared for the 1980 SIETAR Summer Institute.

*Enfermé en lui-même, enfermé plus pré-
cisément dans les boucles retroactives de son
système nerveux, l'homme s'est conçu séparé
de l'univers qu'il observait et croyait exister
en dehors de lui, sans être vraiment conscient
de ce qu'il le pénétrait jusqu'à la moindre de
ses particules élémentaires. Il s'est ainsi conçu différent du monde qui l'entourait, isolé,
observateur de ce monde, sans bien réaliser
que c'était encore ce monde qui s'observait en
lui.*

— *Henri Laborit*
L'Agressivité Détournée
Union Générale d'editions,
Paris, 1970.

"Trapped within himself or more precisely,
trapped within the retroactive loops of his own
nervous system, Man has perceived himself as
separated from the universe, disregarding the
modeling of his own being by the same
universe. He has defined human nature as
autonomous from the world without realizing
that in watching the world it was still himself
that he was observing."

— Free translation
by
Pierre Casse.

Foreword

Dear Trainer and Consultant:

This book is an invitation to explore something which is close to you: your mind, or, more exactly, your *cross-cultural mind.*

It is our contention that, by its own nature and structure, the mind is cross-cultural, meaning that it has the capacity to understand other people, comprehend the world in a meaningful way, and, even more, cope with its own internal dialectics.

To understand other people requires a minimum of commonality. We have it. All human beings do actually share something in common: a *psyche*. That psyche is "programmed" differently according to the cultures which exist (or have existed) around the world. Furthermore, the content of the psyche varies in relation to the individual genetic inheritance as well as the situational experiences he or he has gone through. This fact does not contradict the idea that the *basic structure* of the human psyche is the same for all human beings. Deep down inside our psyche, it seems that we can find a set of what the Swiss psychologist C.G. Jung called the *ARCHETYPES* which make you and me alike and capable of reciprocal understanding.

To understand the world is easy since we are part of the world. The problem is that we sometimes have a tendency to forget it on the one hand and deny it on the other. Why such a reaction? It looks like a characteristic of human nature to be able to separate itself from the parts which make up what we are as well as from the whole which, in a way, possesses us. This continuous process can be attributed to the human drive toward identity, and the fulfillment of what one actually *is*. Everything goes as if one had to be different in order to be and to exist. Despite this phenomenon (or maybe because of it), we are without any doubt capable of understanding nature in its broad sense since when we observe the world it is still man that we look at, and *vice versa*. Furthermore, it seems that human beings, because of that very belongingness, have the magic power of influencing the world, and through it, themselves and their fate. Jung used to tell the story about a Chinese rainmaker who, when called by a village in order to make rain, simply withdrew for three days, asking only for some bread and water. After four days, the rain fell. Amazed and grateful, the villagers asked him how he did it. He answered: "I withdrew into myself and put myself in order; and when I am in order the world around me must naturally come into order too, and then the drought must be followed by rain." [1]

---

[1] C.G. Jung, quoted by J. Jacobi, *The Way of Individuation*, London: Hodder & Stoughton, 1967.

To understand oneself is maybe the most challenging endeavour that we face. The ongoing dialogue between the unconscious and the consciousness is by its very nature intercultural. The unconscious uses an esoteric and symbolic language that the consciousness cannot readily understand. Moreover, when it is understood, it is not unconscious anymore. It has been assimilated by the consciousness, which must employ its own "cultural code"—the symbols—to monitor the signals and meanings coming from the depth of the psyche. We are like a group of blind people trying to find our way in the darkness of our own psyche. It is us and it is not. We understand and at the same time we don't. We progress and yet do not have the impression that we learn anything. This is the intrinsic element of the cross-cultural mind.

The implication of the three above comments is simple. There is no need for you and me to go around the world to experience some kind of cross-cultural adventure. Just stay where you are. Talk and listen to the person next to you. The interaction is cross-cultural. Watch the world and discover its "truth." The confrontation between what actually is and your perception of what is or what seems to be is also intercultural.

But there is a simpler way. Do not move. Just close your eyes and listen to that internal dialogue. You know that "little voice" which is saying: "do" and "don't." You are at the center of a cross-cultural interaction. Observe your cross-cultural mind at work. It is fascinating, isn't it? Can you recognize the conversation between the left side and the right side of your mind? — "Do it now!... Wait a minute, don't you remember your past experience... I like it... I want it... Fine, but plan in advance, organize yourself... What for?... It's not going to work anyway... Well, look at the facts...

It is quite possible that the proposed exploration will lead you nowhere. However, there is the chance that in going through the experience, you will get lucky and have the opportunity to meet your own shadow, which is nothing else than you and the other combined in one: the transcultural mind. What an exploration!

Preface to the Second Edition

A reviewer of the first edition of this book wrote that "Pierre Casse has prepared an appetizing cookbook." A good test of a cookbook is whether it works i.e., whether it can help someone who is not a professional cook to produce dishes which are liked and are asked for again. In this case, the "professional cook" is normally a sociologist or psychologist. I am neither and yet I have directed several times some of the workshops described here, alone or with an associate (often, but not always, Pierre), in the US, in Africa, in Asia. Usually, the majority of participants have said that they liked it and have asked for more such exercises either for themselves or for colleagues.

The secret of this particular cooking is a combination of courage and prudence. Courage because it does seem strange to stand up and start talking about matters which are often considered too personal to discuss, matters which are of great value to oneself and yet may make another smile or laugh. Prudence because one has to know one's limits, and to accept that one must learn to walk before trying to run, especially when the first successes could make one believe that the whole exercise is very simple. It is not, and I learned early that if I tried to go too fast or to be too ambitious, I had to expect painful bruises to my ego.

This is a cookbook for the professional trainer and for the person who has experience to pass on to others but does not know how to do it. Having started only with my experience, I would say to those who want to do the same: start modestly by conducting a few workshops under the guidance of someone who has done it successfully, and be reasonably cautious before you try to do it alone. Each workshop is a new happening, enormously enjoyable because of the changes from workshop to workshop. It is also difficult for us who are without degree in sociology or psychology because we know little of the scientific or theoretical framework in which the workshop has been conceived.

But then, if there are such difficulties why should we, seasoned professionals such as economists, engineers, lawyers, financial analysts, technical specialists, want to conduct this kind of workshop? Why not leave them to sociologists or psychologists? First, because these workshops present in a systematic way a good part of the experience on the human relation aspects of our respective jobs that we have acquired unsystematically by trial and error. Second, because we understand the substantive problems of our colleagues in our profession, we are capable to show them the interaction between the process and the task, and the solutions we can propose are much more credible and effective than those a sociologist or psychologist could suggest. Last but not least, because conducting such workshops can be an extremely enjoyable and fruitful experience for both leaders and participants.

Having started with individual workshops, one is soon tempted to go beyond, to do more. And it is possible to assemble a number of these workshops plus some other material (preferably things related directly to your own profession) to create a 2-3 day workshop. In my experience, these workshops are successful when we obeserve the following conditions: (i) include the workshop in a larger course for professional upgrading directed by someone who is recognized as experienced in the field, (ii) define very clearly realistic objectives for the workshop within the course and within the professional life of the participants and (iii) associate closely two workshop leaders, one, a sociologist or psychologist, and the other, a professional whose business experience is of great interest to the participants. The interaction between the two workshop leaders and the course director can create strong dynamics encouraging everyone to work much harder and discover much more about oneself and one's relation with others.

And this, finally, is probably the best aspect of this book: it provides a practical guide to discover many things about oneself and one's relation with others and, the more it is used, the more one feels the need to know more about oneself. In other words, Pierre gives us here both a motivation and a means to follow the prescription given 25 centuries ago by Socrates and much earlier even in the East: Know thyself. This ancient prescription is still very much needed today and, it is safe to predict, it will continue to be needed in centuries to come. I hope you will enjoy following it as I have.

René H. Springuel
Program Coordinator for Africa
Economic Development Institute
World Bank

January, 1981

Introduction

This handbook for cross-cultural trainers and consultants does not propose to cover all topics related to intercultural reality. Rather, it focuses on a set of very well identified issues, including the cross-cultural adjustment process. It does so from a fresh perspective, which is to make cross-cultural confrontations work for people, or, more exactly, to help people make it work for them. [2]

Another point I would like to make is that "culture shock" is everywhere. There is no need to move to an esoteric, strange culture to experience it. It occurs each time that a contradiction or confrontation between various values, beliefs, and assumptions is experienced. It can be superficial and unnoticed. Sometimes it is drastic and leads to some kind of psychological trauma. It can be caused by the change of the value system of an organization as well as by the discovery of one's own real self. In all cases it is characterized, as it has been defined by the French sociologist E. Durkheim, as a *state of anomie*. Something does not fit anymore. It is time for a change....

This book is primarily *process oriented*. It attempts (a) to help people who are interested in the field ask some of the right questions, and (b) to assist them in constructing their own training or consulting instruments so that they fit their particular situations.

My approach is based on two interrelated assumptions:

1. There is no absolute truth.

It is indeed up to each individual to find out what his or her truth is. Today and tomorrow. The search must be ongoing. It cannot stop since the dynamics of the world never stop. What is true today will be obsolete and untrue tomorrow. What is allright for one individual is not necessarily so for another. What is effective for one situation is not automatically so for any situation. In short, everything is relative. What counts, at least from a training viewpoint, is to help individuals discover what their relative truths are.

2. To learn how to learn is the answer.

The main objective of any intercultural training program must be to help people *learn how to learn.* That is to say, "to learn how to adjust to different situations, environments and settings.

The theory I advocate is the "double loop" learning approach (see next section) applied to cross-cultural issues.

---

[2] One of the basic assumptions which underlie my approach is that the intercultural experience can be very rewarding; that it is (if properly handled or managed) an opportunity for self-discovery and personal growth.

This handbook provides *exercises, theoretical inputs, readings* and *references* for further explanation in relation to five main themes:

1. Discovering intercultural realities.

2. Learning how to cope in a cross-cultural setting.

3. Practical guidelines for cross-cultural action.

4. Basic concepts and principles on "managing" intercultural interaction.

5. Assessing intercultural training and learning effectiveness.

Trainers and consultants should feel free to use all the exercises and other training instruments as they wish. I only ask that they quote their references as accurately as possible as I have tried to do myself.

I want to conclude this introduction by thanking all my students and trainees, who in the last fifteen years have helped me "make a dream come true." I equally want to express my gratitude to the Society for Intercultural Education, Training and Research (SIETAR), which not only gave me the idea for this project but has also supported it until the end.

I wish to acknowledge the work of Ms. Jean Ponchamni, who typed and edited the first draft of the manuscript. A special thanks to Ms. M. Bussat, who created and produced the six extraordinary photographs which illustrate the main parts of the book, to Ms. Jane Gouveia, who worked on all the graphics and sketches, and, last but not least, Mr. Stephen Anspacher, who believes in the book and was courageous enough to go ahead with its publication. Without all these people, this creative act would not have taken place. I am very grateful to them all.

Pierre Casse
Washington, D.C.
May, 1979

Author's note to the Second Edition

I would like to share with readers some of the comments that I have received from those who have not only read but used the first edition of this book.

It seems that the key common words are: It works! (See the Preface to the Second Edition written by Mr. R.H. Springuel of the Economic Development Institute of the World Bank).

Most people who wrote or spoke to me about the book stressed the practicality of its format. They liked the way the workshops were presented with their aims, objectives, simulations, case studies, exercises and related conceptual inputs.

Many trainers and consultants involved in intercultural activities pointed out the usefulness of the references and suggested readings. It appears that the book triggered some motivations to read further and explore some selected issues in more depth.

A few people even mentioned the fact that the materials included in the fifteen chapters had, in many cases, to be adpated to learning situations and perceived that need as an incentive to intercultural creativity. I did like that very much. I still strongly believe that it is the best way to use the book.

Maybe the most interesting reaction I have received so far is the request from managers who have attended some of the workshops in various countries (in Asia and Europe, for example) to organize them in their own institutions.

Last but not least, I have also received provocative comments from readers who reacted to the theoretical (especially psychological) elements of the book. If I understand them correctly, it seems that I went either too far or not far enough in presenting models interpreting the intercultural realities. I need some time to think about this . . . .

In the same line, some people were slightly lost not being able to decide if the book is for practitioners or for academics. I *can* answer that question: it is, of course for both.

I now want to apologize for two major mistakes which slipped my attention when the book was first published. On page 32 of the original edition, one should have read "transpersonal *unconscious*" and "cosmic *unconscious*" in the graphic (instead of *"conscious"* in both instances); also, on page 159 of that edition, the matrix should have been scaled from 20 to 100 (and not from 80 to 400). Both errors have been corrected in the present edition.

You will notice that a new chapter has been added. It deals with the marketing of intercultural training. I wrote it because some readers told me that to have the good ideas is not enough, one also has to be able to "sell" them to the right people and institutions. What is the use of a good book which remains on the shelf? What is the use of a workshop which is not implemented? The point is well taken ... let's go out and market what is so needed nowadays: the promotion of intercultural empathy and understanding. Let's be pro-active. Good luck.

Pierre Casse
Washington, D.C.
January, 1981

Learning how to learn.

The 'practical' man, if he is to become an effective trainer, must learn to conceptualize the cross-cultural learning experience in terms applicable to experience-based learning.

— R. Harrison & R.L. Hopkins

The double-loop learning process as described by C. Argyris in his book, *Increasing Leadership Effectiveness,* [3] is particularly appropriate for cross-cultural training which addresses itself to people who:

1. do not know what or how to learn;

2. do not know that they do not know what or how to learn; and

3. live in a world which does not support the questioning of basic cultural assumptions.

The process is organized around four phases: **discovery, invention, production,** and **generalization.** Each phase also has a learning cycle of its own *(Figure 1).*

Figure 1. The double-loop learning process

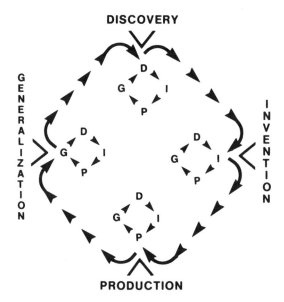

[3] Adapted from Argyris, C., *Increasing Leadership Effectiveness*, New York: John Wiley & Sons, 1976, p. 217. Reproduced with permission.

The existence of learning cycles within learning cycles implies that learners have to go through four steps for each phase of the mainstream process. In practical terms, it means that learning how to learn requires a maximum of competency in each of sixteen different types of behavior (*Figure 2*).

Figure 2. Learning how to learn: A matrix

PHASES	STEPS			
DISCOVERY	1 Discover that they do not know how to discover what they want to discover	2 Invent how to discover	3 Produce behavior needed for discovery	4 Generalize about effective discovery processes
INVENTION	5 Discover that they cannot invent what they want to invent	6 Invent how to invent	7 Produce the invention	8 Generalize about effective invention processes
PRODUCTION	9 Discover that they cannot produce what they want to produce	10 Invent how to produce	11 Produce the production	12 Generalize about effective production processes
GENERALIZATION	13 Discover that they cannot generalize what they want to generalize	14 Invent how to generalize	15 Produce the generalization	16 Generalize about effective generalization processes

The workshop method.

The method I recommend is the *workshop* methodology which is inspired by the experiential learning process as it has been promoted by the psychologist K. Lewin.

It consists of placing the participants in experiential situations where their "me" finds itself engaged and the experience offers them a particularly significant learning context. This fundamental pedagogic principle, expressed by C. Rogers[4], emphasizes *total* learning by engaging not only the intellectual but also the emotional level. Fully responsible for their own learning, the participants are called upon to draw lessons from their experience (here and now) which seems most relevant. Through its principles and dynamism, the experiential learning method constitutes an excellent tool in the service of *training by objectives*.

---

[4] Rogers, C.R., *Freedom to Learn*, Columbus: Charles E. Merrill, 1969.

The pedagogic method can be described as follows *(Figure 3)*: an exercise, selected and presented by a facilitator, permits the group of participants to experience a certain situation (Phase I), to detect a series of problems (with the aid of theoretical inputs if necessary), analyze their causes and consequences (Phase II), search for possible solutions (Phase III), and to test these solutions (Phase IV) either in an intermediate way, which returns the group to a deeper investigation of the problems (Phase II), or more definitely (final test) which brings the participants to the selection of a new theme of research or training module (Phase I).

Each phase of the training process encourages the members of the group to learn how to learn, according to the process first described by K. Lewin, *i.e.,* "defreezing—moving—refreezing." The process of discovering becomes itself the object of the training and the role of the facilitator or trainer is to help the group go as deeply as possible into that specific field of learning how to learn. His principal contribution, besides the preparation of the training program is to create and maintain within the group a climate of confidence in themselves and in their capacity to discover and learn. The pedagogic (or andragogic) method can integrate different training techniques into the scheme. Thus, the facilitator can use the case method, role-playing, T-group, cultural assimilator, videotape self-confrontation, contrast technique, etc.

Setting the stage.

May I suggest that the trainer who intends to design and implement cross-cultural training programs have a first look at the following three learning tools:

1. Is cross-cultural training magic?

2. A competency matrix for cross-cultural trainers.

3. A self-rating instrument for intercultural trainers.

1. Is cross-cultural training magic?

The Prince and the Magician [5]

Once upon a time there was a young prince who believed in all things but three. He did not believe in princesses, he did not believe in islands, and he did not believe in God. His father, the king, told him that such things did not exist. As there were no princesses or islands in his father's domain, and no sign of God, the prince believed his father.

---

[5] Reprinted from *The Magus* by John Fowles, Dell Publishing Co., pp. 499-500. Used by R. Bandler and J. Grinder in their book, *The Structure of Magic*, Science and Behavior Books, Inc., Palo Alto CA 94306, 1975, p. xiii.

**Figure 3. Diagram of an experiential learning model:
The workshop methodology**

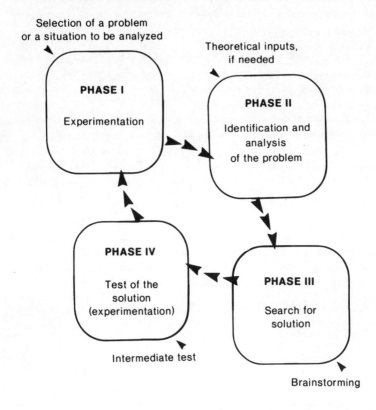

But then, one day, the prince ran away from his palace and came to the next land. There, to his amazement, from every coast he saw islands, and on these islands strange creatures whom he dared not name. As he was searching for a boat, a man in full evening dress approached him along the shore. "Are those real islands?" asked the young prince. "Of course they are," said the man in evening dress. "And those strange creatures?" "They are all genuine and authentic princesses." Then God must also exist!" cried the prince. "I am God," replied the man in evening dress, with a bow.

The young prince returned home as quickly as he could. "So, you are back," said his father, the king. "I have seen islands, I have seen princesses, I have seen God," said the young prince, reproachfully.

The king was unmoved. "Neither real islands, nor real princesses, nor a real God exists." "I saw them!" "Tell me how God was dressed." "God was in full evening dress." "Were the sleeves of his coat rolled back?" The prince remembered that they had been. The king smiled. "That is the uniform of a magician. You have been deceived."

At this, the prince returned to the next land and went to the same shore, where once again he came upon the man in full evening dress.

"My father, the king, has told me who you are," said the prince indignantly. "You deceived me last time, but not again. Now I know that those are not real islands and real princesses, because you are a magician."

The man on the shore smiled. "It is you who are deceived, my boy. In your father's kingdom, there are many islands and many princesses. But you are under your father's spell, so you cannot see them."

The prince pensively returned home. When he saw his father he looked him in the eye. "Father, is it true that you are not a real king, but only a magician?" The king smiled and rolled back his sleeves. "Yes, son, I am only a magician." "Then the man on the other shore was God." "The man on the other shore was another magician." "I must know the truth—the truth beyond magic." "There is no truth beyond magic," said the king.

The prince was full of sadness. He said, "I will kill myself." The king, by magic, caused death to appear. Death stood in the door and beckoned to the prince. The prince shuddered. He remembered the beautiful but unreal islands and the unreal but beautiful princesses. "Very well," he said, "I can bear it."

"You see, my son," said the king, "you, too, now l ⸴ to be a magician."

Questions for the reader:

1. Do we create our own reality?

2. Do people believe that what they see is reality?

3. Is it true that in order to see what our construction of reality is, we need to be confronted with other "realities?"

4. Are real and unreal relative?

5. Aren't you a magician?

Some tentative answers to these questions are given in Chapter 2, "Paradigms for Human Survival." The key thing to be observed (and eventually discussed) is that human beings perceive, discover and create their realities according to the "cultural maps" or paradigms they have in their minds.

Different beliefs, values and assumptions lead to various constructions of the natural and social worlds. Any individual has the extraordinary potential to generate a special, unique construction of what is, so that his or her needs are met. The magic is that the "program" can be changed. The world is defined by our cultural and psychological program. At the same time, our own identity depends on the way we program ourselves. We are what we are. We can be what we decide to be.

As Plato pointed out, we are still like human beings living in caves and watching, with fascination, the shadows of our own movements on the walls. The magic of human life is maybe to identify new shadows and beyond that, to learn how to turn around, face the entrance to the cave, and see what the "real" world looks like. As John O. Stevens put it, "We are on the threshold of a quantum jump in human experience and capability."[6]

Please see "A Competency Matrix for Cross-Cultural Trainers," found on page xxiii.

Questions for the reader:

1. Are the categories put into the matrix relevant?

2. Is the role identification complete?

3. Can you add at least three categories under knowledge?

4. Can you select the five skills which are the most important for cross-cultural training?

5. Is "learning by doing" a belief?

---

[6]   John O. Stevens, author of *Awareness* and editor of *Gestalt Therapy Verbatim* and *Gestalt Is*.

(2) A competency matrix for cross-cultural consultants and trainers (Figure 4)

ROLE REQUIREMENTS	KNOWLEDGE	SKILLS AND BEHAVIOR	ASSUMPTIONS AND VALUES
ROLE IDENTIFICATION		**RELATED TO PEOPLE AND PROCESSES** (TO BE ABLE)	**BELIEFS IN**
To design, conduct and evaluate cross-cultural training programs To train trainers in cross-cultural relations To advance the field of cross-cultural training	COMMUNICATION INTERCULTURAL RELATIONS INTERNATIONAL RELATIONS TRAINING SOCIOLOGY SOCIAL PSYCHOLOGY ANTHROPOLOGY - ORGANIZATION DEVELOPMENT GROUP DYNAMICS ANDRAGOGY	■ to act as a facilitator ■ to practice empathy ■ to listen ■ to ask questions in a non-threatening way ■ to use various training methods ■ to recognize people's learning styles ■ to answer questions in a non-threatening way ■ to involve people in a research/training project ■ to help people to know themselves better (as individuals—as products of various cultures) ■ to deal with change ■ to make clearer presentations and be factual ■ to reassure in identifying support systems for people involved in a change process ■ to understand theories of group processes ■ to help people to clarify their training needs, strengths and weaknesses ■ to help people to learn how to learn, how to teach ■ to be flexible and adjust to people's needs ■ to encourage and support a self-directed learning process ■ to work in a team	■ cross-cultural training (its usefulness) ■ cultural difference ■ cultural similarities ■ the importance of processes *versus* content ■ the existence (and importance) of cultural assumptions, values ■ the fact that people can change ■ the possibility of controlling and improving cross-cultural interactions ■ the willingness of people to learn more about themselves ■ learning by doing ■ self-directed learning ■ the uniqueness of people ■ the need to adjust cultural guidelines to each participant's expectations ■ the necessity to live actual experiences in other cultures ■ that cultures are not superior or inferior to other cultures, only *different from.*
		RELATED TO IDEAS (TO BE ABLE)	
		■ to set up, organize and implement a research project on cross-cultural relations ■ to identify training needs ■ to design and structure training workshops, seminars or courses ■ to select the appropriate (according to subject matter, people, environment, purpose...) training techniques ■ to design and use simulations, roleplaying, case-studies... as appropriate	■ to keep abreast of development in the cross-cultural field ■ to evaluate the impact of the training program on people ■ to write on the subject ■ to learn from previous intracultural and intercultural experience ■ to set up meaningful training objectives (behavioral changes)

The above matrix represents a first step in designing a competency model for cross-cultural trainers and consultants. It should help the reader to complete the self-rating instrument which follows.

(3) A self-rating instrument for intercultural trainers (Figure 5) [6a]

COMPETENCIES IN CROSS-CULTURAL TRAINING	RATING			
	None	Weak	Fair	Strong
A. GENERAL (capability to)				
1. practice empathy				
2. deal with change				
3. help people learn how to learn				
4. communicate				
5. motivate				
*6. _____				
7. _____				
8. _____				
9. _____				
10. _____				
B. SPECIFIC (capability to)				
1. assess cross-cultural training needs				
2. set up intercultural training objectives				
3. design programs				
4. select appropriate teaching methods				
5. evaluate training outcome				
*6. _____				
7. _____				
8. _____				
9. _____				
10. _____				
* Add your own (at least five) [6b]				

According to my own experience in the intercultural training and consulting fields, the five questions raise a critical awareness in terms of what is expected from a trainer responsible for designing and conducting cross-cultural training programs.

Some answers to these questions can be found in Chapter 12, "Training

[6a] Inspired by M. Knowles, *Self-Directed Learning*, New York: Association Press, 1975.

[6b] For a more in-depth analysis, see "A Self-Development Process for Training and Development Professionals," *Training and Development Journal*, May 1979, pp. 6-12.

in Other Cultures." Ten intercultural specialists were consulted in the compilation of the matrix.

The reader is now asked to go one step further and assess his or her strengths and weaknesses as a cross-cultural trainer and consultant. Five items should first be added under general and specific skills. Then, a rating should be attributed to each listed skill (put a check in the corresponding column) so that by the end of the exercise a profile is established.

My advice is to *downgrade* all the results before making any decision regarding an action plan for improving one's own effectiveness. In other words, the reader should be "tough" on himself or herself, and what has been rated strong should become fair, fair should become weak, weak is now lacking, and none should be seen as seriously missing.

The **action plan** which will follow can be organized around five themes:

1. Performance areas to be considered;

2. Actions to be taken to improve existing situations (see Chapter 15, "Assessing Intercultural Training Effectiveness"—Workshop 17);

3. Identification of potential obstacles;

4. Outline of preventive actions;

5. Definition of indicators of progress and accomplishment.

Ideally, the action plan should be presented to another trainer who will play the "devil's advocate" role so that all themes are thoroughly examined and cross-checked.

Suggested Preliminary Readings:

Batchelder, D. and E.G. Warner (eds.), *Beyond Experience. The Experiential Approach to Cross-Cultural Education.* Brattleboro, VT: Experiment Press in cooperation with SIETAR, 1977.

Benedict, R., *Patterns of Culture.* New York: Mentor Books, 1960.

Brislin, R.W. and P. Pedersen, *Cross-cultural Orientation Programs.* New York: Gardner Press, Inc., 1976.

Casmir, F.L. (ed.), *Intercultural and International Communication* Washington, DC: University Press of America, 1978.

Cole, M. and S. Scribner, *Culture and Thought: A Psychological Introduction.* New York: John Wiley & Sons, Inc., 1974.

DeCrow, R., *Cross-Cultural Interaction Skills: A Digest of Recent Training Literature, ERIC* Syracuse, NY: Clearinghouse on Adult Education, February, 1969.

Harrison, R. and R.L. Hopkins, "The Design of Cross-Cultural Training: An Alternative to the University Model," *The Organizational Psychology: A Book of Readings*, D.A. Kolb, I.M. Rubin and J.M. McIntyre. Englewood Cliffs, NJ: Prentice-Hall, Inc., 1971, pp. 27-45.

Hoopes, D.S., "What is an Intercultural Workshop?" in *Readings in Intercultural Communication, Vol. 1.* SIETAR publication, 1975.

Kluckhohn, C., *Culture and Behavior.* New York: The Free Press, 1962.

Kohls, L.R., *Survival Kit for Overseas Living.* Chicago: Intercultural Network/Systran Publications, 1979.

Mead, M., *Male and Female.* New York: William Morrow & Co., Inc., 1967.

Peace Corps, *Guidelines for Peace Corps Cross-Cultural Training.* Washington, DC: Peace Corps Office of Training Support, 3 vols., 1970.

Pedersen, P. and D. Hoopes, "Research in Evaluating the Objectives of the Intercultural Communications Workshops," in *Readings in Intercultural Communication, Volume III* SIETAR, 1973.

Prosser, M.H., *Major Books on Intercultural Communication.* Pittsburgh, PA: Intercultural Communications Network of the Regional Council for International Education, 1972.

Samovar, L.A., *Intercultural Communication Research: Some Myths, Some Questions.* Paper delivered at the Fourth Annual SIETAR Conference, Phoenix, AZ, 1978.

Weeks, W.H., P.B. Pedersen & R.W. Brislin (eds.), *A Manual of Structured Experiences for Cross-Cultural Learning.* Washington, DC: SIETAR, 1977.

TRAINING FOR THE
CROSS-CULTURAL MIND

*A Handbook for
Cross-Cultural Trainers and Consultants*

Je pense donc je suis.
— Descartes

I know that I know nothing.
— Socrates

Not knowing that one knows is best.
— Lao Tzu

1 *DISCOVERING*

Chapter 1

THE PHENOMENOLOGY OF CULTURE

Subjective culture is a cultural group's characteristic way of perceiving the man-made part of its environment.

— H.C. Triandis

In most cases it is helpful to develop a working definition of culture before analyzing intercultural relations. The idea is not to have an in-depth analysis at this stage [7] but to give a chance to a group of trainees to experientially define the meaning of culture. The *BaFa BaFa* exercise, which is an integrated simulation which enables participants to experience at first hand the creation of culture and the dynamics of cultural relations, is certainly appropriate for this purpose [8]. Hereunder is a workshop that I have developed and tested. It deals with *PROBLEM-SOLVING ACROSS CULTURES*. This workshop also provides a good opportunity for the group to set up its own micro-culture right at the outset of the training program. It can be used as a warm-up stage in the training process. This can be effectively analyzed at the end of the workshop.

WORKSHOP 1. [9]

1. Aim: To experience the meaning of culture (subjective culture) as well as intercultural relations using a problem-solving approach.

2. Objectives: Participants will:

(1) analyze two basic and different ways to handle problem-solving (conceptual framework: theoretical inputs 1 and 2);

---

[7] We shall do it when we approach cultures as paradigms for survival (p. 26).

[8] *BaFa-Ba-Fa: A Cross-Cultural Simulation*, by R.G. Shirts of Simile II, 1150 Silverado, La Jolla, CA 92037.

[9] We are grateful to Dr. J. Mobley, who has created a program on "value options" and gave me the idea of the training process for this workshop.

(2) identify three approaches to cross-cultural interaction (conceptual framework: input 3);

(3) examine the dynamic of a culture in terms of problem-solving (conceptual framework: input 4).

3. Process:

(a) Ask the participants to fill out the following self-assessment exercise on the problem-solving modes (10-15 minutes):

This self-assessment exercise is intended to give you some information regarding the way in which you approach problems. It will also help you analyze a few different cultural patterns related to problem-solving. Be as spontaneous as possible in answering. Focus on what you believe right now and not on what your choice *should* be. Read each "value orientation" and check the appropriate number to the right of the sentence knowing that the meanings of the numbers used are:

> 7: I **strongly agree**
> 5: I **agree**
> 3: I **disagree**
> 1: I **strongly disagree**

1. Problems are fun 7 5 3 1
2. I perceive problems as opportunities 7 5 3 1
3. I avoid problems 7 5 3 1
4. I ignore problems 7 5 3 1
5. I see problems as potential sources of conflicts 7 5 3 1
6. I'm serious about problems 7 5 3 1
7. I see problems in their totalities 7 5 3 1
8. I focus on the parts of a problem 7 5 3 1
9. I perceive problems in a static way 7 5 3 1
10. I define problems as dynamic realities 7 5 3 1
11. I take problems as part of a whole 7 5 3 1
12. I like to deal with personal problems (intra) 7 5 3 1
13. I enjoy handling interpersonal problems 7 5 3 1
14. I like to cope with impersonal problems 7 5 3 1
15. I like to solve problems alone 7 5 3 1
16. I like to solve problems in teams 7 5 3 1
17. I am factual in solving problems 7 5 3 1
18. I am intuitive in solving problems 7 5 3 1
19. I plan when I have to solve problems 7 5 3 1
20. I am quick in solving problems 7 5 3 1
21. I am careful in solving problems 7 5 3 1
22. I am bold in solving problems 7 5 3 1
23. I like to be rewarded when a problem is solved 7 5 3 1
24. I know for sure when a problem is well solved 7 5 3 1
25. I keep a record for solved problems 7 5 3 1
26. I like to pre-test potential solutions to problems 7 5 3 1
27. I started to realize that there are problems to be solved
    early in life 7 5 3 1

28. I like to feel fully responsible when solving problems 7 5 3 1
29. I am looking for help when confronted with problems 7 5 3 1
30. I am ready to assist others involved in solving problems 7 5 3 1
31. I enjoy solving problems 7 5 3 1
32. I create problems 7 5 3 1
33. I complain about problems 7 5 3 1
34. I look for causes when solving problems 7 5 3 1
35. I believe in chance (good luck) when solving problems 7 5 3 1
36. I look in any past to apply the right method to solve problems . 7 5 3 1
37. I use theories to solve problems 7 5 3 1
38. I observe other people to know more about how to solve problems 7 5 3 1
39. I use the trial and error approach to solve problems 7 5 3 1
40. I focus on follow-through 7 5 3 1
41. I always look for ways for improving 7 5 3 1
42. I use one basic approach to solve problems 7 5 3 1
43. I use a combination of approaches to solve problems 7 5 3 1
44. I perceive problem-solving as a win-lose situation 7 5 3 1
45. I am emotional when dealing with problems 7 5 3 1
46. I associate problem-solving with power 7 5 3 1
47. I compete with others when solving problems 7 5 3 1
48. I differentiate between problems to be solved by men or women 7 5 3 1
49. I blame others for the existence of problems 7 5 3 1
50. I am aggressive when solving problems 7 5 3 1

OTHERS:

51. _____ 7 5 3 1
51. _____ 7 5 3 1
52. _____ 7 5 3 1
53. _____ 7 5 3 1
54. _____ 7 5 3 1
55. _____ 7 5 3 1

(b) Five blank cards are given to each individual who selects and writes down:

□ the two items that he or she likes most;

□ the two items that he or she likes least; and

□ one item that he or she added to the list.

Between five and ten minutes are needed for this part of the workshop.

(c) When ready, participants can trade their cards with one another (they must try to get rid of cards they do not like and acquire new cards with items they do like). This phase lasts between fifteen and 45 minutes according to the size of the group. By the end of the trade-off, each participant should have at least two cards left in his or her hand. (Some people will be stuck with cards that they do not like.)

(d) The group members are now asked to go around in the room and identify people who share more or less their main assumptions (likes *and* dislikes) regarding problems. When it is done, they meet and clarify what they have agreed upon, namely, how to define and approach problems (fifteen minutes). In so doing, they have created a set of MICRO-CULTURES.

(e) After fifteen minutes, the facilitator or trainer asks the group to brainstorm and come up with *five guidelines* to solving problems according to their basic assumptions. (The guidelines are written down on a flipchart.) Ten minutes are allowed for this phase.

(f) A problem is given to the group which has to solve it and at the same time stick to their guidelines. The process goes like this:

1) the instructions are given to the participants, who read them (five minutes);

2) the groups perform with or without leaders (it is up to the facilitator to decide). It is recommended that groups be asked to designate a member who will make sure that the guidelines are applied during the exercise (30 minutes); and

3) debriefing the subgroups (what have we learned from this exercise?) (fifteen minutes).

THE PROBLEM
Bomb Shelter Exercise
Instructions

An atomic war has just started and your group is safe in a bomb shelter which means that you will survive. There is still room for three persons. Please make a choice among the list attached of the three individuals you are going to invite into your group. You have 30 minutes to accomplish this task.

Bomb Shelter Exercise
Waiting List

☐ a Catholic priest	☐ a worker (building)
☐ an engineer	☐ a pastor
☐ an architect	☐ a teacher (primary school)
☐ a poet (woman)	☐ a physician (general)
☐ a social worker	☐ a specialist in electronics
☐ an agronomist	☐ a mechanic
☐ a politician	☐ a journalist
☐ a general	☐ a businesswoman
☐ a banker	☐ an economist
☐ a psychologist	☐ a child (boy, ten years old)
☐ a surgeon (woman)	☐ a policeman
☐ a language specialist	☐ a specialist in nutrition (woman)

(g) Participants must now meet with members from other "cultures" and reach a consensus on a common way to define and approach problems (30 minutes).

(h) The debriefing of the entire workshop is critical. It should last at least 45 minutes and focus on the following themes:

1) What is a culture? What is a subjective culture?

2) Of what is a culture made up?

3) Ideal versus actual values?

4) What are some of the key "problems" which surface when several cultures meet?

5) What are the different ways to manage cross-cultural relations?

Previous discussions with workshop participants have emphasized the fact that a culture is the product of the interaction between people having different values, beliefs and assumptions regarding self, others, nature and spiritual matters.

The interaction with others seems to activate new *patterns of human conduct* within the participants. This is a creative act. The tension which underlies the process varies from one group to another. However, it seems that it diminishes when the group is able to reach a consensus on a set of values and ways of behaving. Then one can say that a micro-culture is born.

It has been stressed in most discussions that the conflict between different ways of approaching problems has something positive in itself: it forces the group or micro-culture to review and revise its well-established patterns.

4. Total time for the workshop: About three hours.

5. Conceptual Framework:

Three theoretical inputs can be made at the end of the workshop. The facilitator should be very careful to avoid overloading the group with new information. He or she should also make sure that the workshop experiment as well as the theories are clearly related to cultural field experiences.

INPUT 1

Problem-Solving: The Systematic versus the Small Project Approach

THE SYSTEMATIC APPROACH	THE SMALL PROJECT APPROACH

1. clarify information
2. identify objectives as well as performance standards (criteria for success)
3. analyze strategies
   ☐ various options
   ☐ pros and cons
4. set up an action plan (who does what, how, when, etc.)
5. action
 	
(the entire process should be *reviewed* on an on-going basis)
	1. action
	2. *REVIEW* of the results of the experiment (did it work? strengths and weaknesses? adjust the approach
	3. elaboration of an action plan (more pilot-projects, more testing, improving using a step-by-step approach)
	4. a strategy is defined (it actually comes out of the experiments)
	5. definition of objectives (finally objectives and priorities are clarified)

The group can be asked to react to the following questions:

(a) Can you relate the two approaches to cultural realities?

(b) When do people use which approach?

(c) Can we combine the two approaches?

Groups have been able to identify the need to use the systematic approach in a cultural environment characterized by the availability and accuracy of information whereas the small project one is particularly justified when there is a lack of data or when these are unreliable.

Many discussions have also suggested that to start with the small project approach and switch to the systematic process when the situation is clarified makes a lot of sense.

INPUT 2

Differences Between Logical and Creative Problem-Solving [10]

CHARACTERISTICS	LOGICAL	CREATIVE
1. PROBLEMS	Well-defined	Ill-defined
2. TYPES OF THINK-ING	Convergent (analytical)	Divergent (open-ended)
3. PROCESS:		
a. FACTS	Most important	Not critical
b. PROBLEM FORMULATION	One statement (incl. "must" criteria)	Many statements (incl. only minimal constraints)
c. IDEAS	Few ideas	Many ideas (variety of techniques)
d. EVALUATION	Accept only ideas fitting criteria	Many criteria (use to reshape strange ideas)
e. ACTION	Corrects situation	New challenges
4. APPLICABILITY	Cause-related	All types of situations, opportunities
5. RESULTS	Predictable, measurable, re-establishes *status quo*	Risky, probability of major breakthrough

Questions to the group:

(a) What are some of the basic cultural assumptions which underlie the two processes?

(b) What about other cultural approaches towards problem-solving (*e.g.*, the "do-nothing" approach)?

(c) Characterize a culture which denies the existence of problems.

[10] This chart is from M.O. Edwards, "Comparison of Logical and Creative Problem Solving," *Bulletin on Training*, Vol. 4, No. 1 (Jan.-Feb. 1979), BNA Communications, Inc. Reproduced with permission.

Many cultures perceive the problem-solving process as constructive and rewarding. A problem is an opportunity! The basic assumption which underlies this position is that if a problem can be identified and worked out, the end result is an *improved situation*. Some other assumptions or beliefs typical of this cultural paradigm are related to the fact that there is a solution to each problem and that the application of logic will automatically lead to the ideal solution.

Other cultures do not like to talk about problems. As a matter of fact, they do not perceive and register problems. Problems are shortcomings, things that one does not talk about. Besides, there are problems for which no solution exists...or for which there are many solutions. To solve a problem is not necessarily an improvement. In those cultures it is also belived that *time* solves most problems: "Just wait and you will see your problems disappear...."

INPUT 3

K. Lewin's "Force Field Analysis" Applied to Cultural Change [11]

CULTURAL DRIVING FORCES:

Values, Beliefs, Assumptions

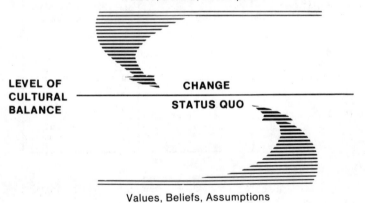

LEVEL OF CULTURAL BALANCE   **CHANGE**

STATUS QUO

Values, Beliefs, Assumptions

CULTURAL RESTRAINING FORCES:

[11] Lewin, K., "Quasi-stationary Equilibria and the Problem of Permanent Change," in W.G. Bennis and R. Chin (eds.), *The Planning of Change*, New York: Holt, Rinehart & Winston, 1969, pp. 235-238.

To change the cultural equilibrium one can:

(a) change the cultural driving forces (ask the group to find illustrations);

(b) change the cultural restraining forces (as above);

(c) change both sets of forces at the same time (as above).

It is suggested that this would be applied to the group itself and that a comparison be made between the group as it was at the beginning of the workshop and as it is at the end.

Three different ways to create "third cultures:"

☐ **Compromise:** One of the cultures gives up something;

☐ **Synthesis:** The two cultures agree on something they can live with;

☐ **Creative:** They create something which goes beyond their actual cultural identities.

6. Handouts and readings:

(a) Handouts:

Ewing, D.W., "Discovering your Problem-Solving Style," *Psychology Today,* December, 1977.

Lewin, K., "Force Field Analysis," *The 1973 Handbook for Group Facilitators,* pp. 111-113.

Sherwood, J.J. and F.M. Hoylman, "Utilizing Human Resources: Individual versus Group Approaches to Problem Solving and Decision-Making," *The 1978 Annual Handbook for Group Facilitators,* pp. 157-162.

Strodtbeck, F.L., "Values and Beliefs in Cross-Cultural Interaction," in *Overview of Intercultural Education, Training and Research, Vol. 1, Theory,* D.S. Hoopes, P.B. Pedersen and G.W. Renwick (eds.), SIETAR, September, 1977.

Triandis, H.C., "Culture Training, Cognitive Complexity and Interpersonal Attitudes," in *Readings in Intercultural Communication, Vol. III,* The Intercultural Communication Network of the Regional Council for International Education, 1973.

(b) Readings:

Brown, I.C., *Understanding Other Cultures,* Englewood Cliffs, NJ: Prentice Hall, 1963.

Cole, M. and S. Scribner, *Culture and Thought,* New York: John Wiley & Sons, Inc., 1974.

Condon, J.C. and F. Yousef, *An Introduction to Intercultural Communication*, Russell R. Windes (ed.), New York: 1975.

deBono, E., *The Use of Lateral Thinking*, London: Penguin Books, 1967.

Downs, J.F., *Cultures in Crisis*, Beverly Hills, CA: Glencoe Press, 1971.

Durkheim, E., *Les règles de la méthode sociologique*, PUF, Paris: 1968.

Fisher, B.A., *Small Group Decision Making: Communication and the Group Process*, New York: McGraw-Hill, 1974 ("The Decision Making Process," pp. 124-152.

Johnson, D.W. and F.P. Johnson, *Joining Together*, ("Problem Solving," pp. 257-275), Englewood Cliffs, NJ: Prentice-Hall, 1975.

Kluckhohn, C., *Mirror for Man*, New York: McGraw-Hill Book Co., 1943.

Kluckhohn, C., *Culture and Behavior*, New York: The Free Press, 1962.

Patton, B.R. and K. Giffin, *Problem-Solving Group Interaction*, New York: Harper & Row Publishers, 1973.

Seelye, H.N., *Teaching Culture*, Skokie, Ill.: National Textbook Co., 1976.

Wagner, R., *The Invention of Culture*, Englewood Cliffs, NJ: Prentice-Hall Inc., 1975.

White, L.A., *The Science of Culture*, New York: Farrar, Strauss & Giroux, 1975.

WORKSHOP 2. [12]

1. Aim: To give an opportunity to the participants to experiment, observe and analyze a transfer process from a cross-cultural perspective.

2. Objectives: Participants will:

(1) Define the concept of transfer across cultures (conceptual framework: input 1).

(2) Analyze the various phases of the transfer process (conceptual framework: input 2).

3. Process:

Phase 1. The group is split into three sub-groups. Two sub-groups are the performers and the third one plays the role of the observers. The two groups of performers are separated (they cannot see or hear each other), whereas the observers can move freely between the two other teams but without interfering in the exercise.

---

[12] The exercises used in this workshop have been borrowed and adapted from E. deBono, *The Five-Day Course in Thinking*, London: Pelican Books, 1967.

Instructions for Team 1 (Performers)

Using only the four knives, construct a platform on top of the three glasses which are upside down and separated by a distance slightly superior to the length of a knife. No part of any knife may touch the ground. The platform has to be more or less in the middle of the three glasses and must be strong enough to support a full glass of water. [13]

Instructions for Team 2 (Performers)

Using only the four knives, construct a platform on top of the two glasses which are upside down and separated by a distance slightly superior to the length of a knife. No part of any knife may touch the ground. The platform has to be more or less in the middle of the two glasses and must be strong enough to support a full glass of water. [14]

Instructions for Observers

Observe the different approaches people use to solve the problem.

Phase 2. Usually Team 1 is able to solve the problem first (if not, the facilitator should help them solve it). When it happens, the facilitator stops the exercise and asks the two teams of performers to select one representative. It is then explained to everybody that the representative of the team who was able to solve its problem is going to meet the representative from the other team and help him/her solve the problem. The two representatives meet in the middle of the room so that everybody can watch what's happening. The instructions to the observers are: "Observe the interaction between the two representatives who, so far, do not know that the problem to be solved is different from the problem already solved by Team 1."

Phase 3. After fifteen minutes, the representative from Team 1 is asked to leave (having or not solved the problem). A new problem is then given to the representative from Team 2 to check if he or she has learned anything from the interaction.

Instructions for the Representative of Team 2

Using only the four knives, construct a platform on top of the four glasses which are upside down and separated by a distance slightly superior to the length of the knife. No part of any knife may touch the ground. The platform has to be more or less in the middle of the four glasses and must be strong enough to support a full glass of water. [14a]

Everybody observes the validity of the transfer (if any).

---

[13] Facilitators will find the solution in *Figure 6.*

[14] Facilitators will find the solution in *Figure 7.*

[14a] Facilitators will find the solution in *Figure 8.*

Figure 6. Solution to the **"three glass"** problem

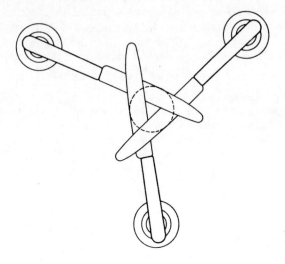

Figure 7. Solution to the "two glass" problem

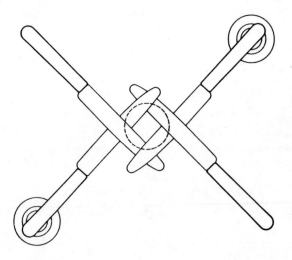

Figure 8. Solution to the "four glass" problem

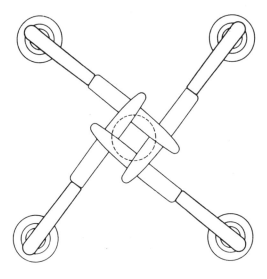

Phase 4. The debriefing is organized around five issues (analyzed from a cross-cultural perspective: see input 1).

(a) the transfer process itself;

(b) learning styles;

(c) motivation;

(d) communication; and

(e) helping relationship.

4. Time: Two hours.

5. Conceptual Framework:

INPUT 1.

The transfer between cultures can be defined as the process by which an individual who belongs to a certain culture tries to share something (issues, techniques, principles, methods, technologies, etc.) with someone else who does not share his or her ways of thinking, feeling and behaving.

The five issues to be taken into account when analyzing the transfer process are:

a. **The transfer process itself** (see input 2).

b. **The learning styles involved in the process** (see "Learning Styles Inventory"[15]).

c. **The motivations of the partners involved** (see "Work and the Nature of Man"[16]).

d. **The communication dimension of the process** (see "International Communication: A Reader"[17]).

e. **The helping relationships** (see "The Skilled Helper"[18]).

INPUT 2.

The Transfer Process

1. What is to be transferred?

   A. Too often the emphasis is on the *solution of an immediate problem.*

   B. What is important is to transmit a *provision* for handling similar problems.

   C. In many cases, the priority is to transfer a way of learning (learning how to learn, how to be creative, how to solve new problems).

2. Success criteria?

   A good transfer can be seen when the recipient of the help is capable of accomplishing new tasks independently without further help.

3. How does one transfer?

   The transfer of a problem can go as follows:

   Phase 1. The partners get acquainted.

   Phase 2. The counterpart defines the problem. The specialist asks questions.

   Phase 3. The counterpart explains what has already been done to solve the problem. The specialist asks questions.

---

[15] "Learning Styles Inventory," in *Organizational Psychology: An Experiential Approach*, by D.A. Kolb, I.M. Rubin, and J.M. McIntyre, Englewood Cliffs, NJ: Prentice-Hall, 1971, pp. 21-42.

[16] F. Herzberg, *Work and the Nature of Man*, Cleveland: World Publishing Co., 1966. See also Maslow, A., *Motivation and Personality*, New York: Harper & Bros., 1954; and McClelland, D., *The Achieving Society*, New York: The Mac-Millan Co., 1961.

[17] Samovar, L.A. and R.E. Porter, *Intercultural Communication: A Reader*, Belmont, CA: Wadsworth Publishing Co., 1972.

[18] Egan, G., *The Skilled Helper—A Model for Systematic Helping and Interpersonal Relating*, Monterrey, CA: Brooks/Cole Publishing Co., 1975.

Phase 4. The specialist explains what he/she knows about the problem. The counterpart asks questions.

Phase 5. Specialist and counterpart work together solving the problem. [19]

☐ Vertical approach.

☐ Lateral approach.

☐ Other approach.

Phase 6. Evaluation and review of the lessons to be learned from the experience.

6. Handouts and Readings.

(a) Handouts:

The Maslow Need Heirarchy, The 1972 Yearbook for Group Facilitators, p. 125.

Maslow's Need Hierarchy Motivation: A Feedback Exercise, in the 1973 Annual Handbook for Group Facilitators, pp. 43-45.

"Developing Cross-Cultural Learning Skills," D. Batchelder in *Beyond Experience: The Experiment in International Living,* Brattleboro, VT, 1977, pp. 155-158.

"The Broken Squares Exercise: A Handbook of Structured Experiences for Human Relations Training, Vol. 1." J.W. Pfeiffer and J.E. Jones, Iowa: University Associates Press, 1969.

"The Transferability of Western Management Concepts and Programs: An East African Perspective," J.R. Moris, in *Education and Training for Public Sector Management in the Developing Countries,* New York: Rockefeller Foundation, March, 1977.

"Consultation or Control? The Cross-Cultural Advisor-Advisee Relationship," R. Morrill, *Psychiatry,* Vol. 35, August 1972, pp. 264-280.

"Personal Counseling Across Cultural Boundaries," by C.H. Clarke (paper presented at the International Communication Association conference), Montreal: April, 1973.

"The Johari Window: A Model for Soliciting and Giving Feedback," *The 1973 Annual Handbook for Group Facilitators,* p. 114.

"Conditions Which Hinder Effective Communication," *The 1973 Annual Handbook for Group Facilitators,* p. 120.

---

[19] See E. deBono, *Lateral Thinking (Creativity Step by Step),* New York: Harper Colophon Books, 1970.

"Human Needs and Behavior," *The 1975 Annual Handbook for Group Facilitators,* p. 123.

"Dimensions of the Consultant Job, *Journal of Social Issues,* 1959, XV, (2).

Three Patterns of Behavior," McBer & Co., Cambridge, MA.

"An Exercise of Imagination," created by D. McClelland and published by McBer & Co., Cambridge, MA.

"Is Help Helpful," (p. 20) and "Feedback: The Art of Giving and Receiving Help," (p. 18), in *Reading Book for Laboratories in Human Relations Training,* NTL, 1972, edited by C.R. Hill and L.C. Porter.

Rotter, T., "External Control and Internal Control," in *Psychology Today,* June, 1971.

(b) Readings:

Arensberg, C.M. and A.H. Niehoff, *Introducing Social Change: A Manual for Americans Overseas,* Chicago: Aldine Publishing Co., 1964.

Blake, R.R. and J.S. Mouton, *Consultation,* Reading, MA: Addison-Wesley, 1976.

Foster, R.J., *Examples of Cross-Cultural Problems Encountered by Americans Working Overseas: An Instructor's Handbook,* Alexandria, VA: HumRRO, May 1965.

Lassey, W.R. (ed.), *Leadership and Social Change,* Iowa: University Associates, 1971.

Lippitt, G.L., *Visualizing Change (Model Building and the Change Process),* NTL-Learning Resources Corporation, Fairfax, VA: 1973. See *Models for Cultural Adaptation Training* (pp. 126-150).

Lippitt, G.L. and D.S. Hoopes, *Helping Across Cultures,* published by the International Consultants Foundation, Washington: 1978.

Miller, S., E.W. Nunnally and D.B. Wackman, *Alive and Aware (How to Improve your Relationship through Better Communication),* Minneapolis: Interpersonal Communication Programs, Inc.

Seurat, S., *Réalités du transfert de technologie,* Masson, Paris, 1978.

WORKSHOP 3.

1. **Aim:** To explore the different dimensions of culture shock, its various facets and cultural interpretations as well as its historical background.

2. **Objectives:** Participants will:

(1) Identify and analyze two sets of cultural assumptions and values which affect the perception of culture shock (conceptual framework: input 1).

(2) Examine some of the *causes* and symptoms of culture shock (conceptual framework: input 2).

3. **Process:**

(a) Ask the participants to answer the following questions (on their own or in subgroups):

☐ Is it true that culture shock has always existed?

☐ What are the main causes of culture shock?

☐ What are its main manifestations?

☐ What are some of its cultural forms?

☐ Is culture shock good? bad? or ...?

(b) Participants share their viewpoints.

(c) Split the group again into two sub-groups and ask them to comment on the following statements (one for each group):

"Culture shock is a form of personality maladjustment which is a reaction to a temporarily unsuccessful attempt to adjust to new surroundings and people."

— Sven Lundstedt
"Personality Determinants and
Assessment," *Journal of Social
Issues* July 1963, p. 3.

"When the individual is plunged into a fast and irregularly changing situation, or a novelty-loaded context, however, his predictive accuracy plummets. He can no longer make the reasonably correct assessment on which rational behaviour is dependent."

— Alvin Toffler
Future Shock, London:
Pan Books, Ltd., 1970, p. 319.

(d) *Provide* an exercise to the group as a whole so that they can *experience* the situation described by Alvin Toffler. Participants share their reactions when the exercise is over.

Instructions for Participants

You have 25 minutes to summarize the key points made by Alvin Toffler in his book *Future Shock* (the book is given to the group) applying the following rules:

(a) a new leader has to be appointed every five minutes;

(b) nobody can look at anyone during the entire exercise;

(c) everybody has to whisper;

(d) the group must move to another spot in the room every ten minutes; and

(e) the task will be redefined by the facilitator "from time to time."

(e) A final exercise consists of giving the following text and picture *(Figure 9)* to the group and asking the participants to relate them to culture shock from a cross-cultural perspective:

"Thus change is conceived of partly as the continuous transformation of the one force into the other and partly as a cycle of complex phenomena, in themselves connected, such as day and night, summer and winter. Change is not meaningless—if it were, there could be no knowledge of it—but subject to the universal law, too."

The *I Ching* or *Book of Changes*.
The Richard Wilhelm translation rendered
into English by Gary F. Baynes
Bollingen Series XIX, Princeton University
Press, 1977, p. lvi.

4. Time: Between two and three hours.

Figure 9.

5. Conceptual Framework:

INPUT 1.

Two different sets of assumptions about culture shock can be identified and discussed with the group:

Figure 10. Cultural assumptions and values affecting our perception of culture shock

SET 1	SET 2
1. Culture shock exists.	1. It does not exist. It is an invention of social scientists.
2. Culture shock is negative.	2. Culture shock is positive.
3. Culture shock is caused by external factors.	3. Culture shock is caused by internal factors.
4. Culture shock is a one-time experience.	4. Culture shock keeps repeating itself.
5. Some people are more predisposed to experience culture shock than others.	5. Everybody experiences culture shock.
Others. (To be added by participants.)	*Others.* (To be added by participants.)

The five preceding exercises are aimed at clarifying the very nature of culture shock through discussions and experiences. The above matrix intends to pinpoint some of the cultural assumptions and values which influence people's perception of culture shock.

INPUT 2.

Extract from *Culture Shock and the Problem of Adjustment to New Cultural Environments*, by Dr. Kalvero Oberg (see handout for complete reference):

"Culture shock is brought on by the anxiety that results from losing all our familiar signs and symbols of social intercourse. These signs or cues include the thousand and one ways in which we orient ourselves to the situations of daily life: when to shake hands and what to say when we meet people, when and how to give tips, how to give orders to servants, how to make purchases, when to accept and when to refuse invitations, when to take statements seriously and when not. Now these cues, which may be words, gestures, facial expressions, customs, or norms, are acquired by all of us in the course of growing up and are as much a part of our culture as the language we speak or the beliefs we accept. All of us depend for our peace of mind and our efficiency on hundreds of these cues, most of which we *are not consciously aware.*

"Now when an individual enters a strange culture, all or most of these familiar cues are removed. He or she is like a fish out of water. No matter how broadminded or full of good will he may be, a series of props have been knocked from under him. This is followed by a feeling of frustration and anxiety. People react to the frustration in much the same way. *First, they reject the environment which causes the discomfort, 'The ways of the host country are bad because they make us feel bad.'* When Americans or other foreigners in a strange land get together to grouse about the host country and its people, you can be sure they are suffering from culture shock. Another phase of culture shock is *regression.* The home environment suddenly assumes a tremendous importance. To an American everything American becomes irrationally glorified. All the difficulties and problems are forgotten and only the good things back home are remembered. It usually takes a trip home to bring one back to reality.

"Individuals differ greatly in the degree in which culture shock affects them. Although it is not common, there are individuals who cannot live in foreign countries. Those who have seen people go through a serious case of culture shock and on to a satisfactory adjustment can discern steps in the process.

"During the first few weeks, most individuals are fascinated by the new. They stay in hotels and associate with nationals who speak their language and are polite and gracious to foreigners. This honeymoon stage may last from a few days or weeks to six months, depending on circumstances. If one is a very important person, he or she will be shown show places, will be pampered and petted, and in a press interview will speak glowingly about the progress, good will, and international amity, and if he returns home may well write a book about his pleasant if superficial experience abroad.

"But this 'Cook's tour' type of mentality does not normally last if the foreign visitor remains abroad and has seriously to cope with real conditions of life. It is then that the second stage begins, characterized by a hostile and aggressive attitude toward the host country. *This hostility evidently grows out of the genuine difficulty which the visitor experiences in the process of adjustment.* There is mail trouble, school trouble, language trouble, house trouble, transportation trouble, shopping trouble, and the fact that people in the host country are largely indifferent to all these troubles. They help, but they just don't understand your great concern over these difficulties. Therefore, they must be insensible and unsympathetic to you and your worries; the result, 'I just don't like them.' You become aggressive, you band together with your fellow countrymen and criticize the host country, its ways and its people. But this criticism is not an objective appraisal but a derogatory one. *Instead of trying to account for conditions as they are through an honest analysis of the actual conditions and the historical circumstances which have created them, you may talk as if your experiences are more or less created by the people of the host country.* You take refuge in the colony of your countrymen and its cocktail circuit, which often becomes the fountainhead of emotionally charged labels known as stereotypes. This is a peculiar type of invidious shorthand which caricatures the host country and its people in a negative manner. The 'dollar grasping American' is a mild form of stereotyping. The use of stereotypes may salve the ego of someone with a severe case of culture shock, but certainly does not lead to any genuine understanding of the host country and its people. This second stage of culture shock is in a sense a crisis in the disease.

"As the visitor succeeds in getting some knowledge of the language and begins to get around by himself, the beginning of his adjustment to the new cultural environment is taking place. He may still have difficulties but he takes a 'this is my cross and I have to bear it' attitude. Usually in this stage, the visitor begins to become interested in the people of the host country. His sense of humor begins to assert itself. Instead of criticizing, he jokes about the people and even cracks jokes about his or her own difficulties. He or she is now on the way to recovery. And there is also the poor devil who is worse off than yourself whom you can help which in turn gives you confidence in your ability to speak and get around.

"In the final stage of adjustment, the visitor accepts the customs of the host country *as just another way of living.* He can operate within the new milieu without a feeling of anxiety, although there are moments of strain. Only with a complete grasp of all the cues of social intercourse will this strain disappear. *For a long time the individual will understand what the national is saying, but he is not always sure what the national means.* With a complete adjustment, you not only accept the foods, drinks, habits and customs, but actually begin to enjoy them. When you go on home leave, you may even take things back with you, and if you leave for good, you generally miss the country and the people to whom you have become accustomed."

This excellent paper summarizes the key symptoms of culture shock:

(1) First one gets the experience of being lost in a strange environment;

(2) At the same time, one experiences frustration and anxiety;

(3) Then, one has a tendency to reject the environment which creates the discomfort (at this stage many people regress in the sense that they idealize their home culture);

(4) Next, one experiences some hostile and aggressive attitudes towards the host culture;

(5) Some people take refuge in some kind of "cultural ghetto" (the "colony syndrome" reaction);

(6) One starts to adjust in learning about the new culture, getting interested in the people and being able to put things into perspective.

(7) Finally, the visitor accepts the values, beliefs and assumptions of the new culture as "another way" of constructing reality.

All the above points should be discussed and related to the previous exercises.

6. Handouts and Readings:

(a) Handouts:

"Culture Shock and the Problem of Adjustment to New Cultural Environments." (an edited talk by Dr. Kalvero Oberg, anthropologist, Health, Welfare and Housing Divison, United States Operations Mission to Brazil), published by the Foreign Service Institute, Washington, D.C.

"Culture Shock and its Effects on Aid Programmes," by E.D. Wittkower in *Going Abroad: A Guide By, For and About Canadians*, CIDA, Ottawa, 1970.

"Culture Shock and the Cross-Cultural Learning Experience," by P.S. Adler in *Readings in Intercultural Communication, Vol. II*, p. 6.

"Building New Cultures," by R.H. Useem, Michigan State University.

(b) Readings:

Durkheim, E., *Suicide*, New York: A Free Press Paperback, 1951. (p. 241, "Anomie Suicide.")

Friedman, M. and R.H. Rosenman, *Type A Behavior and Your Heart*, New York: A Fawcett Crest Book, 1974.

Rhinesmith, S.H., *Bring Home the World*, New York: Amacom, 1975.

Selye, H., *Stress without Distress*, New York: A Signet Book, 1974.

Triandis, H.C., *The Analysis of Subjective Culture*, New York: John Wiley & Sons, Inc., 1972.

CULTURES: PARADIGMS FOR HUMAN SURVIVAL

A paradigm is a shared set of assumptions. The paradigm is the way we perceive the world, water to the fish. The paradigm explains the world to us and helps us to predict its behavior. When we are in the middle of the paradigm, it is hard to imagine any other paradigm.

— A. Smith

What is a culture? It is basically the product of any human association. We meet, we communicate, we interact and in so doing we create cultures (E. Durkheim). A culture is a paradigm for human survival. It enables human beings to survive. It is basically the product of the interaction between different minds or psyches. It comes from inside as well as outside. It is changing. It is a process and a product. A culture is what we are.

WORKSHOP 4.

1. Aim: To reinforce the participants' awareness regarding cultural realities using a provocative approach.

2. Objectives: Participants will:

(1) Analyze some aspects of the cultural dimension of the human psyche (conceptual framework: input 1).

(2) Experience the day-to-day construction of cultural realities (exercises).

(3) Discuss the statement: "Each individual is a culture in himself or herself" (conceptual framework: input 2).

3. Process:

(a) Have the group read and comment on the following two statements:

"The development of man's psyche and his inherently social way of life thus are bound to each other. Both are the affirmative results of the poor physical equipment with which the human species emerged in the process of evolution. To survive, men needed to use resources other than those available to the individual organism alone. He needed to band together in groups; and he needed to use his mental powers in turning his environment to account. Both of these go together, psyche and society; neither is possible without the other and each bears the marks of the other through and through."

— Ira Progoff *(The Death and*
Rebirth of Psychology, "Alfred Adler
and the Wholeness of Man," pp. 53 and 54.)

"The aim of Jung's theory of the archetypes is to identify and describe those patterns of behavior that are generic to human species in the same way that nest-building is generic to birds...the archetypes signify not 'innate ideas' as he has often been misinterpreted to mean, but simply propensities that are part of human nature just as building dams is part of beaver nature. These archetypal properties are present in the human seed merely as possibilities of action. They are constantly present in the species, and whether or in what manner they will actually be exposed in any given individual depends on the situation of time and place, and on a host of special factors."

— Ira Progoff *(ibid.*
"C.G. Jung at the Outpost
of Psychology," pp. 165-166.)

(b) Ask the group to react to L. Leshan's statement and go through the proposed exercises:

Statement: "It is that what we see and hear around us is at least as much our invention as it is our discovery; that we contribute so much to the existence of the reality of the world we know that we can never separate what we create from what is already 'out there.' From this the next step inexorably follows: there are other ways of creating our contribution to what is real and thereby changing reality. The next step is even harder: We each have a responsibility for creating and maintaining the universe we live in; what the world is like is to a large—and as yet unknown—degree up to us."

— L. Leshan,
Alternate Realities, p. 3.

Issues to be Discussed:

(1) We perceive and discover the world according to our cultural models or maps;

(2) We create "the world" as well as we discover it;

(3) We are *responsible* for creating the world in which we live.

Exercise:

"Would you like to watch yourself creating reality? There is an old, simple method to gain a glimpse of yourself doing this. Take a stick with a knob on the end, something like a walking stick. Hold it straight out in front of your right eye. Close your left eye. Looking straight ahead, slowly move the walking stick in an arc to the right. There is a spot on the retina known as the 'blind spot' that does not have receptors for vision. Soon the knob will be in front of it and you cannot see it. It becomes invisible to you. Since, however, you invent reality as much as you discover it, and the notion of a blank 'hole' in the space you observe does not fit into your ideas as to what is 'out there,' you will not leave a blank space where the knob is. Watch—still looking straight ahead—as you fill in the hole. The edges grow together to fit the background. Whatever colors, lines, etc., are in the background complete themselves to fill in the hole. Shortly it is not there any more. You have erected the 'natural, logical' pattern to fill it in."

— L. Leshan (p. 7).

Another exercise consists of showing the following picture *(Figure 11)* and asking the participants to describe what they see: a meaningless patchwork, a map, a painting...the picture of a man with a beard? After a while, the following description can be given to the group:

"It is the face of a man and it is turned towards you, and occupies the middle third of the upper half of the picture. The top of the picture cuts across the brow so that the top of the head is not shown. The face is lit from the observer's right-hand side so that the eyes are the shadow and the cheeks and chin brightly illuminated. His hair and beard are long, but the chin is clean-shaven and there is a white spot catching the light just above the middle of the picture. A white cloth covers the right shoulder and slopes across the breast; the left shoulder is turned a little away from you and the right upper sleeve is a black area in the lower left part of the picture."

— M.L. Johnson Abercrombie,
*The Anatomy of Judgement: An
Investigation into the Processes
of Perception and Reasoning*, London:
Hutchinson, 1960, p. 25.

For those who cannot "see" the drawing in Figure 11, Figure 12 can be used.

Issues to be discussed:

(1) Identify a set of common reactions towards ambiguity.

Figure 11. The Hidden Man.

Figure 12. The Hidden Man Revealed.

(2) We see what we *want* to see. We create our realities.

(3) Our perceptions are functions of our states of consciousness.

(4) Interpretations are often combined with judgments.

(5) Our past experiences influence our constructions of reality.

(c) Ask the participants to identify three different assumptions regarding the *meaning of work* and discuss their impact on the way people construct reality. The three assumptions can be:

(1) *Work is a moral obligation.* It is painful but it has to be done. One has no choice....

(2) *Work is enjoyable.* It provides pleasure and joy. People should never stop working.

(3) *Work is an opportunity for growth.* Working leads to the actualization of potential, self-development...

(d) L. Leshan contends that one shifts realities all the time. He also believes that the switching process can be managed or controlled.

The group is asked:

(1) To identify the switching process (*i.e.*, our construction of reality largely depends on what we focus upon. If we change our focus we automatically change our construction!) See Leshan, "Do we already know how to shift realities?"

(2) To learn how to control the shifting process. An effective way to experience this is to give the group a "problem-solving" or "decision-making" exercise, and ask them to *monitor* their working construction of reality, *control* the assumptions, values and beliefs which influence the group process, *choose* the cultural framework they want to use in order to achieve the objectives they have selected. (This leads to a discussion on how to assess the intrinsic value of a cultural paradigm.) An instrument we recommend is the "Kidney Machine: Group Decision-Making" exercise (in the *1974 Annual Handbook for Group Facilitators*, p. 78).

4. **Time:** Between three and four hours.

5. Conceptual Framework:

INPUT 1
The Cultural Dimension of the Human Psyche

For C.G. Jung the psyche is basically made of two components: the conscious and the unconscious. *(Figure 13)* Historically speaking, the unconscious comes first and contrary to what many psychologist believe, C.G. Jung claims that at the time of birth it is already fully "charged" with potential patterns of human life that he named *archetypes*.

At the same time that the child is going to develop his or her consciousness through the work of the ego, an activation process is going to take place. Through education and personal experiences (*i.e.*, contacts with already well defined and structured world), the child actualizes some of the archetypes which then become *symbols* or cultural patterns. This actualization, when started, never stops. The ego, or center of consciousness, ensures that the interaction between the inner and outer worlds leads to an unfolding process which enables the individual to become more humane, more cultural and also more unique.

Figure 13. The psyche: the conscious and unconscious parts

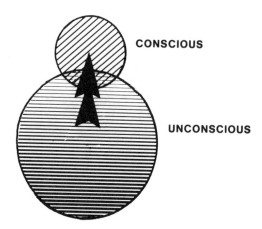

CONSCIOUS

UNCONSCIOUS

C.G. Jung identifies three basic levels in the unconscious, namely the personal unconscious, collective or transpersonal unconscious, and cosmic unconscious. *(Figure 14)* The personal unconscious relates to the individual's past and history. It comprises repressed emotions, feelings and ideas which were accumulated by the individual during childhood and following adult experiences. It is part of the person's uniqueness.

The collective or transpersonal unconscious is made up of all "value orientations" created and shared by all human beings on earth in response to ecological and historial challenges.

The cosmic unconscious is the deepest level of the unconscious and is directly connected with nature and the cosmos. It makes man part of the universe and the universe part of the human psyche.

The transpersonal unconscious of any individual virtually possesses the capacity to produce any kind of pattern of human life in any cultural form one can think of if activated the proper way.

Figure 14. The nature and structure of the unconscious

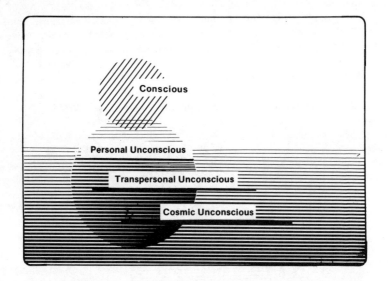

INPUT 2

Each individual is a culture in himself or herself (a model).

The key issues according to the model are:

□ Societies actualize different sets of universals according to their needs. In other words, to survive they "select" among the archetypes those which seem more appropriate to respond to the limitations, constraints and challenges of the environment. (The notion of *SELF* is interpreted differently in different societies.) [20]

---

[20] See E.C. Stewart, *American Cultural Patterns: A Cross-Cultural Perspective,* SIETAR, 1978, pp. 66-74.

INPUT 3

Each individual is a culture in himself or herself (a model)

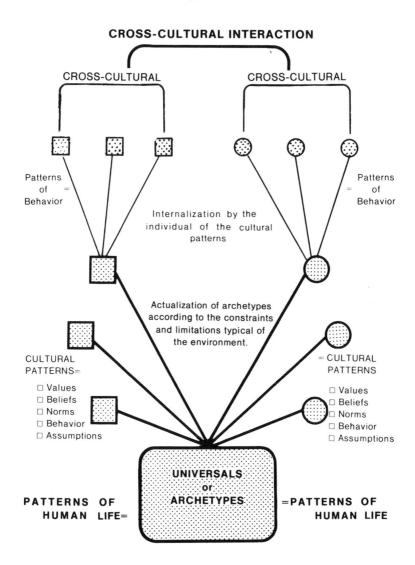

See J. Jacobi, *Complex Archetype Symbols in the Psychology of C.G. Jung,* Princeton: Bollingen Series, 1971.

☐ Actualized universals or *cultural patterns* become sometimes obsolete, inadequate. In order to survive, the society must go back to the storage of universals and activate a new set of archetypes. (A new notion of *SELF* can thus appear in the society.)

☐ Individuals internalize the cultural patterns of their society (values, beliefs, assumptions...) in different ways. People are different.

☐ Since individuals internalize the cultural patterns differently, there is no need for anybody to leave his or her culture in order to experience some kind of cross-cultural interaction. As a matter of fact, each time that two persons meet they are involved in an intercultural communication.

☐ If the model is right, one can find in each individual: (a) what is u-nique and particular to that individual (one cannot find two people completely alike); (b) what is shared with some other people (the values, beliefs, assumptions typical of the culture or micro-culture to which the individual belongs); and (c) what is typical of the human species (the universals of archetypes).

☐ According to this model, cultures and psyches are intimately related. All cultural possibilities exist in any individual psyche. A very few archetypes are used or actualized.

☐ All individuals (human beings) share something in common: the universals or *archetypes* which are the natural products of the human psyche and consist of patterns of human life. They determine what human beings can be and cannot be.

☐ The dialectical interaction between individuals and societies can be described as follows:

"Jung maintains the basic thesis that a society can continue to function effectively only by providing its individuals with meanings in which they can have a living faith. Only then can the psychic energies be directed out into the world and into the socially productive enterprises which a community requires. If a culture fails to maintain psychologically effective symbols, its individuals withdraw from the social areas of life and turn into themselves in search of new meanings." [21]

☐ Through the interaction with other people one can actualize new cultural patterns and activate new universals or archetypes and in so doing become more "humane."

---

[21] I Progoff, *Jung's Psychology and its Social Meaning,* New York: Anchor Books/ Doubleday, 1973, p. 199.

6. Handouts and Readings

(a) Handouts:

"Assumptions about the Nature of Man," *The 1972 Annual Handbook for Group Facilitators*, p. 119.

"Alternatives to Theorizing," *The 1976 Annual Handbook for Group Facilitators*, p. 143.

"Beyond Cultural Identity: Reflections on Cultural and Multicultural Man," by P.S. Adler in *Topics in Culture Learning, Vol. 2*, 1974, East-West Center, Honolulu, HI, pp. 23-40.

"Breaking Out of the Double Bind," G. Bateson, interviewed by D. Goleman, *Psychology Today*, 1978.

(b) Readings:

Bateson, G., *Steps to an Ecology of Mind (A Revolutionary Approach to Man's Understanding of Himself)*, New York: Ballantine Books, 1972.

Berger, P.L. and T. Luckmann, *The Social Construction of Reality*, New York: A Doubleday Book, 1967.

Berger, P.L. and B. Berger, *The Homeless Mind*, New York: Random House, 1973.

Berger, P.L., *Pyramids of Sacrifice*, New York: Anchor Press, 1974.

Castaneda, C., *The Teachings of Don Juan: A Yaqui Way of Knowledge*, New York: Pocket Books, 1975.

Edinger, E.F. *Ego and Archetype*, Baltimore, MD: Penguin Books, 1972.

Hall, E.T., *Beyond Culture*, Garden City, NY: Anchor Books/Doubleday, 1976.

Harding, E., *Psychic Energy: Its Source and its Transformation*, Princeton University Press: Bollingen Series, 1973.

Hegel, G.W.F., *The Phenomenology of Mind*, New York: Harper & Row, 1967.

Ingalls, J.D., *Human Energy*, Reading, MA: Addison-Wesley, 1976.

Jacobi, J., *The Psychology of C.G. Jung*, London: Yale University Press, 1973.

Jung, C.G., *Man and His Symbols*, New York: A Windfall Book/Doubleday, Inc., 1964.

Leshan, L., *Alternate Realities*, New York: Ballantine Books, 1976.

Ornstein, R.E., *The Psychology of Consciousness*, New York: Penguin Books, 1972.

Pearce, J.C., *The Crack in the Cosmic Egg*, New York: Pocket Books, 1977.

Piaget, J., *The Child's Construction of Reality*, London: Routledge & Kegan Paul Ltd., 1955.

Progoff, I., *Jung, Synchronicity and Human Destiny*, New York: A Delta Book, 1973.

Schumacher, E.F., *A Guide for the Perplexed*, New York: Harper & Row, 1977.

Smith, A., *Powers of Mind*, New York: Ballantine Books, 1971 ("This Side of Paradigm," pp. 19-56).

Chapter

3

THE SEARCH FOR MEANING

Man's search for meaning is a primary force in his life and not a 'secondary rationalization of instinctual drive'.

— V.E. Frankl

Meanings are not in words; they are in people. The word "dog" does not bark. The map is not the territory. The map does not represent the entire territory. [22] Human beings are always in search of meaning. Sometimes they stick to socially, culturally approved meanings. They resist change. At other times, they look for new interpretations or new ways of using old words. This process seems to be the grassroots of "human development."

A receptive mind encounters something in nature; the object out there is gradually drawn into the thinking subject; reflection occurs, hypotheses are put forard and tested, a pulse of excitement becomes audible; suddenly, everything coalesces, time stands still for a moment, an image is born out of matter and spirit.

— Paul Gray
writing on L. Thomas's
book *The Medusa and
the Snail, Time,*
May 14, 1973.

WORKSHOP 5.

1. Aim: Reflect upon the need for human beings to attribute meanings to words (very often without being aware of the existence of this process and its impact on human behavior) and to confuse words with realities.

2. Objectives: Participants will:

(1) Experience their very subjective ways of attributing meanings to words (exercises).

---

[22] Korzybski, A., *Science and Sanity,* The International Non-Aristotelian Library Publishing Co., 1933.

(2) Become more aware of the discrepancy which exists between what is, what is perceived and what is said of what is perceived (conceptual framework: input 1).

(3) Analyze two different ways of perceiving (conceptual framework: input 2).

(4) Examine a theory on representational systems (conceptual framework: input 3).

3. Process:

(a) Participants react to an excerpt from the dialogue between Alice and Humpty-Dumpty: [23]

— "I don't know what you mean by 'glory'," Alice said.

— Humpty Dumpty smiled contemptuously: "Of course you don't— till I tell you. I meant there's a nice knockdown argument for you."

— "But 'glory' doesn't mean 'a nice knockdown argument'," Alice objected.

— "When I use a word," Humpty Dumpty said, in rather a scornful tone, "it means just what I choose it to mean—neither more nor less."

— "The question is," said Alice, "Whether you can make words mean so many different things."

— "The question is," said Humpty Dumpty, "which is to be master— that's all."

(b) Ask the group to discuss the following four statements:

The question arises, what do we mean by a real name? The answer is that there is no such thing. Our belief in real names originates in a kind of semantic illusion, sometimes referred to as the principle of identity. One of mankind's deepest intuitions is to respond to the symbols he invents as if they 'are' whatever it is that he invented them to symbolize...with a few variations, people from all kinds of cultures invent names with an almost magical dimension.

— Neil Postman

We want to do something, and a definition is a means of doing it. If we want certain results, then we must use certain meanings (or definitions). But no definition has any authority apart from purpose, or to bar us from other purposes.

— I.A. Richards

Meaning may be regarded as an approximate synonym of pattern, redundancy, information, and 'restraint,' within a paradigm of the following sort: Any aggregate of events or objects, (*e.g.*, a sequence of phonemes, a painting, or a

---

[23] Carroll, Lewis (Charles Dodgson), *Alice's Adventures in Wonderland, Through the Looking Glass,* and *The Hunting of the Snark,* The Modern Library, 1925, pp. 246-247.

frog, or a culture) shall be said to contain 'redundancy' for 'pattern' if the aggregate can be divided in any way by a 'slash mark,' such that an observer viewing only what is on one side of the slash mark can guess with better than random success, what is on the other side of the slash mark. We may say that what is on one side of the slash contains information or has meaning about what is on the other side.

— G. Bateson

Serious breakdowns in communication can be attributed to the false assumption that there is meaning in the message, rather than only in the source and receiver...Words do not mean at all. Only people mean, and people do not mean the same by all words.

— D. Berlo

(c) Ask each participant to write a short sentence on the "meaning of culture shock" or on the "meaning of meaning." Next, everybody *unpacks* [23a] each word of the sentance, meaning:

□ each word is examined and defined using free associations (what would you have meant?).

□ alternative words are looked for (what would you have said instead?).

□ freewheel reactions are encouraged (what is each word leading to?).

When each participant has accomplished the unpacking, trios are set up and some sharing takes place.

The purposes of the entire exercise are both to discover that words are loaded with *psychic energy* and that multiple meanings are contained in the words used in day-to-day conversation (including intra-conversation).

(d) Participants read the statement below and answer two questions:

(1) Relate the "reification" process to your own experience. [24]

(2) Analyze the relationship between reification and culture shock.

Man, the producer of a world, is apprehended as its product, and human activity as an epiphenomenon of non-human processes. Human meanings are no longer understood as world-producing but as being, in their turn, products of the 'nature of things.' It must be emphasized that reification is a modality of consciousness, more precisely, a modality of man's objectification of the human world. Even while apprehending the world in verified terms, man

---

[23a] We call this exercise the *unpacking exercise.* I am grateful to Professor O. White of the University of North Carolina for having given me the opportunity to experience this approach and to learn a great deal from it.

[24] *Reification* is the process by which human beings understand and perceive the products of their activities as if they were something other than human products.

continues to produce it. That is, man is capable paradoxically of producing a reality that denies him.

— P.L. Berger and T. Luckman

(e) *By-passing exercise.* By-passing is the process by which one assumes that someone who says something means what one would have meant if one had said the same thing. In most cases, one is wrong and one is not aware of the discrepancy. As N. Postman puts it:

> All communication depends, to some extent, on projection. In order to make any sense at all of what people are saying, we must assume that they are using words roughly in the same way we do. We put other people in our skins, so to speak, and, therefore, to some extent, all our conversations are dialogues with ourselves, creations of our own imagination.

And he adds:

> Since communication depends on an assumption of shared, predictable meanings, we are easily lead to believe that words, themselves, have meanings, and fixed ones at that. But if there is anything certain in the whole field of human talk, it is that words do not have meanings. People do. And because people are different and perceive their purposes in different ways, the meanings they assign to words are not only not fixed by have wide validity.

Illustrations can be provided by:

(1) Giving a sentence to the group (*i.e.,* "each individual is a culture in himself or herself") and asking the participants to check the meaning of the sentence with the facilitator.

(2) Asking each participant to write down a sentence which relates to culture shock (a personal experience, reaction, perception), exchange that sentence with another member of the group who has to give his or her own interpretation of the sentence so that the eventual distortion and discrepancy can be pinpointed. The exercise is repeated a second time with the other person's sentence.

(3) Splitting the group into trios and having them do the following:

☐ Select a topic for discussion.

☐ One member starts to speak about the topic and systematically repeats himself or herself saying: "what I mean is..."

☐ Another member listens and systematically asks the question, "what do you mean?"

☐ The third member plays the role of the observer and watches the impact of the process upon (a) the people involved in the communication, and (b) the quality of the exchange.

4. Time: Between two and three hours.

5. Conceptual Framework:

INPUT 1

The "General Semantics" Model [25]

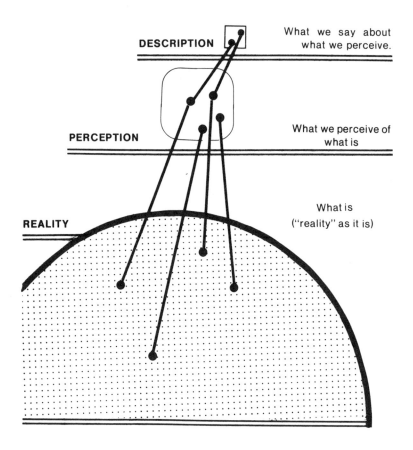

DESCRIPTION — What we say about what we perceive.

PERCEPTION — What we perceive of what is

REALITY — What is ("reality" as it is)

[25] Bulla de Villaret, H., *Introduction à la Sémantique Générale de Korzybski*, Le Courrier du Livre, Paris, 1965, p. 53-63.

There are several biases and distortions in perceiving reality and teaching about it:

(1) We always miss a great deal of what's going on around us.

(2) We leave out many things we see when we talk about our perceptions to other people.

(3) People who listen to us only hear parts of what we say.

(4) Listeners leave out many details of what we said when they have to repeat it.

A few key issues to be discussed:

☐ The more abstract we are the farther we are from "reality."

☐ What I say is not what I saw. What you say about an event is not what happened.

☐ Most people are not conscious of the fact that they distort "reality."

☐ Since we create our own experience of reality, we can change or modify it at will.

☐ Past experiences have a great influence on our construction of realities.

☐ We never can perceive everything of what's going on.

INPUT 2
Two Different Ways of Perceiving (C.G. Jung's Model)

According to C.G. Jung, there are two different ways of perceiving or getting information from the inner or outer world into our psyche.

The Psychic Compass: Two Perceiving Functions

SENSES

INTUITION

(a) *Senses.* We can use our five senses to identify reality (we hear, see, smell, touch and taste. When we approach a situation using our sensing function, we try to be as factual, objective, neutral, accurate as possible. We focus upon the facts. We try to understand what is as it is. We are present-oriented.

(b) *Intuition.* We can also use our imagination to observe what's going on. In this case, we use our imagination and go beyond the facts to guess the ultimate realities. We look for possibilities and opportunities which are inherent to the situation. We project ourselves into the future.

A few issues to be discussed:

□ Each individual possesses the two perceiving functions in his or her psyche.

□ One cannot use the two functions at the same time.

□ There is a function that one feels more comfortable with and that one uses more often. It is the *dominant* function.

□ The dominant perceiving function has been reinforced by the culture to which the individual belongs.

□ Perceptions can be cross-cultural by the simple fact that one handles data differently.

□ One can learn to reinforce the use of the less used perceiving function.

INPUT 3
A Theory on Representational Systems

J. Grinder and R. Bandler have designed a new approach towards understanding our construction of realities. They call it "representational systems or other maps for the same territory." [26] The four representational systems are:

(1) *The Visual System.*

The construction of reality is based upon (a) visual representations or pictures that we make out of the information we receive, and (b) the selection of the visual components of the observed situation.

In order to identify the visual system, ask the following *questions:*

□ Do you make pictures in your head? [27]

---

[26] Grinder, J. and R. Bandler, *Frogs into Princes (Neuro Linguistic Programming), Real People Press, MOAB, 1979, p. 25.*

[27] Shorr, J.E., *Go See the Movie Inside Your Head,* New York: Popular Library, 1977.

☐ Can you visualize (or see) what I am talking about?

(2) *The Kinesthetic System.*

This system is characterized by the body *sensations* that an experience creates within ourselves.

Questions:

☐ What do you feel when you are speaking?

☐ Are you "in touch" with what someone else is saying?

(3) *The Auditory System.*

Perceptions are based on audition or auditory inputs (sounds).

Questions:

☐ Do you hear sounds and voices in your head?

☐ Can you hear what I say inside your head?

(4) *The Language or Linguistic Respresentational System.*

This means that we use language to describe the three other representational systems.

Questions:

☐ Check the words or predicates (especially the verbs, adjectives, and adverbs) that you use most. Are they words such as see, hear, listen, touch, feel, look, say, talk, read, tell, show ? These words give you some clue about your utilization of the three main representational maps that all human beings possess.

Key issues to be discussed:

☐ Human beings can shift from one representational system to another (I make pictures out of the sounds that I hear).

☐ The four "input channels" are needed to have a more or less accurate, objective representation of reality.

☐ Intuitive people have a tendency to over-use the linguistic system.

☐ Sensing people like to use the visual and auditory systems.

☐ People have a representational system that they value more than the others.

☐ Representational systems are culturally biased:

—*Some cultures are, for example, more* visual *than others.*

—*The way the operational system is used is particular to the culture* (e.g., Zen people hear and see things that nobody else notices).

6. Handouts and Readings:

(a) Handouts:

"The Awareness Wheel," *The 1976 Annual Handbook for Group Facilitators,* p. 120.

"Meaning and Behavior: Communication and Culture," by E.S. Glenn, in *Intercultural Communication: A Reader,* Samovar and Porter (eds.), Belmont, CA: Wadsworth Publishing Co., 1972, pp. 123-141.

"People Who Read People," by D. Goleman, in *Psychology Today,* July, 1979.

"Neurolinguistic Programming: The Answer to Change?" by D. Maron in *Training and Development Journal,* October 1979, pp. 68-71.

(b) Readings:

Bandler, R. and J. Grinder, *Frogs into Princes,* Real People Press, 1979.

Capra, F., *The Tao of Physics,* Boulder, CO: Shambhala, 1975.

Cameron-Bandler, L., *They Lived Happily Ever After,* Cupertino, CA: META Publications, 1978.

Fabun, D., *Three Roads to Awareness,* Beverly Hills, CA: Glencoe Press, 1970.

McCoy, J.T., *The Management of Time,* Englewood Cliffs, NJ: Prentice Hall, Inc., 1959.

Penfield, W., *The Mystery of the Mind,* Princeton, NJ: Princeton University Press, 1975.

Sapir, E., *Culture, Language and Personality,* Berkeley, CA: University of California Press, 1943.

Singer, J., *Boundaries of the Soul (The Practice of Jung's Psychology),* New York: Anchor Books, 1973.

Thomas, L., *The Lives of a Cell (Notes of a Biology Watcher),* New York: Bantam Books, Inc., 1974.

Whorf, B.L., *Language, Thought and Reality,* Cambridge, MA: MIT Press, 1956.

4

THE MEANING OF COMMUNICATION

Definitions are not statements of fact, they do not describe the physical cal words, they have no moral value, they cannot be considered correct or incorrect. Definitions are expressions that suggest the meaning a person intended to attach to a word or other symbol.

— D. Berlo

Defining is *giving* sense to something. Defining is also looking for meanings. There are two different cultural ways to define defining: either you look for what is already there or you "load" it with what you *believe* it is.

Communication is the process by which two individuals "try" to exchange a set of ideas, feelings, symbols meanings.

Intercultural communication is the process by which two individuals who do not belong to the same culture "try" to exchange a set of meanings. The mere fact that the two individuals do not belong to the same culture implies that they do not share the same assumptions, beliefs, values, or, to put it differently, the same ways of thinking, feeling and behaving. This phenomenon makes the communication process much more difficult and challenging than we think.

WORKSHOP 6.

1. Aim: Clarify the intercultural dimension of the communication process.

2. Objectives: Participants will:

(1) Analyze two illustrations of cultural differences and their impact on communication (exercises);

(2) Examine three approaches regarding intercultural communication (conceptual framework: input 1).

3. Process:

(a) Below is the description of two opposite ways of perceiving the world.

☐ analyze the impact of each assumption on the way people communicate.

☐ examine the communication process between two individuals who disagree on how to perceive the world.

☐ seek other cultural options regarding the perception of the world.

EXTROVERT WAY	INTROVERT WAY
1. There is a world "out there." An objective world. It exists by itself.	1. There is no world "out there." Everything is subjective. Everything exists in people's minds.
2. Development requires going out there, understanding the world in scientific terms and coming up with the right techniques and methods in order to manage the world.	2. Development requires a better understanding of the way one constructs realities so that we become more able to "manage" our own cultural paradigms.
3. To manage the world implies to plan, organize, and above all, control the dynamics of the situations one has to deal with.	3. To manage one's own psychological and cultural constructions of realities implies self-awareness, psychic understanding and control.

(b) Two sets of assumptions about the meaning of life are presented to the group, which discusses them (see next page).

Participants are asked to:

☐ discuss the two models in terms of their respective "advantages and disadvantages."

☐ design a "self-assessment exercise" which would help people determine what their dominant paradigm is.

☐ examine the implications of switching from one paradigm to another.

☐ use the same two models but replace the word "life" with "development."

4. Time: About two hours.

THE MEANING OF LIFE: TWO CULTURAL PARADIGMS

| THE STAIRCASE MODEL | THE ROLLER COASTER MODEL |

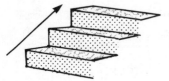 

PREMISES

The goal in life is to reach the top of the staircase.

In order to get there one has to work hard, be patient, think positively, endure temporary hardship, persevere through adversity, look for support.

There will be pain along the way but at the end of the process are roads to the top of the staircase and one can at least *enjoy*.

One can choose.

One can control the process.

One is responsible for the outcome.

Planning is critical.

BASIC ASSUMPTIONS

Permanence is the only good. The golden room at the top of the staircase is what counts.

To speed up the process is the key to success.

Good things are those which lead toward the top.

Just as there is one permanent place to ascend to, there is one permanent *self* who lives forever.

PREMISES

Life is like a roller coaster. It goes up. It goes down. It never stops. It never runs backwards.

One does not control the ride. One does not even know what's ahead.

Enjoy the ride is the key rule.

If one is down, it is not too bad because what is down must come up.

If one is up, one is careful because one knows that what is up must come down.

The process (journey) is what counts. One is not responsible.

One flows with the forces. One doesn't choose.

BASIC ASSUMPTIONS

Change is the only permanence.

There is no golden room.
You do not speed up. You just ride the roller coaster.

Good things exist everywhere. But they do not last.

To survive and enjoy life, one needs a mobile, changing *self*.

5. Conceptual Framework:

INPUT 1

Three maps to look at intercultural communication.

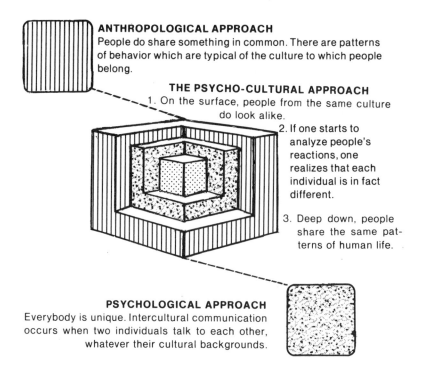

ANTHROPOLOGICAL APPROACH
People do share something in common. There are patterns of behavior which are typical of the culture to which people belong.

THE PSYCHO-CULTURAL APPROACH
1. On the surface, people from the same culture do look alike.
2. If one starts to analyze people's reactions, one realizes that each individual is in fact different.
3. Deep down, people share the same patterns of human life.

PSYCHOLOGICAL APPROACH
Everybody is unique. Intercultural communication occurs when two individuals talk to each other, whatever their cultural backgrounds.

6. Handouts and Readings:

(a) Handouts:

Porter, R.E. and L.A. Samovar, *Intercultural Communication Research: Where do we go from here? Readings in Intercultural Communication*, Pittsburgh, PA: The Intercultural Communication Network of the Regional Council for International Education, Vo. III, 1973, p. 2.

Porter, R.E., "An Overview of Intercultural Communication, in Samovar & Porter, *Intercultural Communication: A Reader*, Belmont, CA: Wadsworth Publishing Co., 1972, p. 3.

Singer, M.R. "Culture: A Perceptual Approach in Readings in Intercultural Communications," Vol. 1, SIETAR, p. 11.

Readings:

Berlo, D., *The Process of Communication (An Introduction to Theory and Practice)*, San Francisco: Rinehart Press, 1960.

Rhinesmith, S.H., *Cultural-Organizational Analysis (The Interrelationship of Value Orientations and Managerial Behavior)*, Cambridge, MA: McBer & Co., 1970.

Smith, A.G. (ed.), *Communication and Culture (Readings in the Codes of Human Interactions)*, New York: Holt, Rinehart & Winston, 1966.

Chapter

5

COMMUNICATING ABOUT COMMUNICATION

Honest and sincere men in the field continue to fail to grasp the true significance of the fact that culture controls behavior in deep and pointing ways, many of which are outside of awareness and therefore beyond conscious control of the individual.

— E.T. Hall

Communication is a situation in which people participate, rather like the way a plant participates in what we call its growth.

— N. Postman

Communication is more than communication: Culture is communication (E. Hall). Communication is by its very nature intercultural as we have seen before. Two remarks are in order: (a) we must realize that after many years and even centuries of research on communication between human beings, we still don't know why we do not understand each other, and (b) the "miracle" is that despite the fact that we don't know that we don't know, we are still able to communicate and get along with other peple. Therefore, it would seem that we know more than we think. The problem is maybe that we do not know that we know!

Using the "American approach" (meaning a more *factual* way of talking about communication), let us examine five facts regarding intercultural communication.

WORKSHOP 7.

1. Aim: To examine five facts about communication and their impact on cross-cultural interaction.

2. Objectives: Participants will:

(1) Analyze five facts which are closely related to intercultural communication (exercises).

(2) Relate their workshop experiences to three communication models (conceptual framework: inputs 1, 2, and 3).

3. Process:

(a) *Fact No. 1: PURE COMMUNICATION IS IMPOSSIBLE.*

By this it is meant that it is impossible for any individual to transfer 100% of what is in his or her mind into somebody else's mind. Participants are asked to comment upon the following illustrations which document the above statement.

☐ *What I say is not what I mean.* (There is always a gap between what I would like to say and what I actually say; the words that I use do not "translate" exactly the thoughts that I have; sometimes my thoughts are not clear and I clarify them in going through the process of explaining something to another person.)

☐ *What you hear is not what I say and certainly not what I mean.* (Meanings are not in words but in people. Consequently, the same words can have completely different meanings.)

☐ *I attach* experiential *and* emotional *connotations to words.* (A good and powerful exercise consists of asking the participants to identify words which are emotionally loaded for them.)

☐ *The meaning of what I say is a function of the* "semantic environment" *to which I belong at the time I say it.* Semantic environments are made up of situations in which we are involved and the rules by which we are expected to behave. From a cross-cultural point of view, it should be noticed that (a) situations or semantic environments are differently identified by different people. (A workshop can be perceived as a T-group exercise by someone and as a seminar involving no sensitivity training whatsoever by someone else.) (b) The rules which are typical of the identified situation are very often loosely interpreted.

Two exercises can be proposed to the participants in the workshop:

(1) Participants are asked to define the rules typical of a few semantic environments, *i.e.*, talking in the street, meeting someone for the first time, talking about politics, religion, development, asking for a promotion (the approach should be intercultural and comparative in the sense that identical situations should be selected so that the variations in terms of the cultural rules can be analyzed).

Specific suggestions can be addressed by the group:

☐ What do you say in an elevator? in a church?

☐ Find a dichotomy between what is said in a situation and what is supposed to be said. (The dichotomy will presumably be due to the difference between the purposes of the situation and the intentions of the individual.)

☐ Identify the two semantic environments to which the following sentences relate:

— 1 want to be responsible for my own development.

— I want to be responsibile for my own development.

— Obey orders.

— Take initiative.

☐ Find examples of conflicts between two semantic environments which occupy the same space-time.

(2) Each participant describes a situation he or she knows without using any of the terms which are typical of the semantic environment (education, technical assistance, management, intercultural communication, etc.).

(b) Fact No. 2: WE COMMUNICATE ALL THE TIME.

We never stop sending messages to other people and receiving signals from them. In most cases we are not aware of this fact and consequently we do not control the process.

Exercises to become aware of our silent language:

☐ Tell the group to be silent and stop thinking for one minute. The exercise illustrates that (a) it is almost impossible not to think (that leads to the question: "who is in charge?") and (b) that there are many things which exist in the environment of which we are not aware in our "normal" states of existence. (We screen all the time.)

☐ Ask them not to think about "THE PINK ELEPHANT."

☐ Define words which exist in one language and not in another (*background* in French, *detente* in English)

☐ Analyze idiomatic expressions such as "off the top of my head," "beating around the bush," "to bite the bullet," "to get the picture," "to have a ball"....

☐ Participants are asked to interlock their fingers, check which thumb is in the upper position, switch to the other position and become aware of their uneasiness (most gestures are performed unconsciously).

☐ Analyze what we say to other people through the way we dress, wear jewelry, touch each other, carry our bodies, look at each other (eye contact), manipulate space, time.

☐ The following *case study* is given to the group:

The school day ended. Tired Miss Larson took her classroom problems home with her and shared her concerns with friends at an informal cocktail party; shared her frustration over teaching English in the Ethiopian government school: "For three years, I've tried to get those dear little girls to behave like normal human beings, to have some pride, to hold up their heads, look me in the face, and answer a question in a voice I can hear without straining. They're so bright; they learn as fast as the children back home, but they're hopeless, absolutely hopeless. They just can't seem to learn to behave with human dignity. For all the good I've done here, I might as well have stayed home in Iowa and continued to teach there." The school day ended. Kebedetch walked stiffly home. The strange steel she had forced into her neck-muscles seemed to have spread throughout her body. She felt rigid, brave and frightened. Entering the *gojo* (small house or hut), Kebedetch was greeted warmly. Father asked the usual, daily question: "What did you learn today?" Kebedetch threw back her head, looked her father in the eye, and proclaimed in a loud, clear voice, "Ethiopia is composed of twelve provinces plus the Federated State of Eritrea...." Momma and Poppa talked late that night. What had happened to Kebedetch? She was no longer behaving as a normal human being. "Did you notice how she threw back her head like a man?" asked Poppa; "What has happened to her shyness as a woman?" "And her voice," added Momma, "How happy I am that our parents were not present to hear a daughter of ours speak with the voice of a foreigner." "She showed no modesty; she seemed to feel no pride. If she were normal, she would be ashamed to raise her head like that, being a girl-child, and to speak so loud as that," Poppa added with a deep sigh. "Kebedetch has learned so much," said Momma, "She knows more than I, and this has given me great joy. But if her learnings are making of her a strange, ungentle, beast-like person, I do not want her to learn more; she is my only daughter." Poppa pondered. Finally he shook his head and spoke. "You are right, Mebrat, our daughter must not return to school. The new education is not good, but only the strongest can survive. I had hoped Kebedetch could learn and remain normal and gentle, could become a woman of dignity. The frightening behavior or hers tonight has convinced me. She has lost her sense of pride, lost her sense of shame, lost her dignity. She must never return to the school. We shall try to help her find herself again.

> — E. Lord in *Examples of Cross-Cultural*
> *Problems Encountered by Americans*
> *Working Overseas: An Instructor's*
> *Handbook*, Alexandria, VA: HumRRO, May 1965,
> pp. 2-27.

Issues to be discussed: Identify and analyze the different meanings and values attached to the body language.

☐ Express the following set of feelings and emotions only using gestures: **anger, sadness, trust, joy**

☐ The tone of the voice as well as the emphasis we place on the words have special meanings. Analyze the following sentence as if the emphasis were placed on each word at a time: I LIKE MY JOB

I like my job = there are other people who do not like their jobs.

I **like** my job = do you have the impression that I don't like my job?

I like **my** job = it is my property; I might not like another job.

I like my **job** = there are other things that I do not like.

(c) *Fact No. 3: WE SEE THINGS WHICH DO NOT EXIST.*

We discover things according to the *cultural map* we have in our minds. Sometimes our model leads us to see things which do not exist.

Exercises:

☐ Ask the participants to join the nine points with four straight lines without lifting up their pencils:

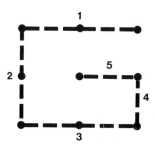

For the sake of the exercises, it is important that the trainer show beforehand what is meant by "joining the nine points." The demonstration can go as follows:

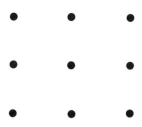

This is wrong because one more than four straight lines were used. Give up to three minutes to the group to solve the problem. The solution is given and the reactions of the participants are discussed and commented upon.

(1) *Solution to the problem:*

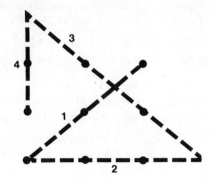

(2) *Analysis of the group's reaction:*

—You went out of the frame. It is unfair.

—Which frame? Nobody said that there was a frame.

—Well, yes, the facilitator did indeed put a frame into the participants' minds when showing how to solve the problem (demonstration).

—We see things (frames) which do not exist.

—We perceive according to the cultural paradigm that we have.

—Our paradigm comes from our educational and cultural as well as psychological experiences.

—To see anew requires a re-consideration of our cultural paradigm.

□ The group analyzes the following two statements:

...we are all somewhat in love with our ways of talking about the world, whatever deformities such talk might have, and it takes some doing to convince any of us that our favorite sentences often betray our best interests.

— N. Postman

No one can tell anything 'like it is.' In the first place, 'it' isn't anything until someone names it. In the second place, the way in which 'it' is named recalls not the way it is but how the namer wishes to see it or how he is capable of seeing it. And think, how it has been named becomes the reality for the namer and all who accept the name. But it need not be our reality.

— N. Postman

□ The group must transform the Roman numeral IX into six, adding only one line.

Solution: **S** ix

☐ Participants are asked to find an answer to the following problem:

"Many years ago when a person who owed money could be thrown into jail, a merchant in London had the misfortune to owe a huge sum to a money-lender. The money-lender, who was old and ugly, fancied the merchant's beautiful teenage daughter. He proposed a bargain. He said he would cancel the merchant's debt if he could have the girl instead. Both the merchant and his daughter were horrified at the proposal. So the cunning money-lender proposed that they let Providence decide the matter. He told them he would put a black pebble and a white pebble into an empty money-bag, and then the girl would have to pick out one of the pebbles. If she chose the black pebble she would become his wife and her father's debt would be cancelled. If she chose the white pebble she would stay with her father and the debt would still be cancelled. But if she refused to pick out a pebble, her father would be thrown into jail and she would starve. Reluctantly the merchant agreed. They were standing on a pebble-strewn path in the merchant's garden as they talked, and the money-lender stooped down to pick up the two pebbles. As he picked up the pebbles, the girl, sharp-eyed with fright, noticed that he picked up two black pebbles and put them in the money-bag. He then asked the girl to pick out the pebble that was to decide her fate and that of her father.

Imagine that you are standing on that path in the merchant's garden. What would you have done if you had been the unfortunate girl? If you had to advise her, what would you have advised her to do?
— E. deBono. *The Use of Lateral Thinking*, London: Jonathan Cape, Thirty Bedford Square, 1967, pp. 11-12.

Issue to be discussed:

When trying to solve the problem, stop from time to time and analyze the *basic assumptions* that you have and which prevent you from finding a solution.

A possible solution:

The girl in the pebble story put her hand into the money-bag and drew out a pebble. Without looking at it she fumbled and let it fall to the path where it was immediately lost among the others. "Oh, how clumsy of me," she said, "but never mind—if you look into the bag you will be able to tell which pebble I took by the colour of the one that is left."

☐ Another excellent illustration of the fact that we sometimes see things which do not exist is the "Herman Grid." *(Figure 15)*

Look at the squares and you will see gray dots appearing at the intersections of the horizontal and vertical white lines.

Figure 15. The Herman Grid

Also look at *Figures 16* and *17:*

— Are the two grays identical? (Yes, they are.)
— Are the lines parallel? (Yes, they are.)

Figure 16. Are the two grays identical?

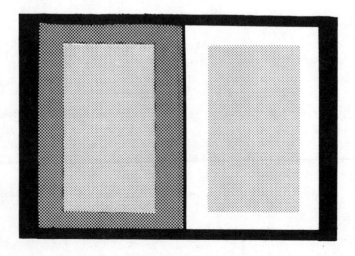

Figure 17. Are the two lines parallel?

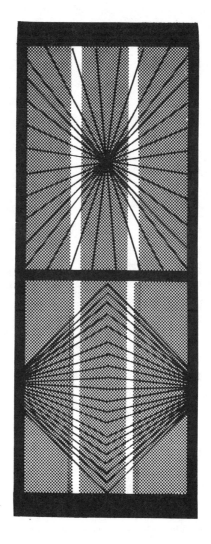

(d) *Fact No. 4: WE DO NOT SEE THINGS WHICH EXIST.*

Two exercises can be used in order to illustrate the fact that there are things which exist and of which we are not aware:

☐ Participants read the three statements which are reproduced on a flipchart or blackboard.

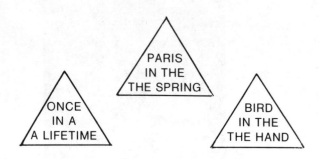

(After R. Books in *The Anatomy of Judgment: An Investigation into the Process of Perception and Meaning,* Hutchinson of London: J. Abercrombie, 1960, p. 28.)

Most people do not see the duplication of the article in each statement (Paris in **the the** spring; Once in **a a** lifetime; Bird in **the the** hand).

Issues to be discussed:

—We see what we want to see;

—We perceive according to what we have been trained to see;

—We always try to make sense out of what we see;

—We see what fits our map.

☐ The second exercise is called "look for the bird." *(Figures 18 and 19).*

To perceive the bird in this picture the eye needs to classify some parts of the pattern as background and some as the animal. If may be that the pictorial recognition difficulties observed in some cultures are essentially of this nature. More complex problems arise when a picture makes several mutually exclusive classificatory schemes possible.

— *Illusion in Nature and Art,*
edited by R.L. Gregory and E.M. Gombrich,
London: Duckworth, 1973, p. 160.

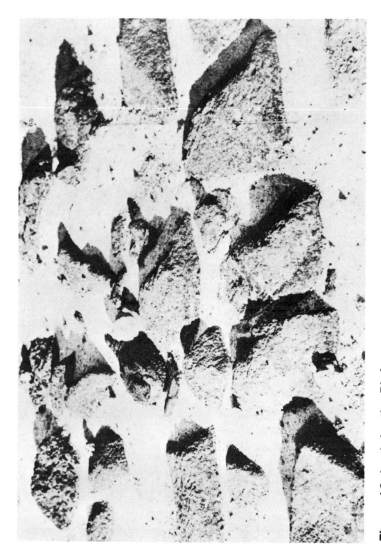

Figure 19. Look for the Bird.

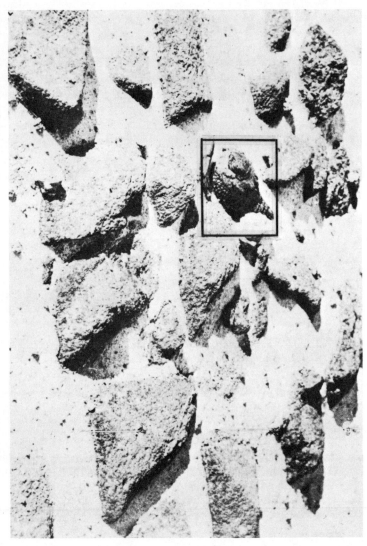

Figure 20. The Bird Identified.

(e) *Fact No. 5: WE PERCEIVE DIFFERENTLY.*

Ask the group to look at the picture in Figure 20 and see the old and young ladies who are represented. After a couple of minutes, the trainer checks with the group who can see the young lady, the old one, or both. A participant who can see both is then asked to explain to those who can see only one where the other face is. The trainer maintains some tension during the exercise by (a) requesting the participant who tries to show where the two faces are to continue his or her effort until *everybody* in the group can see what he or she sees, and (b) by saying from time to time: "By now, everybody should be able to see both." The following points are discussed during the de-briefing session:

(1) Perceptions are always different. Sometimes the gap between two individuals' perception is small. Sometimes it is huge. Most of the time people are not aware of the existing perceptual gap.

(2) It is not easy to explain to others what we see so naturally ("it is obvious").

(3) It is not easy to perceive exactly what somebody else sees despite our efforts to practice *empathy*.

(4) Points two and three bring up frustration and value judgments ("Are they stupid that they cannot see what I see?" or, "What's wrong with him or her that I cannot understand the explanation and see what's there on the picture?")

(5) Participants are able to observe the "group think phenomenon." The more people can see both faces, the more difficult it becomes for people to admit that they are still unable to see what the others can see. After a while, the social or group pressure becomes such that some people say that they can see even when it is not true.

□ The same points can be made with the picture in Figure 21.

□ The second exercise is a classic. The facilitator askes for five volunteers. All leave the room with the exception of one, who has a look at the following picture *(Figure 22)* and prepares himself or herself for the next phase of the exercise.

Volunteers are brought back into the room, one by one. The first volunteer explains to the second what the picture is all about. The second to the third and so on until the fifth participant, who is asked to explain to the group (observers) what the picture is all about. The observers are entitled to look at the picture during the entire exercise.

Issues to be discussed:

(1) We change or distort the meaning of what we look at.

(2) We select things when observing a situation (we screen or subtract elements of the picture).

(3) We add up things which do not exist (we see things which are not "out there").

Summary of the five facts which influence intercultural communication:

(1) Pure communication is impossible.

(2) We communicate all the time.

(3) We see things which do not exist.

(4) We do not see things which do exist.

(5) We perceive differently.

The conclusion is that we *construct* or *create* our realities regarding communication as we do for other processes (as treated in Chapter 2).

4. Time: Two or three hours.

5. Conceptual Framework:

INPUT 1

The Distortion of Information when Communicating [28]

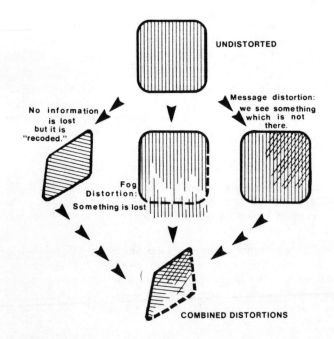

---

[28] "The Distortion of Information," by J.R. Kirk and G.D. Talbot, in *Communication and Culture* (A. Smith, ed.), pp. 308-321.

Figure 20. Where are the two ladies?

Picture designed by the American psychologist E.G. Boring.

DEPICTION OF THE OLD LADY

DEPICTION OF THE YOUNG LADY

Figure 21. What do you see?

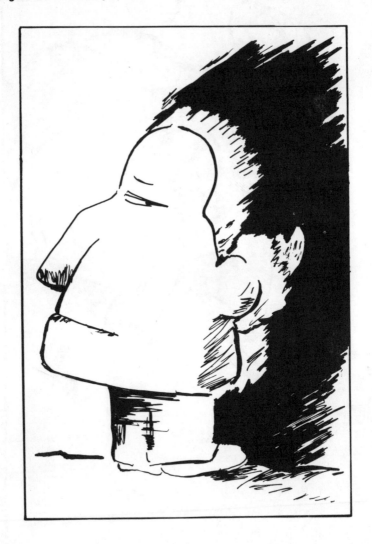

Eskimo or Indian?

Figure 23. At the Door.

INPUT 2

A Communication Model

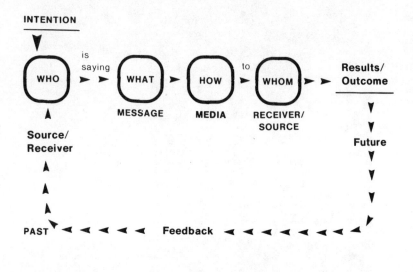

The *effectiveness* of the communication process is a function of (D. Berlo):

— the communication skills of the partners involved.
— their attitudes.
— their knowledge and knowhow.
— their status (the social system).
— their cultural norms (including the ones regarding communication).

INPUT 3

A Cross-Cultural Communication Model

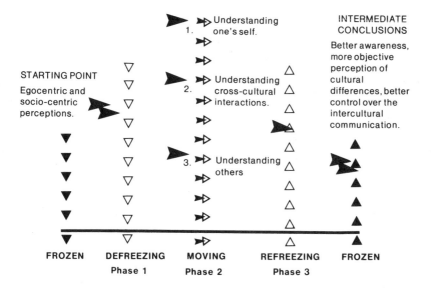

6. Handouts and Readings:

(a) Handouts:

Brewer, M.D., *Perceptual Processes in Cross-Cultural Interaction: An Overview of the State-of-the-Art*, Santa Barbara, CA: University of California, February 1977.

DiPietro, R.J., *The Function of Language in Cross-Cultural Interactions: An Overview*, Chicago: SIETAR Conference, February 1977.

Hall, E., "How Cultures Collide," in *Psychology Today*, June, 1976.

Hall, E., "Learning the Arabs' Silent Language," in *Psychology Today*, August, 1979.

Hall, E., "The Silent Language," in *Overseas Business*, HBR, May-June 1960.

Levis, G., *Preliminary Overview: Nonverbal Communication and Inter-cultural Education*, New Mexico: University of New Mexico, 1977.

"Nonverbal Communication and the Intercultural Encounter," *The 1975 Annual Handbook for Group Facilitators*, p. 155.

Singer, M.R., "Culture: A Perceptual Approach," in *Readings in Inter-cultural Communication (Vol. 1)*, Regional Council for International Education, University of Pittsburgh (D. Hoopes, ed.).

Stewart, E.C., *Outline of Intercultural Communication*, Washington, DC: The BCIU Institute, American University, Winter 1973.

(b) Readings:

Fast, J., *Body Language*, Philadelphia: M. Evans & Co., Inc., 1970.

Goffman, E., *The Presentation of Self in Everyday Life*, New York: Anchor Books, 1959.

Gregory, R.L., *The Intelligent Eye*, New York: McGraw-Hill, 1970.

Hall, E.T., *The Silent Language*, New York: Anchor Books, 1959.

Hall, E.T., *The Hidden Dimension*, New York: Anchor Books, 1959.

Hayakawa, S.I., *Language in Thought and Action*, New York: Harcourt, Brace, 1949.

Knapp, M.L., *Nonverbal Communication in Human Interaction*, New York: Holt, Rinehart & Winston, 1978.

Miller, G.A., *The Psychology of Communication*, New York: Basic Books Publishers, 1967.

Morris, D., *The Human Zoo*, New York: McGraw-Hill, 1969.

Morris, D., *Manwatching (A Field Guide to Human Behavior)*, New York: Harry N. Abrame, Inc., Publisher, 1977.

Morris, D., *The Naked Ape*, New York: McGraw-Hill, 1967.

Nierenberg, G.I. and H.H. Calero, *How to Read a Person Like a Book*, New York: Cornerstone Library, 1971.

Ruben, B.D., D.J. Kealey, and J.B. Askling, *Cross-Cultural Effectiveness: Interpersonal and Group Communication Dimensions*, paper presented at the Third Annual Conference of the Society of Intercultural Education, Training and Research, Chicago, 1977.

Smith, E.C. and L.F. Luce (eds.), *Toward Internationalism. Readings in Cross-Cultural Communication*, Rowley, MA: Newbury House Publishers, Inc., 1979.

Sommer, R., *Personal Space (The Behavioral Basis of Design)*, Englewood Cliffs, NJ: Prentice-Hall, Inc., 1969.

Relating ideas is one of the central functions of innovation. The creative act takes place in three stages:

☐ *conscious information gathering and relating*
☐ *unconscius assimilation and interpretation accompanied by psychosomatic symptoms, discomfort, restlessness, etc.*
☐ *the "aha" of insight and surge of elation and spirits.*

— J.T. McCay

2   *INVENTING*

Chapter 6

CULTURE SHOCK REINVENTED

In discussing culture shock, we are actually referring to the *cross-cultural adjustment process.*

Cross-cultural adjustment is defined as a process which any individual (or group of individuals) has to experience to function effectively (but without alienation) in a setting that does not recognize all or parts of the assumptions and behavioral patterns that he or she takes for granted. Some implications of this definition are:

1. The adjustment process varies from one individual to another and from one organization to another.

2. Adjustment is a continuous, ongoing process. It never stops.

3. The end process nearly always results in both a change in the individual and the setting. All realities are altered.

4. Ideally, the process should allow the individual to achieve his goals and find satisfaction while the basic organizational expectations are fulfilled.

5. If we accept the idea that *any organization is a culture,* then any transfer from one organization to another has a cross-cultural dimension. In fact, if one acknowledges that a cultural entity constantly undergoes changes, then we must admit that cross-cultural adjustment is always necessary.

6. A key question is: where does adjustment end and alienation begin?

7. A major concern for any culture is maintaining the right degree of uniformity so that a minimum of stability and continuity is reached without preventing individual self-expression. [29]

8. All individuals and organizations have their own definitions of "adjusted" and "non-adjusted."

9. Each organization possesses its own inherent methods of helping (or "forcing") new employees adjust to the existing value system.

---

[29] Gardner, J.W., *Self-Renewal (The Individual and the Innovative Society)*, New York: Harper & Row, 1963.

10. Adjusting requires the practice of conflict-resolution.

The major adjustment problems (and opportunities) encountered by most people moving into a new cultural environment can be related to three types of confrontations or conflicts:

One's Own Culture:

A majority of people are not aware of the impact of the culture to which they belong on their personal values, activities, thinking and behavioral patterns. They usually do not realize, or accept, that they are the living product of a culture. As R. Benedict said, "It is hard to be conscious of the eyes through which one looks." [30]

Conflicts with the Organizational Culture:

The new employee does not understand that the is entering into a culture with its own structure, dynamics and value system. Moreover, very little has prepared him to approach or "decode" the new cultural environment in a systematic way.

Conflicts with Others:

Quite often, the individual experiencing a feeling of loss or bewilderment when joining the new organization has difficulty with the dynamics of cross-cultural communication. Uneasiness, engendered when events are beyond comprehension, hampers his effectiveness and so, caught between value conflicts, he tends to survive more through trial and error than by controlling the process.

To sum up, it appears that many individuals have not been trained to master a process they must continually confront. It is painful and it is costly. It prevents growth and self-actualization. Without awareness and preparation, the adjustment phenomenon is generally perceived as a threat to basic and psychological security. That perception generates defensiveness and resistance and it certainly is not healthy for the individual or the organization.

WORKSHOP 8.

1. **Aim:** *Figure 23* summarizes the aim of the culture-shock workshop.

2. **Objectives:** Participants will work on a set of interrelated knowledge, skills, values, assumptions and behavior according to the following matrix. The four inputs in the conceptual framework will *document* the various stages of the workshop.

---

[30] Benedict, R., *The Chrysanthemum and the Sword (Patterns of Japanese Culture)*, New York: New American Library, 1974.

Figure 23. Cross-cultural workshop: Learning objectives [31]

Key Learning Areas \ Subject Matter	Culture Shock	Adjustment Process
KNOWLEDGE	1. To become aware of the existence of culture shock and its consequences.	2. To understand some of the key aspects of the adjustment process.
SKILLS	1. To be able to recognize culture shock and its symptoms.	2. To be able to apply a set of core skills in order to ease the adjustment process.
VALUES / ASSUMPTIONS	1. Culture shock exists and affects our attitudes, behavior and performance.	2. The adjustment process can be eased and taken advantage of.
BEHAVIOR	1. To avoid, to flee, fight, become too dependent and adjust.	2. To demonstrate a capacity to select the right reactions when confronted with an unusual or ambiguous situation.

3. Process:

(a) After a short introduction which sets up the key concepts to be used in the workshop and "warms up" the participants, a group exercise is provided so that they can either experience or observe the reactions (behavior) of people having to go through some aspect of culture shock. At that stage, participants are not aware of the goal. The trainer asks for six to eight volunteers who sit in the middle of the room (fishbowl format). The instructions for the participants are given to observers first and next to the participants/volunteers. People sitting in the middle of the room are reminded that they have to speak up so that everybody can hear what they say.

Instructions for the Volunteers/Participants:

1. Please analyze the psychological and cultural phenomena which occur in your small group—here and now.

---

[31] Basically, the workshop is an awareness program. Nevertheless, the structure of the learning process is such that it offers an opportunity to go beyond the awareness level for those who wish to do so.

2. You can freely express all the things you are feeling in relation to the given task.

3. The group must not study what is irrelevant to that which is happening right now.

4. The group is free to decide how much time you devote to the exercise.

Instructions for the Observers: [32]

Please observe the reactions of the participants who are plunged into an *unusual situation*. Attached you will find:

1. The instructions for the participants who are going to carry out the experiment (see page 79).

2. An evaluation grid which can help you to observe what is happening in the group (see *Figure 24*).

Figure 24. Evaluation grid.

ITEMS	IDENTIFICATION OF THE PARTICIPANTS' REACTIONS (WHO DID IT—WHAT DID HE/SHE DO?)
1. Curiosity, interest in the task.	
2. Embarrassment, feelings of insecurity.	
3. Frustration, aggressiveness.	
4. Speaking of another subject.	
5. Trying to accomplish the task.	

---

[32] An alternative consists of giving the participants' instructions to the observers and offering them the opportunity to join the group of volunteers during the exercise if they feel like helping. They can come and go as they wish (chairs should be made available for that purpose); volunteers cannot leave.

(b) When the exercise is over (it takes between ten and thirty minutes according to the groups), a structured discussion in subgroups made up of observers and volunteers/participants is organized around two issues:

SITUATION	REACTIONS
Using adjectives, please characterize the situation into which the volunteers/ participants have been placed.	Having characterized the situation, please identify some of the volunteers'/ participants' reactions *vis-a-vis* the situation.
The situation was: 1. 2. 3. 4. 5.	The participants: 1. 2. 3. 4. 5.

This phase lasts between twenty and thirty minutes. Hereunder is a sample of what subgroups came up with in previous seminars. All comments are shared between the four or five sub-groups. The result of their discussion is written down on a piece of paper (flip-chart), posted on the wall, and presented to everybody by a spokesperson.

(c) When the subgroups' reactions are all recorded, the trainer steps in and organizes the learning process as follows:

1. Presentation of a *model* regarding the cross-cultural or culture shock process;

2. the presentation is made in a step-by-step manner so that

3. the theory can be related to what happened during the exercise as well as to

4. What happens to someone who has to move from one culture to another [33].

---

[33] It can be from one organizational or cultural setting to another.

SITUATION	REACTIONS

The situation was:
■ confusing
■ unclear
■ artificial
■ unusual
■ strange
■ challenging
■ frustrating
■ embarrassing
■ disorganized
■ ambiguous
■ conflicting
■ a waste of time
■ stressful
■ amusing
■ enjoyable
■ unfair
■ dangerous
■ unexpected
■ disappointing
■ undefined
■ tense
	The volunteers/participants:
	■ were silent
	■ laughed
	■ tried to clarify the instructions
	■ were ill at ease
	■ looked for leadership
	■ sought support
	■ were patient
	■ were lost
	■ expressed feelings of
	  - inferiority
	  - insincerity
	  - inadequacy
	■ were passive
	■ were nervous
	■ were talkative
	■ tried to identify their objectives
	■ withdrew
	■ did not do what they were supposed to do
	■ smiled
	■ talked about the observers

Hereunder is a description of what can be said and discussed with the group.

STAGE 1. FIRST CONTACT.

Explanation: Pre-conceived ideas have a tremendous impact on the way one reacts when joining a new cultural environment. They always exist. The higher the expectations, the more the chance one has to be disappointed. Pre-conception should be identified and controlled.

The first reactions have been identified by psychologists and social psychologists as spread on a spectrum which goes from being *excited* to *ill at ease* with a sort of *"wait and see"* position in between. The reactions depend on the individuals, their personalities and cultural backgrounds. Someone can be excited at the beginning of the joining process and become terribly upset after a while. Another individual can remain cool and just curious during the entire adjustment. The very nature or expression of the excitement and uneasiness will also vary from one culture to another.

STAGE 1: First contact.

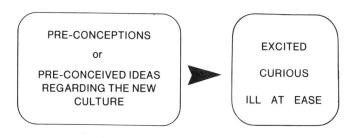

PRE-CONCEPTIONS
or
PRE-CONCEIVED IDEAS
REGARDING THE NEW
CULTURE

EXCITED

CURIOUS

ILL AT EASE

Illustrations: Before joining the group in the middle of the room, volunteers/participants had some pre-conceived ideas about the exercise in which they were going to be involved, *i.e.*, it was going to be about cross-cultural communication, it would be easy, funny, etc. What a shock for most of them to realize that the instructions were unclear, undefined, not easy to understand. Some of the volunteers perceived the unclearness of the instructions as a *challenge*. They were excited about handling the task. Others felt uncomfortable and expressed their uneasiness in a non-verbal way (smiling, laughing, being silent, fidgeting on their chairs,...). Some others were just waiting to "take note" or become involved in the discussion.

Real Life Situation: Participants are asked to meet in trios and relate what has been said so far to their personal, past or present experiences. A general discussion follows.

STAGE 2. FIRST ATTEMPT TO ADJUST.

Explanation: After the initial reactions, the individual makes his first attempt to adjust to the new cultural setting. He is immediately confronted with three problems:

1. He receives demands from the environment for which, to his amazement in most cases, he has *no ready-made answer.* The situation can indeed be embarrassing since he does not know what to say, what to do, or how to say it and do it.

2. The solution is, of course, to adjust the existing behavioral patterns or create some brand new ways of coping. This leads to the second prob-

lem which is characterized by the fact that the individual's behavior does not deliver what it was intended to. In other words, the reactions from the environment are not quite expected.

3. The third problem is related to the fact that the newcomer tries to observe and understand what is going on in the new social system he now belongs to and it seems to him that what people do does not make any sense.

STAGE 2: First attempt to adjust

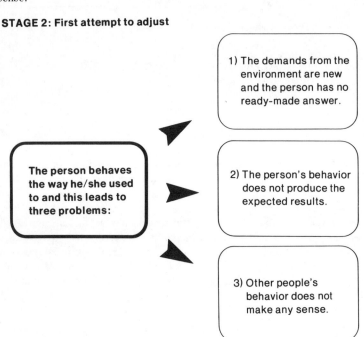

The person behaves the way he/she used to and this leads to three problems:

1) The demands from the environment are new and the person has no ready-made answer.

2) The person's behavior does not produce the expected results.

3) Other people's behavior does not make any sense.

Illustration: Back to the exercise, it could be seen that some volunteers were taken aback by the strangeness of the situation. "To analyze the psychological and cultural phenomena occuring in the group—here and now " is not a situation with which most people are familiar (especially if the task has to be accomplished in from of several observers). It can be frustrating for the participants to become aware of the fact that they have no answer for the question. They did not know how to cope, how to behave. Very shortly after the beginning of the simulation, some people took a risk. They improvised and tried out a few behaviors to overcome the stress of the situation. And much to their surprise, what they said did not trigger the expected results. There were silences, ngeative reations from the other volunteers or, worse, unexpected questions regarding what they had just mentioned ("you said that you feel awkward; can you explain to us the reasons for your feeling?   ). This is without mentioning that neither the trainer nor the observers manifested their support. Another typical problem is that people in the group started to behave in a way which did not make any sense, at least for some of the volunteers ("Let me tell you a story of what happened to me five years ago," "the situation is clear: we need a leader," "what about expressing all our feelings in an 'up-front' manner ").

Real life situation:

Participants meet again in trios and discuss the three points (above) from an experiential viewpoint.

STAGE 3. CONFRONTATIONS CREATING STRESS.

Explanation: The confrontation with the new cultural setting can lead to some emotional reations which are by all means healthy. They signal to the individual the need for further action in order to "survive." They can sometimes become too extreme and lead to what psychologists call an *identity problem.* The individual feels (very strongly) that he or she has to prove something not only to the people around but mainly to himself or herself.

STAGE 3: Confrontations creating stress.

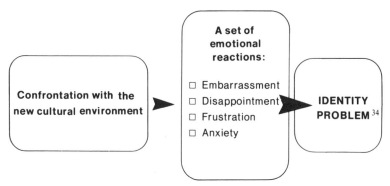

Illustration: Participants are referred to what they came up with during their subgroup discussions when they talked about the volunteers' reactions *vis-a-vis* the situation.

Real life situation: Participants fill out the self-assessment exercise on the following page. A discussion focussing on the two extremes of the

---

[34] Regarding the identity problem, read E.H. Erikson, *Insight and Responsibility,* New York: W.W. Norton & Co., 1964.

scale (20 being the minimum and 80 the maximum) follows:

☐ What if the anxiety is too low?

☐ What if the anxiety is too high?

SELF-ASSESSMENT EXERCISE
(CSA)

Instructions: Read each statement below and check the appropriate box to indicate how you feel regarding your present situation at work. There are no
right or wrong answers. Don't think too much; answer spontaneously.

	Not at all	Somewhat	Above Average	Very much so
1. I feel comfortable	☐	☐	☐	☐
2. I am tense	☐	☐	☐	☐
3. I feel secure	☐	☐	☐	☐
4. I feel calm	☐	☐	☐	☐
5. I feel upset	☐	☐	☐	☐
6. I feel discourgaged	☐	☐	☐	☐
7. I feel depressed	☐	☐	☐	☐
8. I feel on top	☐	☐	☐	☐
9. I feel anxious	☐	☐	☐	☐
10. I feel rested	☐	☐	☐	☐
11. I feel lost	☐	☐	☐	☐
12. I am relaxed	☐	☐	☐	☐
13. I feel nervous	☐	☐	☐	☐
14. I feel disappointed	☐	☐	☐	☐
15. I feel frustrated	☐	☐	☐	☐
16. I feel optimistic	☐	☐	☐	☐
17. I feel challenged	☐	☐	☐	☐
18. I am worried	☐	☐	☐	☐
19. I feel excited	☐	☐	☐	☐
20. I feel happy	☐	☐	☐	☐

MEASURING ONE'S OWN LEVEL OF ANXIETY
Score Sheet

Instructions: (a) Relate your selections to the scoring table below; (b)
add up all your scores.

(1)	4	3	2	1	(8)	4	3	2	1	(15)	1	2	3	4
(2)	1	2	3	4	(9)	1	2	3	4	(16)	4	3	2	1
(3)	4	3	2	1	(10)	4	3	2	1	(17)	4	3	2	1
(4)	4	3	2	1	(11)	1	2	3	4	(18)	1	2	3	4
(5)	1	2	3	4	(12)	4	3	2	1	(19)	4	3	2	1
(6)	1	2	3	4	(13)	1	2	3	4	(20)	4	3	2	1
(7)	1	2	3	4	(14)	1	2	3	4					

STAGE 4. COPING WITH STRESS.

Explanation: People who experience some kind of anxiety have three options to recover or control the situation. The positiveness or negativeness of each option is a function of the degree to which it is used. Overdone, the healthy, functional reaction becomes dysfunctional. It has to be pointed out that in each unadapted reaction there is something positive. The individual can flee or withdraw, be aggressive or assertive, give up or adjust. Let's notice that (a) what is good and functional for one individual cannot be so for another; (b) the three options can be used alternatively; and (c) what is functional in one situation can be dysfunctional in another.

STAGE 4: Adjusting for good ... or bad.

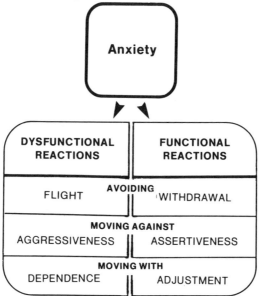

The basic differences between the functional and dysfunctional behaviors are:

FLEEING	WITHDRAWING
I do not try to understand and adjust to the situation which is too painful for me. I just quit. (In case of strong stress, this reaction can be the appropriate one.)	The situation is painful but I want to understand it and adjust accordingly. In order to do so, I get in touch until I cannot stand the process and then I withdraw. After a while, I come back, try again and withdraw when I feel that I have to. And so on until I feel enough control with the situation to stay with it.

BEING AGGRESSIVE
I say what I have to say in a tough mode (I am OK, you are not OK).

BEING ASSERTIVE
I say what I have to in a firm mode (I am OK, you are OK).

GIVING UP
Just tell me what you want and the way you want it and I'll do it (one-way process).

ADJUSTING
I am ready to accept your terms up to a point. Beyond I am not because I believe that I have something to offer to you and the new environment (two-way process).

Illustration: One of the first reactions during the exercise was for the participants to say that there is *no task.* So instead of trying to analyze the psychological and cultural phenomena occuring in the group, they talked about something else, *i.e.,* the purpose of the workshop, the backgrounds of the participants.   At this point it is quite important for the trainer to explain what the task was, using relevant illustration, such as: do we disagree with the group? can we go ahead with an exercise without knowing what the objectives are? do all people look for problems? etc. All the questions are dealt with from a cross-cultural perspective. This was basically fleeing. But from time to time, a member of the group said: "This is not what we are supposed to do. Our task is to talk about what is occuring here and how and we are not supposed to study what is irrelevant to what is happening." This was withdrawing and getting in touch again. During their discussion, the volunteers also manifested some mixed feelings (sometimes in a very strong way) about the exercise ("a waste of time"), the facilitator ("he is responsible for this incredible situation"), and the observers ("it is eay for them to judge us"). This was "being on the defensive" (aggressive and assertive). A few members tried very hard to give some sense (theirs) to the unclear instructions and achieve something despite the ambiguity of the whole situation. Some others just gave up ("this is too silly").

Real life situation: Participants meet in groups of four or five and identify behaviors typical of the functional and dysfunctional reactions as presented above. They tap their previous personal experiences to pin-point relevant examples.

Figure 25 summarizes the entire culture shock process. It has to be stressed again that (a) the process is different from one individual to another, and (b) people's reactions vary broadly. And yet it seems that there is a pattern which can be taken into account when trying to adjust to another culture.

Figure 26. The culture shock process.

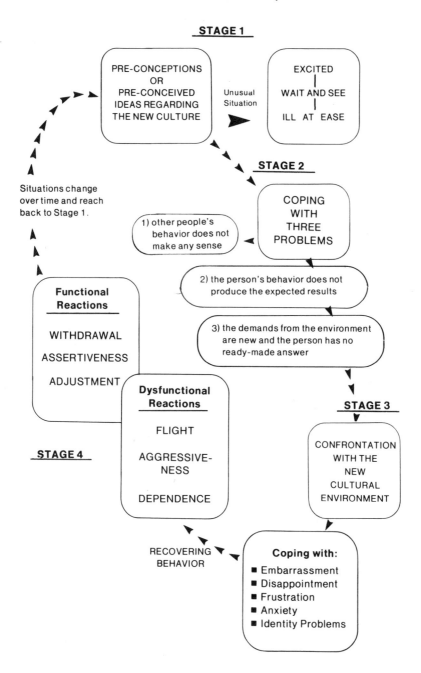

(d) If the participants admit (and they usually do) that culture shock exists and that it is true that when placed in an unusual situation one has a tendency to flee, fight and give up, the next step is to examine with them the possibility of easing the process of facilitating the adjustment. The session is organized as follows:

1) The same subgroups are reconvened. Their task is to brainstorm for twenty or thirty minutes, and set up a list of practical guidelines[35] which can be followed in order to ease the cross-cultural adjustment process. The subgroups are informed that the guidelines have to be as practical as possible because they will have to be tested to see if they work with a new exercise.

2) An exercise is given to the group, which selects two observers before starting its work.

Instructions for participants:

Please freely express your feelings concerning the positive and negative inputs that each member of your subgroup produced during the workshop session. You can organize your task as you wish and decide how much time you need for the exercise.

Instructions for the observers:

Please check the validity of your guidelines. Attached you will find:

1. The instructions for the participants (see above).

2. An evaluation grid which can help you to observe what is happening in the group *(Figure 26)*.

3. All participants meet and share their impressions regarding the guidelines to be used to ease the culture shock process.

4. **Time:** Three to four hours.

---

[35] See **Input 2** on the brainstorming method.
[36] See a sample of guidelines in **Input 4** (p. **93**).

Figure 26. Evaluation grid.

ITEMS	OBSERVATIONS	
	Who did it?	What did he/she do?
1. To what extent did they flee or withdraw?		
2. To what extent did they fight?		
3. To what extent did they try to adjust themselves or just give up?		
4. To what extent did they apply their guidelines?		

5. Conceptual Framework:

INPUT 1

The person who joins a new culture is confronted with three issues which can be summed up as follows:

The Three Dimensions of the Cross-Cultural Integration Process

Related to the Newcomer's Culture	Related to the New Culture the Newcomer is Joining	Related to the Construction of a Third Culture
1. What cultural traits will he/she keep?	1. What cultural traits will he/she adopt as they are?	1. Creating new cultural traits, building upon the differences.
2. What traits will he/she modify according to the new environment?	2. What traits will he/she accept in adjusting to them?	2. Creating new traits from the similarities.
3. What traits will he/she give up?	3. What traits will he/she reject?	3. Cultural synergy: innovation.

INPUT 2
Tips on the Brainstorming Method

The brainstorming method can be split into three main sequences:

1. Every group member expresses his ideas in relation to the given problem (no one is authorized to criticize or evaluate the proposals made by the others).

2. The group—as it goes along—generates a lot of original suggestions (the goal is to get as many ideas as possible).

3. After fifteen minutes, the group selects what seems to be the best ideas (evaluation).

INPUT 3
Identification of the Culture Shock [37]

Problems of personal adjustment to a foreign environment have frequently been referred to as "culture shock." This phenomenon is usually precipitated by the anxiety which results from the sudden loss of familiar surroundings. A person experiences frustration and irritation as he constantly finds his "natural" way of behaving to be in conflict with the life style of those around him. In addition, continual uncertainty and amambiguity about how he should act and react causes a certain amount of discomfort and uneasiness.

Over the years, four distinctive patters of responses to "culture shock" have been identified. These methods of dealing with the new and unfamiliar may be described as "flight," "dependency," "fight," and "adaptation." When a person responds to a new situation through *flight* he rejects those people and things around him which cause his discomfort and withdraws from interaction with them. In each instance, the individual places "blame" either on the local population for a lack of "understanding," or on himself for inadequacy in handling the new experience. The result is that the individual takes some defensive measure such as flight to fellow nationals in a foreign enclave or some other regressive action as a means of removing the threatening atmosphere and reinstate the security of the familiar.

Dependency may be identified by extreme behavior in the opposite direction. In such cases, the individual does not flee from his host culture by joining a foreign enclave, but instead flees from his own national identity by becoming dependent on the host culture. Such behavior, known to

---

[37] Extract of a contribution written by S.H. Rhinesmith and D.S. Hoopes, published in "Reading Materials," Intercultural Communications Workshop, Regional Council for International Education, University of Pittsburgh, Pittsburgh, PA, 2 September 1967.

some as "going native," is also a means of reducing tension. The ultimate effects of denying on's own cultural identity, however, may in the long run be more harmful than beneficial.

Other persons respond to a new culture with hostility and aggression. They become irritated with those around them for making them feel ill at ease and as a result become determined to "show the native how we do it at home." Such individuals *fight* the new environment, trying to change the culture to which they have come, rather than attempting to understand it and respond to it. They tend to assume, often unconsciously, that it is the responsibility of the host culture to adapt to them rather than the other way around, blithely ignoring or unaware of the absurdity of such an expectation.

All of the above three modes of behaviour are really maladjusted reactions to a new environment. In each case, the person will in some way be inhibited from functioning with full effectiveness in a host culture. There are some, however, who begin the slow and painstaking process of cultural *adaptation* and adjustment. These individuals reject neither themselves nor others, but rather try to adapt to the new situation through constant openness to learning and behavioural growth. This requires an ability and desire to *listen* for the responses, both verbal and non-verbal, of those around them. At the same time, these persons must develop an awareness of the messages which they are sending out and the possible interpretations which others might make of them. In short, such individuals refine and expand their skills in interpersonal communication.

INPUT 4.
Practical Guidelines for Easing Culture Shock

Here is a list of practical guidelines that groups identified in various workshops:

☐ Be aware of the existence of culture shock.

☐ Talk about the culture shock symptoms.

☐ Identify as accurately as possible:

　—your assumptions about things, ideas, and people.
　—the assumptions of the new system.
　—the clash between the two sets of assumptions.

☐ Focus on the positive aspects of the adjustment process.

☐ Clarify the expectations of other people as quickly as possible.

☐ Get other people's support.

☐ Move one step at a time.

☐ Establish a two-way communication process.

☐ Look for feedback.

☐ Ask open-ended questions.

☐ Do not lose your sense of humor.

6. Handouts and Readings:

(a) Handouts:

"Defense Mechanisms in Groups," in *The 1972 Annual Handbook for Group Facilitators*, pp. 117-118.

"The Pendulum Swings: A Necessay Evil in the Growth Cycle," *The 1978 Annual Handbook for Group Facilitators*, pp. 143-148.

"Culture Shock Inventory," designed by W.J. Reddin and K. Rowell, marketed by Organizational Tests, Ltd., Box 324, Fredericton, NB, Canada (1970).

"Culture Shock and the Pattern of Adjustment to New Cultural Environments," (an edited talk by Dr. K. Oberg, FSI, Washington, DC).

Singer, M.R., "Identity Issues in Intercultural Communication (Overview Statement)," SIETAR Annual Conference, Chicago, February 1977.

"Culture Shock and the Cross-Cultural Learning Experience," by P.S. Adler in *Readings in Intercultural Communication (Vol. II)*, ed. D. Hoopes, RCIE, June 1972, p. 6-21.

Brislin, R.W., "Increasing the Range of Concepts in Intercultural Communications Research: The Example of Prejudice," paper delivered at the 1978 SIETAR Conference, Phoenix AZ.

(b) Readings:

Adams, J., J. Hayes and B. Hopson, *Transition (Understanding and Managing Personal Change)*, London: Martin Robertson, 1976.

Gaylin, W. *Feelings (Our Vital Signs)*, New York: Harper & Row, 1979.

Levinson, H., *Psychological Man*, Cambridge, MA: The Levinson Institute, 1976.

Selye, H, *The Stress of Life*, New York: McGraw-Hill, 1956.

Selye, H., *Stress without Distress*, New York: Lippincott, 1974.

Tanner, O. and the editors of Time-Life Books, *Stress*, Alexandria, VA: Time-Life Books, 1976.

Toffler, A., *Future Shock*, New York: Pan Books, 1970.

Chapter

7

EXPERIENCING CROSS-CULTURAL CONFRONTATIONS

Utterly futile, therefore, to endeavour by writing to change a man's final inclination, the bent of his mind. You will only succeed in confirming him in his opinions, or, if he has none, drenching him with your own.

— Goethe

The previous chapter was intended to introduce the concept of cross-cultural adjustment. It has been shown that the key step to successful adaptation into an alien cultural environment is first and foremost to *understand* the dynamics of the confrontation between two different ways of constructing reality. Furthermore, it seems that the best way to make people sensitive about this need of understanding oneself as well as others from a cross-cultural perspective is not to talk about it, but to *experience* it̃ either through case studies, simulations, or controlled real-life situations.

WORKSHOP 9.

1. Aim: To give an opportunity to the workshop participants to experience a set of cross-cultural confrontations and in so doing to improve their understanding of the intercultural adjustment process.

2. Objectives: Participants will:

(1) Improve their understanding of cross-cultural confrontations through the analysis of several case studies (cases);

(2) Experience a set of cross-cultural confrontations by role-playing (simulations);

(3) Analyze time management from a cross-cultural perspective (film);

(4) Study the contrast approach created by Dr. E. Stewart;

(5) Pinpoint ways to ease the cross-cultural confrontations (conceptual framework: inputs 1, 2, 3).

3. Process:

(a) Participants are invited to read the following story, answer the four questions, and discuss their ideas in subgroups:

Gordon and Brian had been working in the Honduran village for five days. As theirs was basically a health improvement project, they felt it was advisable to impress upon the villagers the importance of cleanliness. Gordon was to be giving most of the shots; he decided he should look the part of a doctor, so he fashioned a white gown out of an extra sheet he had brought along. The two boys cleaned up the "clinic" to the best of their ability, even to the extent of carefully spraying the whole room with DDT. When the clinic was operating, Brian efficiently took the names of each villager, carefully entered it in his book and instructed the person to line up along the wall and wait to his turn until Gordon was ready. Gordon, for his part, played the role of doctor as he imagined it, to the best of his ability. He meticulously fixed the vaccination in the syringe, assiduously swabbed the arm of the patient, being extremely careful to assure that the spot for the vaccination was scrupulously clean, then professionally injected the needle, performed the vaccination, and sent the villager on his way.

At the end of the day, the two boys were extremely pleased with their performance, both in efficiently vaccinating a large number of people and also in conveying the image of careful antisepsis.

The next day was much the same as the first, except that there seemed to be fewer people to vaccinate. The numbers continued to drop until by the end of the fifth day only a dozen or so people accepted their shot and quickly left. The boys could not understand what was wrong, as they had heard that the people in this village were very cooperative and friendly, but they knew that they had hardly begun to vaccinate everyone in the village. [38]

Questions:

(1) What is the reason for which people drop out in attendance at the clinic? Select the right explanation from among four possible answers presented below:

☐ Hondurans didn't know what to expect. When they found out that vaccinations were painful, the word rapidly spread and people stopped coming to the clinic.

☐ The Hondurans were offended by the boys' brusque manner.

☐ They did not like the smell of DDT.

☐ The villagers had no faith in the vaccinations.

---

[38]   Extract from G.E. O'Brien, F.E. Fiedler and T. Hewett, "The Effects of Programmed Culture Training upon the Performance of Volunteer Medical Teams in Central America," *Human Relations*, Vol. 24, No. 3, pp. 209-231.

The correct answer is: The Hondurans were offended by the boys' brusque manner." While there may not have been any particularly obvious clues in the episode, you should have chosen this alternative as the correct one. In interacting with a Honduran successfully, probably the most important rule is to be friendly. These villagers lead a simple, relatively informal life, and are not used to the cold informality that characterizes much of the American way of life. The boys in this passage did almost everything wrong. Doctors in Honduras generally do not wear white coats. The spraying of the clinic with DDT was an insult and indicated rudeness to the Hundurans. The cold, efficient manner of both boys was foreign to the villagers. Even in the larger urban centers in Honduras, life is very informal. It is even more so in the villages. If you try to make a false impression, the villagers will spot it rapidly and come to avoid you. They expect a friendly interest in themselves as persons and their specific ailments. You can break many other codes of behavior with impunity and be forgiven, so long as you show a genuine interest in them and their problems.[39]

(2) Imagine a *scenario* which would show Gordon and Brian "fleeing" and "withdrawing."

(3) What would fighting and giving up or becoming dependent be in this situation?

(4) Assuming that you have to advise Gordon and Brian on how to adjust, what would you suggest? How would you do it?

(b) Application to real-life situations: a checklist. (Participants work on an individual basis and when ready share their ideas in trios.)

The Joining Process:

Please provide the following information:

1. Recollection of your reaction on the day you learned you were going to join a new culture:

My reaction was:

2. Remembrance of your feelings on the first day you joined.

My feelings were:

3. What your feelings are now, after _____ days in the new setting.

My feelings after _____ days (please complete) were:

4. Describe at least two situations you have encountered in the new cultural environment which you have found unpleasant, and your reactions to them.

Situation 1 (description and reactions):

Situation 2 (description and reactions):

---

[39] Symonds, J., G. O'Brien, M. Vidmar, and J. Hornik, *Honduras Culture Assimilator,* Urbana, IL: Group Effectiveness Research Laboratory, University of Illinois, 1967.

5. Make at least *two suggestions* in order to help people who have to move from one cultural setting to another.

My two suggestions are:

(c) A series of five case studies or critical incidents are given to the group, which handles them in small teams.

CASE ONE [40]

Mrs. A. Jones wanted to have a light bulb installed near the terrace in back of her house. She went to see the local electrician. He promised that he would come the next afternoon. When the electrician failed to show up, Mrs. Jones stopped by again and was assured that the light would be installed the next day. This happened four times before the electrician finally came, and, of course, Mrs. Jones was furious because she had been forced to stay in to wait for him.

The crowning blow occured with the electrician finally arrived. He said that he had forgotten something and then failed to return. Mrs. Jones decided to do without the light.

Questions:

1. How do you explain (in terms of cultural differences) the interactions between Mrs. Jones and the electrician?

2. What is the impact of the electrician's behavior on Mrs. Jones?

3. What would you suggest to Mrs. Jones to solve her problem?

CASE TWO

Mr. and Mrs. Dupont got settled in the new city and decided to have a number of friends over for a party. The invited them over at 8:00 p.m. on a Friday evening for some dinner. After everyone had arrived and had a drink, the guests seated themselves for dinner. Mr. Dupont got up when his wife came in from the kitchen and said, "Let me come out and help you," and he started towards the kitchen door. His wife turned to him and in obvious anger and indignation said, "Be seated, please, this is not your job." Mr. Dupont's wife was cool to him for the rest of the evening and he couldn't understand why.

Questions:

1. How do you explain (in terms of cultural differences) the interaction between Mr. and Mrs. Dupont?

2. What is the impact of Mr. Dupont's behaviour on his wife?

3. What would you suggest to Mr. and Mrs. Dupont to avoid this kind of incident in the future?

---

40 All case studies or critical incidents are borrowed and adapted from the "Greek Cultural Assimalator," designed by T. Mitchell, J. Gagerman, and S. Schwartz.

CASE THREE

When the October PTA [Parent-Teachers Association] meeting of the PLATO school was announced, Mrs. F. Anari decided she would go since she had two boys attending the school. It was her first meeting. When she got there, she was immediately struck by the fact that a number of parents came up and inquired of teachers why their sons and daughters had not been doing well in their classes. A few of the parents were even rude. They said things such as "I know my child is bright and if he got a 'D' on your test then there must be something wrong with the teaching," or "Why do you dislike my child so much?" The teacher was apparently taken aback and not able to answer. The meeting was not very constructive, and Mrs. Anari left the school very upset.

Questions:

1. Is the parents' behavior typical of a certain culture? If yes, which one? Explain.

2. What is the impact of the parents' behavior on (a) the teacher, and (b) Mrs. Anari?

3. According to you, what has to be done in order to improve the relationship between the teacher and the parents?

CASE FOUR

Mr. and Mrs. Smith had just had a baby. Mrs. Smith had brought the child home and was still a little tired so she occasionally asked her neighbor to babysit for a couple of hours. After a few weeks, however, she noticed that her neighbor was taking over more and more duties. She would come in, uninvited, feed the baby, change him or even try to take the baby back to her house. Mrs. Smith told her a couple of times that this was not really necessary but this didn't stop the neighbor. Finally, Mrs. Smith blew up and told the woman to leave and not come back again. Needless to say, the relationship with the neighbors was forever strained.

Questions:

1. Is the neighor's behavior typical of a certain culture? If yes, which one? Explain.

2. How do you understand (in terms of cultural differences) the interaction between the two women?

3. According to you, what can be done to improve their relationship?

CASE FIVE

After staying in Athens for two months in a Greek organization, Sam Williams decided to make some suggestions to the Greek who was in charge. He talked about how effective American supervisors had found the brainstorming technique in getting new ideas. Sam explained that a number of people would get together and the problem or topic of discussion would be introduced. Then everyone would give whatever suggestions came to mind and the best ideas would then be utilized. The Greek supervisor seemed rather hesitant, but since Sam was supposed to be an expert advisor, the supervisor set up a brainstorming session with his Greek subordinates with executive positions. All the men got together at 2:00 p.m. the next afternoon and they began the discussion on a certain topic. However, after a very short time, it was obvious from the long periods of prolonged silence that the process just wouldn't work.

Questions:

1. What is your cross-cultural diagnosis of the situation?

2. What do you think Sam Williams should do?

(d) A very straightforward exercise can be used to illustrate the impact of pre-conceived ideas on intercultural relations.[40a]   The group is split into three teams:

☐ a team of international experts

☐ a team of national authorities

☐ a team of observers.

The following instructions are distributed to the three respective teams:

Instructions for the Team of National Authorities

You are a team of national experts belonging to a developing country.

Yearly flooding of the crops has severely reduced the food supply in a specified region. As a result, there is malnutrition and a high death rate amongst the children. After investigation, it appears that the villagers concerned are indifferent and not ready to solve the problem by themselves.

Please prepare the outline of a plan of action.

You have fifteen minutes to accomplish your task.

Instructions for the Team of International Experts

You are a team of international experts. One of you (Mr./Ms. _____) is going to fly to a developing country and join a team of national experts who are confronted with a dramatic problem.

It seems that yearly flooding of the crops severely reduced the food supply in a specific region of the country. The population is hungry and children are dying.

According to your contacts in the country, it also seems that the national authorities are not very sensitive to the problem, whereas the population has tried to solve it without any success thus far.

Please help Mr./Ms. _____ to prepare himself/herself for the mission.

You have fifteen minutes to accomplish your task.

Instructions for the Observers

Identify the impact of preconceptions on the interaction between the interna-

---

40a   An international expert goes on mission to a developing country with some misleading information regarding the local situation.

tional expert and the national authorities. You have fifteen minutes to set up a checklist to be used for observing the simulation.

After fifteen minutes of preparation, the selected expert meets with the team of national authorities. They have twenty minutes to come up with the outline of action plan. A general discussion (with inputs from observers) on the importance of preconceptions and how to handle them follows. Most groups seem to stress:

☐ to be careful with orientation programs;

☐ to keep an open mind;

☐ to cross-check the information received beforehand;

☐ to be tactful in asking questions;

☐ to be sensitive to others' reactions (verbal and non-verbal);

☐ to be flexible;

☐ to create a climate of trust as quickly as possible;

☐ to reach a common ground in the discussion with the national authorities;

☐ to show interest in the problem at stake;

☐ to watch the impact of what one says on others.

(e) A role-play on experiencing cultural differences. Seven volunteers are required for this role play, which is organized as follows:

1. The theme (for the trainer *exclusively*): The treasurer of a cooperative in a developing country has "stolen" $100 donated by other members of the community. The role play focuses on the reactions of seven people involved in one way or another in the situation: a project manager, an expert in cooperatives, a counterpart to the expert in cooperatives, a community development expert, the counterpart to the expert in community development.

2. The seven volunteers receive their instructions. They have fifteen minutes to prepare themselves (with the facilitator's help if needed) for the role-play. At the same time, the rest of the group prepares itself for the simulation (see their own instructions, below).

3. A table and seven chairs are set up in the middle of the room. Name cards are put in front each role-player with an identification of their role (project manager, expert in community development, etc.).

4. The role-play begins and lasts 30 minutes.

5. The facilitator can reinforce the dramatization of the meeting by giving messages to the project manager, *e.g.*, "the minister of agriculture is very upset about the incident. A drastic decision has to be made and the expert must apologize to the authorities" or "The minister of agriculture has decided that the expert must leave the country."

6. A general discussion is conducted by the facilitator with the assistance of the observers (45 minutes).

Instructions for the Project Manager

You are the Project Manager of an international team, working with farmers' cooperatives in a developing country. You have just heard that one of your experts (the specialist in cooperatives) discovered fifteen days ago that the treasurer of a cooperative had calmly taken $100 which had been donated by other members of the community.

Immediately after the incident, the expert tried to persuade the members of the cooperative that the man should be punished. You know that no one made any move to punish the treasurer.

Hearing all that, you have decided to organize a staff meeting. **You are mainly concerned with:**

1. The future of the project (if such things happen, will it be possible to maintain the cooperative system?);

2. the reaction of the national experts *vis-a-vis* your expert's behavior.

Please prepare your meeting accordingly.

Instructions for the Project Co-Manager

You are the Project Co-Manager of an international team working with farmers' cooperatives in your country. You have just heard that one of the experts (the specialist in cooperatives) discovered fifteen days ago that the treasurer of a cooperative had calmly taken $100 which had been donated by other members of the community. Immediately after the incident, the expert tried to persude the members of the community that the man should be punished. No one made any move to punish the treasurer. You know that the government authorities of the region are not happy about the expert's behavior.

The Project Manager, hearing about the incident, has just called all the team members together for a meeting.

Your position is clear: Whatever the problem may be, an expert (a foreigner) is not allowed to involve himself/herself in a local matter. Your main concern is to decide how to avoid such incidents in the future. Although you know your administration (Ministry of Agriculture, Community Development Service), is already aware of what happened, you have to tell your colleagues that an official report has been made.

Please prepare yourself for the meeting.

Instructions for the Counterpart to the Expert in Cooperatives

You are the counterpart of Mr./Ms. _____ (an international expert, specialist in cooperatives), and member of an international team working with farmers' cooperatives in your country. Fifteen days ago, the expert with whom you are working discovered in a village that the treasurer of the cooperative had calmly taken $100 which had been donated by other members of the community. Immediately after the incident the expert tried to persuade the members of the cooperative that the man should be punished. He talked to the whole village, using persuasion and common sense. No one made any move to punish the treasurer. The Project Manager, hearing about the incident, has just called all the team members for a meeting.

Your position is: You were absent during the incident (working in another village), but you know that the treasurer has used the money to build himself a new house in the same community and that the villagers are just waiting for more money to be collected thinking that they might be the ones to get hold of it.

Please prepare yourself for the meeting.

Instructions for the Expert in Cooperatives

You are a specialist in cooperatives, and a member of an international team working with farmers' cooperatives in a developing country. Fifteen days ago you discovered that in a village the treasurer of a cooperative had calmly taken $100 which had been donated by the other members of the community.

Immediately after the incident, you tried to persuade the members of the cooperative that the man should be punished. You talked to the whole village, using persuasion and common sense. No one made any move to punish the treasurer.

Your Project Manager, hearing about the incident, has just called all the team members for a meeting.

Your position is very clear: If one accepts this kind of thing, then all of the cooperative system will be in jeopardy.

Please prepare your arguments to defend your opinion on this question.

Instructions for the Expert in Community Development

You are a specialist in community development, and a member of an international team working with farmers' cooperatives in a developing country. You know that an incident occurred fifteen days ago in a project supervised by your colleague specialist in cooperatives. That is all you know.

Your Project Manager has just called all the team members for a meeting.

Instructions for the Counterpart to the Expert in Community Development

You are the counterpart of Mr./Ms. _____ (an international expert, specialist in community development), and member of an international team working with farmers' cooperatives in your country. You know that an incident occurred fifteen days ago in a project supervised by your two colleagues, specialists in cooperatives. That is all you know.

Your Project Manager has just called all the team members for a meeting.

Instructions for the Observers

Attached you will find all the instructions for the role-players. You have fifteen minutes to create an "observation grid" that you will use during the role-play. The observation instrument should focus on:

1. What are you going to observe?

2. Who will observe what?

The discussion with the observers shows that at least five major issues can be pointed out and analyzed:

1. The *right* of a foreigner to intervene in local matters (role definition);

2. The meaning of personal versus community property (the notion of *cooperative* itself);

3. Conflict resolution between national authorities and international experts;

4. Different ways to look at managing a project;

5. The concept of *punishment*.

(f). Hereunder is an exercise which provides another opportunity to identify and analyze cultural differences. It is about *time from a cross-cultural perspective*.

Phase 1:

Please pick *three items* from among the list below and analyze the *basic cultural assumptions and values* which underlie them:

☐ Respect other people's time.

☐ Budget your time.

☐ Have a good time.

☐ Time is life.

☐ Take your time.

☐ Use your waiting time.

☐ Your time will come.

☐ Be on time.

☐ Don't waste your time.

☐ It is time-consuming.

☐ The time of your life.

☐ Find the time.

☐ Make the most of your time.

☐ Running out of time.

☐ Time is money.

☐ Save your time.

☐ Good timing.

☐ Kill time.

☐ Beat time.

☐ You will do better next time.

Phase 2:

The group analyzes a list of basic value orientations regarding time:

☐ Time consciousness (time is perceived as a separate reality).

☐ Two conceptions of time: (a) time is standing still and people move; and (b) people are standing still and time moves.

☐ Emphasis is placed on: Past — Present — Future.

☐ Communication and time: Warming up — Peak — Decline.

☐ Pace of Life: Slow — Fast.

☐ Handling one thing at a time or several things at a time.

☐ Time is valuable and should not be wasted.

☐ Time is a commodity. It can be bought, sold, saved, spent, lost, made up, and measured.

☐ States of life: Infancy, childhood, adolescence, youth, middle age, old age.

☐ Emphasis on: Youth — Middle Age — Old Age.

☐ Present is already Past — Future never comes.

☐ The components of American time — the minutes, the hours — have to add up (it provides *order;* it serves as a link that chains events together).

☐ Depth is a necessary component of time: there is a past on which the present rests.

☐ The need to *quantify* time.

☐ Subjective impressions regarding time (time passing rapidly or slowly according to urgency.

Phase 3:

The first ten minutes of the movie designed by Lakein, "The Time of Your Life," [41] can be shown to the group. Basic cultural assumptions about time are identified and discussed.

Phase 4:

Participants characterize the "notion of time" typical of their own culture(s) [or any culture(s) you are interested in]. Criteria to be used:

Where is the greatest emphasis placed? (Past — Present — Future)

What is the pace of life? (Slow — Fast)

Is time perceived as a resource to be managed?

---

[41] This film is distributed by the Cally Curtis Company, 1111 North Las Palmas Avenue, Hollywood, CA 90038.

Others: _____

_____

Participants assess the impact of the above on:

Planning (determining objectives, selecting priorities and the work to be done).

_____

_____

Organizing (dividing the work into manageable functions).

_____

_____

Motivating (influencing people so that they perform in a desired way).

_____

_____

Innovating (dealing with change).

_____

_____

Delegating (giving responsiblities and authority to other people).

_____

_____

Phase 5(a):

Identify *three* things related to time management that you have learned from the cross-cultural examination and that you want to put to some use:

1. _____
2. _____
3. _____

Phase 5(b):

Pinpoint a few *obstacles* which will prevent you from improving as decided above:

_____

_____

(g) *The contrast American approach.* Created by Dr. Edward Stewart, this approach consists of constrasting two cultures through a critical incident which involves two individuals, one from the group who, after a short briefing, is ready to play a role, and an actor [42] who has

---

[42] There are two reasons that *only actors* shold be used in the contrast American approach. As E. Stewart explains them, they are:

"(1) Ethical: The contrast American part requires that someone consistently tap primordial sentiments that are not always used in face-to-face interaction in American life. The procedure, therefore, involves an ethical dilemma. An actor

been trained to bring up cultural differences during the simulated interaction. The exercise goes like this:

(1) the facilitator introduces the simulation to the group (10 minutes);

(2) the simulation takes place in front of the group (15-20 minutes);

(3) the trained role-player leaves the room and the facilitator and the group interview the remaining person;

(4) the facilitator, the group and the role-player interview the trained actor;

(5) conclusions are drawn from the exercise.

Hereunder are two illustrations of the approach: [43]

(A) Mr. Smith, an expert working in a non-Western country, is hit (not seriously) by a car which he recognizes as Mr. Isphahany's, a high-status local official. Mr. Smith, upset that the car did not stop after the event, seeks out Mr. Isphahany in an exclusive local club. Here is their conversation:

Mr. Smith: Ach! Mr. Isphahany? My name is Mr. Smith.

Mr. Isphahany: Mr. Smith? How are you?

Mr. Smith: I am fine, thank you. I might be a little bit better if it hadn't been for an unfortunate incident which happened just a little while ago.

Mr. Isphahany: What do you mean?

Mr. Smith: As I came into the club I saw a car parked outside. An orange car. Is that your car?

Mr. Isphahany: Of course, it is my car. A beautiful car. Twenty-five thousand dollars.

Mr. Smith: Well—uh—about a half an hour ago, Mr. Isphahany, I was downtown, walking along the street and I was practically run over by a car that looked very much like your car.

Mr. Isphahany: Yes?

Mr. Smith: And I think I saw you driving that car.

Mr. Isphahany: That was my car. You...you are the one who was standing in my path?

---

will have confronted this issue in his work; therefore using only actors in the contrast American role minimizes the ethical risk.

(2) Training: An actor must have the ability to transpose emotions and cognitions into behavior. In other words, the definition of a good actor is a person who is in close touch with his own feelings and ideas and posses the ability to give them quick and spontaneous expression. This is a definite asset in the contrast American. One always knows that one half of the equation will work."

[43] This simulation was recorded at the SIETAR conference in Chicago (1977). Dr. E. Stewart conducted the demonstration. Mr. C. deMello was Mr. Isphahany and Mr. B. Hogan played Mr. Smith's role. The recorded simulation was presented by Dr. E. Stewart and P. Casse to an international group of trainers at a workshop sponsored by the German Foundation for International Development, Bad Honnef, November-December, 1977.

Mr. Smith: Yes, that was me.

Mr. Isphahany: What were you doing over there?

Mr. Smith: I was walking down the street and you practically ran over me with your car.

Mr. Isphahany: You're supposed to walk on the sidewalk here. That's what sidewalks are for.

Mr. Smith: Well....

Mr. Isphahany: The road is meant for beautiful cars like mine to drive on.

Mr. Smith: I was walking on the road because it was impossible to walk on the sidewalk because of the crowd.

Mr. Isphahany: You should still have walked on the sidewalk.

Mr. Smith: You should have been driving more carefully.

Mr. Isphahany: What do you mean, more carefully? You think I didn't drive my twenty-five thousand dollar car carefully?

Mr. Smith: You were not driving carefully half an hour ago, that's for sure.

Mr. Isphahany: You shouldn't have been there first of all in my path; you should have been where the other people walked.

Mr. Smith: Listen, Mr. Isphahany, I'd like to sit down and have a rational discussion with you about this. Alright?

Mr. Isphahany: A rational discussion? What is there to discuss? You are Mr. Smith, I am Mr. Isphahany. Let's shake hands and you go.

Mr. Smith: I am not going. I have something to discuss with you. It is important...and either the two of us discuss it right now alone together or we discuss it at the police station!

Mr. Isphahany: You please sit down. Sit down, I'll discuss with you. You came to the right place to discuss. First of all, who allowed you to come into this exclusive club of ours? You are illegally here and I could arrest you. You know that. Do you have your membership card with you?

Mr. Smith: No, I don't have a membership card. I have been here before as a guest of other members of your club. They happen to be members of the same company I work for and thay are members of your club.

Mr. Isphahany: Do you admit that you are here illegally?

Mr. Smith: Do you admit that you hit me with your car a half hour ago?

Mr. Isphahany: I don't remember hitting you.

Mr. Smith: Mr. Isphahany, I like to...

Mr. Isphahany: If I hit you you must be hurt. Is that right?

Mr. Smith: Yes, . I have a terrible bruise on my leg.

Mr. Isphahany: If you have a bruise on your leg, how come that you are walking then?

Mr. Smith: You can walk with a bruise on your leg. ..

Mr. Isphahany: You have not been hurt. Nothing has happened and you are just trying to extract some money from me, I know. You are an American, aren't you?

Mr. Smith: Yes, I am, but I didn't say anything about money.

Mr. Isphahany: No wonder. You want to claim all the money you can...

Mr. Smith: I didn't say anything about money. I came here because I wanted to discuss with you something which had happened half an hour ago. I think your car was involved. Your were driving your car at that time.

Mr. Isphahany: I was driving the car, sure. I also know that, yes, something happened to you and you fell down yes...but it is not my fault. If you were not present over there I wouldn't have hurt you. Right? So it is your fault, not mine.

Mr. Smith: Mr. Isphahany, I was not seriously hurt.

Mr. Isphahany: Yes, you should be very grateful! You see there is a good thing...

Mr. Smith: I was not seriously hurt and it is not necessary for me to see a doctor because I don't need medical attention.

Mr. Isphahany: You want to see a doctor?

Mr. Smith: I don't want to see a doctor.

Mr. Isphahany: I'll tell you what, I have a very personal physician. I'll call him over here so that when you come tomorrow, he will see you.

Mr. Smith: OK. In the meantime, this is what I want to talk with you about. I was walking along the street and I had to step off the sidewalk into the road because of the crowd on the sidewalk. At that moment, your car, I believe it was your car, was coming down the street very fast....

Mr. Isphahany: Yes, yes.... I always drive very fast....

Mr. Smith: It would have been possible for you to drive out of the way to avoid hitting me. Instead, I think you exercised very little care and practically ran over me. As it was, I jumped out of the way just in time and you bruised my leg. I was not seriously hurt. I don't need medical attention but I want to talk with you about this.

Mr. Isphahany: First of all, it is your fault. How come you're there in that bazaar at that time of the day? Aren't you supposed to be in your office?

Mr. Smith: Aren't you supposed to be in your office, too? What were you doing there?

Mr. Isphahany: Well, I was going for a dinner and I was coming home. This is my office.

Mr. Smith: Well, I was on my way to my office at that time.

Mr. Isphahany: Well, it is not... What kind of a work do you do?

Mr. Smith: That's not the important thing. The important thing is someone has been hit by a car and the driver was not driving carefully. That's what I want to talk to you about.

Mr. Isphahany: You see...you should realize first of all that it is your fault. You stepped aside from the sidewalk. You were in my path. That car is a very powerful car. Even if you pull the brakes it does not stop so easily. It is a machine. You cannot blame a machine. A machine is a machine. So you got hurt. But you were on the road; if you were on the sidewalk this wouldn't have happened... Now, you say you were not very much hurt?

Mr. Smith: Yes.

Mr. Isphahany: You should be very grateful for that. This tells you something. If you are not careful you might have gotten killed. Right?...and you should be happy because I did not kill you. So let's shake hands on that.

Mr. Smith: Before we shake hands, there are just a few things I would like to share with you.

Mr. Isphahany: Well...

Mr. Smith: I have been in your country for a week now and one of the things I have noticed is that people here drive their cars very fast.

Mr. Isphahany: Right.

Mr. Smith: They sometimes go through red lights...they frequently bang into each other's cars. I have seen...

Mr. Isphahany: Red light is only a machine...

Mr. Smith: Have you seen many cars damaging each other in the process of parking. People drive very recklessly. Accidents are almost always happening. All day long.

Mr. Isphahany: Life is like that...full of risks...big adventures.

Mr. Smith: People do not drive like that where I come from and furthermore if someone gets hit by a car, in my country, a policeman is called.

Mr. Isphahany: This is not your country! Why are you telling me all this? This is not your country.

Mr. Smith: I know it is not my country but I am telling you what I think is reasonable. People don't drive their cars here the way they drive them in my country. I am still trying to adjust to the situation.

Mr. Isphahany: It does not matter what happened. The important thing is that you're not dead. Now you adjust. You are in an exclusive club and you are talking to the most powerful man in this club. I am the manager. Yes. You understand? I want to make you a member of my club. I am glad you came to me. I want to extend an invitation....

Mr. Smith: You are inviting me to become a member of your club?

Mr. Isphahany: Yes, very simple: $2,000 membership.

Mr. Smith: What?

Mr. Isphahany: Since you are my friend: $1,000...It is very simple. You see you are away from your country. There is no entertainment for you. Become a member of my club. It is a prestigious club. People of best qualities come over here.

Mr. Smith: May I ask you a question? If you had been walking along the street with your son and the same thing happened to you which happened to me half an hour ago...

Mr. Isphahany: OK. Since you started bargaining...

Mr. Smith: What?...let me make something clear...I am not here to join your club...

Mr. Isphahany: No, no...you have to join, you are my friend. Why not? I am the manager. Why shouldn't you join the club? You see, fate has brought us together, you and me, even though it is in a strange way. You are here now so I am your friend. You are my friend. You don't believe me?

Mr. Smith: What I came here for this afternoon is to find out yes or no...

Mr. Isphahany: You don't believe me...

Mr. Smith: Was that your car? Were you driving that car?

Mr. Isphahany: I was driving my car. Yes, I saw you. I hit you, but I didn't kill you. So, on that basis, let's become friends.

Mr. Smith: That is not the point. The point is: there was an accident which should be reported to the police.

Mr. Isphahany: You want to report to the police? I'll call him right now.

Mr. Smith: You will?

Mr. Isphahany: The chief of police is a personal friend of mine...why don't you do this? This will satisfy you?

Mr. Smith: I think it should be done. Isn't it the custom? Isn't it necessary to call the police when there is an accident?

Mr. Isphahany: I'll tell you what. I will have the chief of police come over here and you can report to him in my presence. He will be happy to hear your story...you see, Fate has brought you here, we cannot let you go without becoming a member: $750...?

Mr. Smith: Let's talk about joining your club another day. That's not what I came here for.

Mr. Isphahany: I want to be your friend. I want to have you as my friend. I speak from the bottom of my heart. You believe me or not?

Mr. Smith: Yes, I believe you, but it is not what I came here to talk about today. I want you to call the chief of police, as you mentioned a few minutes ago, and I would like you to call the doctor, too, because I have some insurance forms that I have to send back to the States and I need some statements from a doctor.

Mr. Isphahany: Everything will be taken care of after you become a member first. That is the first step. I cannot let you go without becoming a member. Believe me. Don't you believe me?

Mr. Smith: Yes, certainly I believe you.

Five cultural issues to be discussed by the group:

(1) The notion of *responsibility* (legal versus fate).

(2) The concept of friendship.

(3) Bribery.

(4) The purpose of the conversation: for the American? for Mr. Isphahany?

(5) The process: A "rational" discussion versus "getting acquainted."

(B) "Mr. Smith, an American advisor for technical development, meets for the first time with Mr. Khan, a land project manager, with whom he is going to work. The purpose of the meeting is simply to get acquainted and for Mr. Smith to check how the project is working, where his help is needed. Mr. Smith's predecessor, Mr. Jones, had worked with Mr. Khan for eight months. Unfortunately, he had no time to brief Mr. Smith about the status of the pro-

ject before leaving the country (he was reassigned to another country)." [44]
The conversation lasts between fifteen and twenty minutes. Two volunteers play the roles, *contrasting* each others' reactions.

The following cultural differences can be pinpointed and discussed:

Mr. Khan focusses upon—

- □ *family*
- □ *social integration*
- □ *convictions that work will be completed whatever happens.*
- □ *attached to his land*
- □ *affiliation oriented*
- □ *enjoys small talk*
- □ *looks for the positive*
- □ *improvisation*
- □ *listen*
- □ *patience*
- □ *intuition*
- □ *impervious, feelings*
- □ *holistic approach*
- □ *quality of relations*

Mr. Smith focusses upon—

- □ *work*
- □ *professional achievement*
- □ *fear that the project is falling behind time schedule*
- □ *enjoys traveling*
- □ *competitive*
- □ *small talk is a waste of time*
- □ *seeks out problems*
- □ *planning*
- □ *talk*
- □ *impatience*
- □ *data gathering*
- □ *systematic evaluation*
- □ *particular approach*
- □ *efficiency*

4. **Time:** Between five and six hours.

5. **Conceptual Framework:**

INPUT 1
Cross-Cultural Awareness: A Contrasting Model

SITUATIONS / REACTIONS	
	1. Problem-solving. 3. Decision making. 2. Conflict resolution. 4. Motivation.
MY REACTIONS	1. Identification of my own reactions regarding each situation. 2. Are they typical of my culture?
THEIR REACTIONS	1. Identification of their reactions regarding the same situation. 2. Are they typical of their culture?
OTHER POSSIBLE REACTIONS	1. Identification of other reactions (imagined or real) 2. Are they typical of other cultures?

---

[44] *cf.* "An Introduction to Issues in Cultural Interaction," *Discussion Leaders' Guide and Program Handbook*, distributed by the Noonmark Associates, 1754 N Street, NW, Washington, DC 20036.

This model can be used in order to reinforce the "learning how to learn" process.

INPUT 2
Two Patterns of Behavior [45]

PATTERN A	PATTERN B
1. *Cognitive consistency:* **Always trying to make sense out of everything (order, structure, logic).**	1. *Openness and tolerance towards ambiguity.* **Openness to experience, flexibility, capability to adjust to various situations.**
2. *Judging:* **Making comparisons evaluations, passing value judgments.**	2. *Descriptive:* **To be descriptive rather than judgmental by describing situations.**
3. *Attributing:* **Giving motives to others as reasons for their behavior.**	3. *Asking:* **Enhancing the capacity to check out assumptions by asking people directly why they did what they did.**

Pattern B is highly recommended for "managing" any kind of cross-cultural interaction.

INPUT 3
The Process of Intercultural Adjustment [46]

Like our values and attitudes, our identities and self-concepts also tend to be frozen into behaviour patterns relevant to our own cultural environment. In an intercultural setting, as we have seen, our identities change. Often, however, our behaviour remains the same. The visitor, in confronting the consequent adjustment problems, sometimes suffers from what Mr. Brewster Smith has aptly called "a circumstance of beleaguered self-esteem." In such a situation he must conquer the anxiety he heels while at the same time developing the capacity to adjust to the new roles and the new learning about himself with are imposed upon him by the new environment.

In undergoing this experience he is involved in a learning process which has been conceptualized by some as a three-phase cycle of "unfreezing — moving — refreezing." Of the three phases, the first is usually the most difficult, requiring the breakdown of ethnocentric biases which have distorted cultural vision for so many years. No matter how much an individual may want to learn, he brings to a new environ-

---

[45] Inspired by C. Argyris and developed by J. Ingalls.
[46] Rhinesmith, S.H. and D.S. Hoopes, *op. cit.*

ment a certain ambivalence and resistance to learning and change. Behaviour change is threatening because it raises questions of personal inadequacies to meet new challenges which might produce failure and ridicule, because it stimulates anxieties over the potential impact of the change on one's concept of one's self, indeed, on the very nature of one's "self."

Once this fear has been overcome, however, a person is ready to learn. The "moving" or second phase refers to the actual process of expanding one's cultural vision through the readjustment of attitudes and perceptions as he becomes more aware of the alternative perspectives which are available to him. This is the phase of actual "learning" when the individual accepts or rejects new experiences and re-evaluates his past and present perceptions in order to form a framework for future behaviour.

In the third phase, "refreezing," the individual "locks in place" his new perceptions and ways of behaving so that regression to a previous mode of behaviour will not readily occur. At this point, we may say that a behaviour of attitudinal "change" has taken place. The extent, nature, and duration of this change, however, depend very much upon the re-enforcements which are supplied thereafter and the extend to which the new perceptions coincide with those held by friends and associates with whom the individual will be working and living from day to day.

The two authors describe the adjustment process as a learning event with three main chronological phases, namely: (1) *unfreezing* or unlearning previous patterns of behaviour; (2) *moving* or expanding ways of looking at the world including self, and (3) *refreezing* or structuring the acquired new cultural events.

6. Handouts and readings.

(a) Handouts

Adler, P.S., *Beyond Cultural Identity: Reflections on Cultural and Multicultural Man,* Honolulu: East-West Center, August 1974.

Klein, M.H., "Preliminary Overview: Adaptation to New Cultural Environments " (presentation at the SIETAR Annual Conference, Chicago, February 1977).

Feldman, M.J., *An Introduction to Issues in Cultural Interaction: Discussion Leaders' Guide & Program Handbook,* Additional material by S.J. Anspacher, D.E. Bittern, and E.C. Stewart. Washington, DC: The Noonmark Associates, 1976.

Kraemer, A.J., "A Cultural Self-Awareness Approach to Improving Intercultural Communication Skills," (pp. 3-13), HumRRO, July 1973 (extract of "Development of a Cultural Self-Awareness Approach to Instruction in Intercultural Communication").

(b) Readings

Berry, J.W., "On Cross-Cultural Comparability," *International Journal of Psychology*, 1969, Vol. 4, No. 2, pp. 119-128.

Fieg, J.P. and J.G. Blair, *There IS a Difference*, Washington, DC: Washington International Center, Meridian House International, 1975.

Harris, P. and R. Moran, *Managing Cultural Differences*, Houston: Gulf Publishing Co., 1979.

Kraemer, A.J., *Workshop in Intercultural Communication: Handbook for Instructors*, Alexandria, VA: HumRRO, June, 1974.

———, *A Cultural Self-Awareness Approach to Improving Intercultural Communication Skills*, Alexandria, VA: HumRRO, April 1973.

Lakein, A., *How to Get Control of Your Time and Your Life*, Hew York: A Signet Book, New American Library, 1973.

Mackenzie, R.A., *The Time Trap (Managing Your Way Out)*, New York: Amacom, 1972.

Stewart, E.C., J. Danielian and R.J. Foster, *Simulating Intercultural Communication through Role-Playing*, Alexandria, VA: HumRRO, May 1969.

Stolurow, L.M., S. Santhai (with the assistance of R. Koopman), *Critical Incidents with Hetero-Cultural Interactions*, Illinois Department of Psychology, University of Illinois, October, 1966.

Strodtbeck, F.L., "Values and Beliefs in Cross-Cultural Interaction (the State of the Art)," presentation at the SIETAR annual conference, Chicago, February 1977.

The best answers for you are within you. Principles, theories, and models can be useful only if they don't trap you.

— S. Herman

Be
As you are
And so see
who you are
and how you are
let go
For a moment or two
of what you ought to do
And discover what you do do
Risk a little if you can
Feel your own feelings
Say your own words
Think your own thoughts
Be your own self
Discover
Let the plan for you
Grow from within you.

— F. Perls

PRODUCING

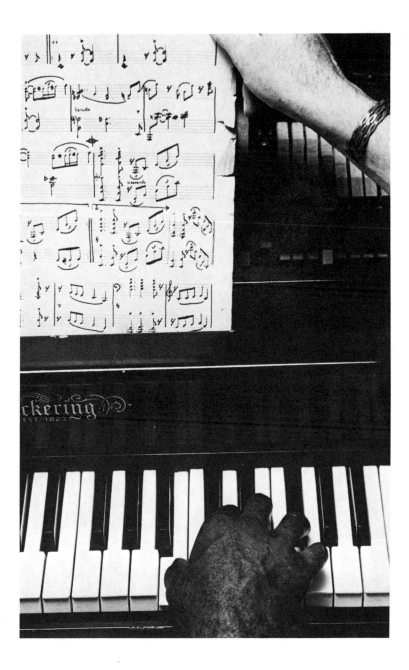

Chapter 8

A GESTALT ORIENTATION TO
INTERCULTURAL UNDERSTANDING

There are different ways of being in the world. You can:

☐ *make a model in your mind of the "right life" and keep trying to live up to it and eliminate the things that seem to interfere with it.*

☐ *be in the middle of what is happening and rejoice at times, suffer at times, rest at times.*

— S. Herman

Too many people have been influenced by the "should-ism" approach to intercultural understanding. Many trainers still believe that there is a set of basic guidelines that everyone should follow in order to be effective when communicating with other cultures. It is not so. The key thing in success in this field as in others is to experience the entire intercultural communication process in its uniqueness and adjust accordingly. The series of exercises which follow is intended to introduce the Gestalt orientation to intercultural understanding. The premise is very simple: in cross-cultural communication there is no rule with the exception of one: there is no rule. That's the rule.

WORKSHOP 10

1. Aim: To introduce the Gestalt way of looking at intercultural communication.

2. Objective: Participants will:

(1) get acquainted with the Gestalt orientation to intercultural communication (exercises and all inputs under conceptual framework);

(2) practice the Gestalt approach (exercises) applied to cross-cultural interactions.

3. Process:

(a) Participants list at least ten "shoulds" or "should nots" which are common in the intercultural communication area (individually first, and then in groups).They agree on a joint list and work in trios, asking the following:

☐ Identify the main sources of the ten agreed upon "shoulds" and "should nots" (education, organization, training, social experiences...).

☐ For each "should" or "should not," write down the behavioral implications.

☐ Examine what you would be naturally tempted to do but that you do not do because of these "shoulds" and "should nots."

☐ Discuss the potential implications of what you would like to do but don't do upon the partners in the cross-cultural communication process.

☐ React to S. Hermann's statement that: "The way to allow yourself to change and grow is to become aware of what you are doing now. It is equally important, too, for you to learn how you stop yourself from doing what you want to do and how you stop yourself from being who you are."

(b) This exercise deals with *fears and hopes* related to cross-cultural interaction. Each member of the group is asked to clarify what he or she fears most when interacting with people who do not belong to the same culture. Next the hopes or expectations are also identified. Participants then share what they are willing to report on. The facilitator writes the various inputs on a flipchart or blackboard using the following format:

FEARS	HOPES
1. to fail	1. to learn something
2. to be misunderstood	2. to grow from the experience
3. to hurt people	3. to adjust
4. to lose face	4. to help others
5. to be rejected	5. to be successful
Others:*	Others:*
6.	6.
7.	7.
8.	8.
9.	9.
10.	10.

*to be completed by the group.

The list is examined from three perspectives:

1. Are the fears and hopes realistic or not? (let's find out through concrete examples).

2. What is the cultural dimension of each fear and hope? (where are those fears and hopes coming from?).

3. What can be done to overcome the fears (if necessary) and build upon the hopes?

(c) A natural extention of the previous analysis is the *If I Were King* exercise. The process goes like this:

□ Participants express *spontaneously* how they would interact with people from other cultures assuming that they have full power (assuming they are kings).

□ What has been said is discussed in terms of (1) the anticipated negative responses from others: are they real or imaginary? (2) the obstacles which prevent the implementation of what people wish to do but don't do; and (3) the required modifications for making the ideas acceptable for both partners.

(d) Ten Gestalt principles are presented to the group, which studies their applicability in the intercultural communication field:

1. Each individual is encouraged *to take responsibility* for himself or herself. The main emphasis is on the recognition and mobilization of individual strength and power. Weak partners are strengthened rather than the strong ones being weakened.

2. Each person sharpens his or her awareness of *what* he or she does and *how*. The here and now, as well as the what and how, are emphasized, not the past or *why*.

3. *Aggressiveness and conflicts* are valued as creative forces. Openness is not recognized as an automatic good thing.

4. The main stress in the communication is placed upon *internal feedback*, and inputs from others are de-emphasized.

5. The capability to choose one's own behavior independently enhanced. The individual's *autonomy* is highly valued.

6. Being "up-front" is healthy even when it implies to be closed. To be able to say "no" is recommended.

7. *Authentic* behavior leads to more genuine relations. To be authentic means that people allow themselves to be as they are.

8. Increasing the individual's competence, whatever the culture, is the primary goal of the Gestalt approach. To help people understand "what they want, how they stop themselves from getting what they want, and what alternatives are available to them.

9. Withdrawing is perceived as something positive which allows us to get our energy back from the contact phases.

10. Confluence and differentiation are equally valued. Separateness, differences and turbulence are essential parts of a full life experience. To get locked into one or the other state (unity versus separation) leads to

problems.

  (e) Self checklist for intercultural contact.

  1. Am I talking about something instead of being authentic?

  2. Am I telling the other person what he or she should do?

  3. Am I saying "I cannot" when I really mean "I won't?"

  4. Am I saying "the group," they, we, when I mean "I?"

  5. Am I focussing on the past whereas the issue is the present?

  6. Am I saying "no" when I mean "no?"

  7. Do I send mixed signals?

  8. Am I able to withdraw when necessary?

  9. Am I "up-front" in my comments?

  10. Do I personalize my interactions with others?

  4. Time: Three hours.

  5. Conceptual Framework:

INPUT 1
The Gestalt "Prayer"

I do my thing, and you do your thing.
I am not in this world to live up to your expectations
And you are not in this world to live up to mine.
You are you, and I am I,
And if by chance, we find each other, it is beautiful.
If not, it can't be helped.

> — F.S. Perls
> Gestalt Therapy Verbatim
> Bantam Books, New York, 1959.

INPUT 2
The Contact Cycle [47]

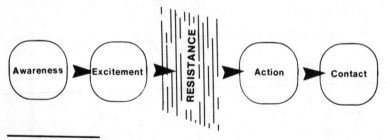

Awareness ▶ Excitement ▶ RESISTANCE ▶ Action ▶ Contact

---

[47] Pfeiffer, J.W. and J.A. Pfeiffer, "A Gestalt Primer," the 1975 *Annual Handbook for Group Facilitators*, p. 183.

1. *AWARENESS:* One realizes that something exists.
2. *EXCITEMENT:* One fantasizes about the prized thing.
3. *ACTION:* One takes some action to come close to the "thing."
4. *CONTACT:* One makes contact with the object.

There are six different ways of preventing (resistance) one's self from acting and having contact with the object (a thing or person or idea):

☐ **Introjection:** values imposed upon us by the cultural environment one belongs to can prevent contact;

☐ *Retroflection:* feeling guilty about what one says or does;

☐ *Attribution:* the opposite of retroflection. Everybody is responsible for what I feel;

☐ *Confluence:* one denies contact to other people by agreeing with everything the other person says;

☐ *Projection:* one says things about others whereas they are true for one's self;

☐ *Deflation:* one does not respond to what the other person says.

INPUT 3
Creative Intercultural Communication:
The Gestalt Approach [48]

Creative intercultural communication requires the integration of two modes of being:

Grabbing hold of and hanging loose.

Being active and living in passive, receptive wonderment.

Analyzing particulars and seeing the whole, the Gestalt.

Being in control and flowing with the process.

Being certain and allowing oneself to experience confusion.

Being serious and playing, having a sense of humor.

Being curious and allowing oneself to float in dullness.

Experiencing wants sequentially and seeing the whole simultaneously.

Naming things and experiencing spatial imagery.

Being intellectual and attending to intuition.

---

[48] Zinker, J., *Creative Process in Group Therapy*, Vantage Books, New York: 1977, pp. 59-60.

6. Handouts and Readings:

(a) Handouts:

Notes on freedom, *The 1972 Annual Handbook for Group Facilitators*, p. 211.

The organizational Gestalt, *The 1978 Annual Handbook for Group Facilitators*, p. 143.

A Gestlat approach to collaboration in organizations, *The 1976 Annual Handbook for Group Facilitators*, p. 239.

A "Shouldlist" Manager, *The 1974 Annual Handbook for Group Facilitators*, p. 146.

Figure and ground, *The 1974 Annual Handbook for Group Facilitators*, p. 131.

(b) Readings:

Hermann, S.M. and M. Korenich, *Authentic Management: A Gestalt Orientation to Organizations and their Development*, Reading, MA: Addison-Wesley, 1977.

James, M. and D. Jongeward, *Born to Win: Transactional Analysis with Gestalt Experiments*, Reading, MA: Addison-Wesley, 1971.

Perls, F.S., *Gestalt Therapy Verbatim*, New York: Bantam, 1969.

Perls, F.S., *Ego, Hunger and Aggression: The Beginning of Gestalt Therapy*, New York: Random House, 1969.

Perls, F.S., R.F. Hefferline and P. Goodman, *Gestalt Therapy (Excitement and Growth in the Human Personality)*, New York: Bantam Books, 1977.

Perls, F.S., *The Gestalt Approach and Eye Witness to Therapy*, New York: Bantam Books, 1976.

Perls, F.S., *In and Out the Garbage Pail*, Moab, UT: Red People Press, 1969.

Polster, E. and M. Polster, *Gestalt Therapy Integrated (Contours of Theory and Practice)*, New York: Vintage Books, 1973.

9

COMMUNICATE
COMMUNICATE
COMMUNICATE

We have language and can build metaphors as skillfully and precisely as ribosomes make proteins. We have affection. We have genes for usefulness, and usefulness is about as close to a 'common goal' for all of nature as I can guess at. And finally, and perhaps best of all, we have music. Any species capable of producing, at this earliest, juvenile stage of its development—almost instantly after emerging on the earth by any evolutionary standards—the music of Johann Sebastian Bach, cannot be all bad.

— L. Thomas

As we have seen in the previous chapters, communication is not an easy thing. It's an art and it requires patience as well as a minimum of skills.

We are different and despite the difficulties we are, after all, able to exchange some meanings (*i.e.*, communicate) from time to time. That is a "miracle:" we can do it. We do it. Genuine communication is a creative art by which you become part of me and I become part of you. Or, to put it differently, it is the process by which you activate something in me and vice versa.

WORKSHOP 11

1. **Aim:** To analyze a set of communication styles, see how intercultural communication can be practically improved and used to help people adjust to new cultural environments.

2. **Objectives:** Participants will:

(1) Analyze four value orientations and their impact on communication styles (self-assessment exercise);

(2) learn how to switch from one style to another (exercise);

(3) learn how to cope with different styles (exercise and conceptual framework: input 1);

(4) Practice four listening and responding styles (exercise and conceptual framework: input 2);

(5) Examine five communication skills and their use across cultures (conceptual framework: input 3).

3. Process:

(a) Participants fill out the self-assessment exercise on communication styles:

Communication Value Orientations: A Self-Assessment Exercise

Please select in each pair of attributes the one which is most typical of your personality. No pair is an either-or proposal. Make your choice as spontaneously as possible. There is no wrong answer.

1. I like action.
2. I deal with problems in a systematic way.
3. I believe that teams are more effective than individuals.
4. I enjoy innovation very much.
5. I am more interested in the future than the past.
6. I enjoy working with people.
7. I like to attend well organized group meetings.
8. Deadlines are important for me.
9. I cannot stand procrastination.
10. I believe that new ideas have to be tested before being used.
11. I enjoy the stimulation of interaction with others.
12. I am always looking for new possibilities.
13. I want to set up my own objectives.
14. When I start something I like to go through until the end.
15. I basically try to understand other people's emotions.
16. I do challenge people around me.
17. I look forward to receiving feedback on my performance.
18. I find the step-by-step approach very effective.
19. I think I am good at reading people.
20. I like creative problem solving.
21. I extrapolate and project all the time.
22. I am sensitive to others' needs.
23. Planning is the key to success.
24. I become impatient with long deliberations.
25. I am cool under pressure.
26. I value experience very much.

27. I listen to people.
28. People say that I am a fast thinker.
29. Cooperation is a key word for me.
30. I use logical methods to test alternatives.
31. I like to handle several projects at the same time.
32. I always question myself.
33. I learn by doing.
34. I believe that my head rules my heart.
35. I can predict how others may react to a certain action.
36. I do not like details.
37. Analysis should always precede action.
38. I am able to assess the climate of a group.
39. I have a tendency to start things and not finish them.
40. I perceive myself as decisive.
41. I search for challenging tasks.
42. I rely on observation and data.
43. I can express my feelings openly.
44. I like to design new projects.
45. I enjoy reading very much.
46. I perceive myself as a facilitator.
47. I like to focus on one issue at a time.
48. I like to achieve.
49. I enjoy learning about others.
50. I like variety.
51. Facts speak for themselves.
52. I use my imagination as much as possible.
53. I am impatient with long, slow assignments.
54. My mind never stops working.
55. Key decisions have to be made in a cautious way.
56. I strongly believe that people need each other to get work done.
57. I usually make decisions without thinking too much.
58. Emotions create problems.
59. I like to be liked by others.
60. I can put two and two together very quickly.
61. I try out my new ideas on people.
62. I believe in the scientific approach.

63. I like to get things done.
64. Good relationships are essential.

65. I am impulsive.
66. I accept differences in people.

67. Communicating with people is an end in itself.
68. I like to be intellectually stimulated.

69. I like to organize.
70. I usually jump from one task to another.

71. Talking and working with people is a creative act.
72. Self-actualization is a key word for me.

73. I enjoy playing with ideas.
74. I dislike to waste my time.

75. I enjoy doing what I am good at.
76. I learn by interacting with others.

77. I find abstractions interesting and enjoyable.
78. I am patient with details.

79. I like brief, to-the-point statements.
80. I feel confident in myself.

(b) *Scoring the self-assessment exercise:* Each *selected item* has to be reported on the four scales reproduced below. In other words, if items 1, 4, 6, have been selected, the same numbers on the four scales should be circled again.

Style 1 = 1−8−9−13−17−24−26−31−33−40−41−48−50−53−57−63−65−70−74−79

Style 2 = 2−7−10−14−18−23−25−30−34−37−42−47−51−55−58−62−66−69−75−78

Style 3 = 3−6−11−15−19−22−27−29−35−38−43−46−49−56−59−64−67−71−76−80

Style 4 = 4−5−12−16−20−21−28−32−36−39−44−45−52−54−60−61−68−72−73−77

Circled items should be added up (not the figures but the number of selected items). The maximum is 20 per style and the total for the four styles should be 40.

(c) *Describing the value orientations:*

Four value orientations have been used to construct this self-assessment exercise. Two assumptions underlie the theory.

☐ the four value orientations can be found in any culture or individual;

☐ the four value orientations have a tremendous impact on the way one communicates.

Style 1 is influenced by the *ACTION* value orientation. People who are strong on this style like action, doing, achieving, getting things done, improving, solving problems.

Style 2 is related to the *PROCESS* value orientation. People who are strong on this style like facts, organizing, structuring, setting up strategies, tactics.

Style 3 is typical of the *PEOPLE* value orientations. Individuals who are people-oriented like to focus on social processes, interactions, communication, teamwork, social systems, motivation.

Style 4 is characterized by the *IDEA* value orientation. People with the idea orientation like concepts, theories, exchange of ideas, innovation, creativity, novelty.

Summary of the four value orientations

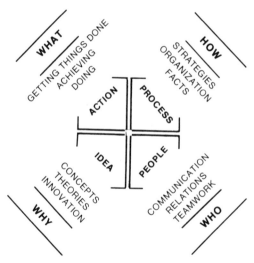

The following remarks should be made at this stage of the process:

(1) Everybody possesses the four value orientations (check with the participants to be sure that nobody has a zero score on any style).

(2) People have a dominant value orientation or a value orientation they feel more comfortable with (ask the participants to focus on their high est score which reflects this dominant value orientation *for the time being!*).

(3) The importance of the value orientations changes according to the *situations* in which people are involved.

(4) Value orientations are influenced by (a) the personality of the individual, (b) his or her cultural background, (c) past experiences, and (d) present situations.

(5) Each individual has the capability to switch from one value orientation to another. However, it has been shown that when a crisis occurs, most individuals switch back to the value orientation they are most used to.

(6) People with even scores have to choose the style they feel is more relevant for themselves. Even scores mean the people ˎ have already some flexibility in shifting from one style to another. They can also appear as confusing to other people.

(d) *Analyzing the impact of the four value orientations on communication styles:*

Participants who share the same dominant value orientation meet together (the group is split into four subgroups) and identify the main characteristics of their communication style. They try to answer the following two questions:

☐ What do we talk about when we communicate? (Content)

☐ How do we do it? (Process)

Figure 27 gives a summary of those characteristics (to be distributed at the beginning of this part of the exercise).

(e) Each subgroup is now asked to prepare a set of guidelines that could be used when one has to cope with different styles:

☐ The action orientation group prepares guidelines to adjust to the process oriented people.

☐ Process oriented people do the same for people oriented individuals,

☐ People oriented individuals for idea oriented persons, and

☐ Idea oriented persons for action oriented people.

The groups share their findings [49] and compare them with the guidelines below *(Figure 28)*, to be distributed when the groups have had a chance to present their guidelines.

---

[49] Videotaped illustrations can be discussed with the group: the four styles, how to recognize them and how to adjust to them. (Created by Drake-Beam and Associates, New York; produced by Rombex Productions, 245 West 55th Street, New York, NY 10019.

Figure 27: Communication styles
(Description of their main characteristics)

FEATURES / STYLES	CONTENT		PROCESS
ACTION	**They talk about:** -Results -Objectives -Performance -Productivity -Efficiency -Moving ahead -Responsibility	-Feedback -Experience -Challenges -Achievements -Change -Decisions	**They are:** -Pragmatic (down to earth) -Direct (to the point) -Impatient -Decisive -Quick (jump from one idea to another) -Energetic (challenge others)
PROCESS	**They talk about:** -Facts -Procedures -Planning -Organizing -Controlling -Testing	-Trying -Analysis -Observations -Proof -Details	**They are;** -Systematic -Logical (cause and effect) -Factual -Verbose -Unemotional -Cautious -Patient
PEOPLE	**They talk about:** -People -Needs -Motivations -Teamwork -Communications -Feelings -Team Spirit -Understanding	-Sensitivity -Awareness -Cooperation -Beliefs -Values -Expectations -Relations -Self-development	**They are:** -Spontaneous -Empathetic -Warm -Subjective -Emotional -Perceptive -Sensitive
IDEA	**They talk about:** -Concepts -Innovation -Creativity -Opportunities -Possibilities -Grand Designs -Issues -Interdependence	-New ways -New methods -Improving -Problems -Potential -Alternatives -What's new in the field	**They are:** -Imaginative -Charismatic -Difficult to understand -Ego-centered -Unrealistic -Creative -Full of ideas -Provocative

Figure 28. Coping with other communication styles

A. Communicating with an idea oriented person:

☐ Allow enough time for discussion.

☐ Do not get impatient when he or she goes off on tangents.

□ In your opening, try to relate the discussed topic to a broader concept or idea (in other words, be conceptual).

□ Stress the uniqueness of the idea or topic at hand.

□ Emphasize future value or relate the impact of the idea on the future.

□ If writing to an idea oriented person, try to stress the key concepts which underlie your proposal or recommendation right at the outset. Start off with an overall statement and work toward the more particular.

B. Communicating with a process oriented person:

□ Be precise (state the facts).

□ Organize your presentation in logical order:
    Background
    Present Situation
    Outcome

□ Break down your recommendations.

□ Include options (consider alternatives) with pros and cons.

□ Do not rush a process oriented person.

□ Outline your proposal (1, 2, 3...).

C. Communicating with a people oriented person:

□ Allow for small talk (do not start the discussion right away).

□ Stress the relationships between your proposal and the people concerned.

□ Show how the idea worked well in the past.

□ Indicate support from well respected people.

□ Use an informal writing style.

D. Communicating with an action oriented person:

□ Focus on the results first (state the conclusion right at the outset).

□ State your best recommendation (do not offer many alternatives).

□ Be as brief as possible.

□ Emphasize the practicality of your ideas.

□ Use visual aids.

(f) *Practicing other styles:*

Participants work in pairs practicing the styles they feel less comfortable with.

(g) *Helping others through intercultural communication skills:*

When trying to help a foreigner ease the cross-cultural adjustment process, it is helpful to keep in mind that:

(1) one cannot solve someone else's problem for him or her. The other person has to come up with his/her own solution to the problem at hand;

(2) what is good for one individual is not necessarily good for another;

(3) what is effective in one situation is not automatically so in another;

(4) people and situations are different. Consequently, decisions about what one should do have to be tailored to the reality of the moment (a *contingency* approach seems to be appropriate);

(5) to learn how to learn is the key to success when trying to adjust to another culture.

Five basic listening and responding *styles* have been identified by social behaviorists. Let us see what they are and how cross-cultural helpers can use them to assist foreigners who go through the culture shock process.

1. The five basic listening and responding styles:

A. *Interpretive:* A response characterized by the fact that the receiver tells the sender what his/her problem is but not what he/she should do about it;

B. *Supportive:* A response that indicates that the receiver wants to reassure the sender, reduce his/her intensity of feeling and show support for what has been already decided or done;

C. *Probing:* A response which leads to further information. The receiver questions the sender and provokes a discussion to clarify the issue at stake;

D. *Understanding:* The receiver paraphrases what the sender said in order to check the accuracy of his/her understanding of what he has said, how the sender sees the problem and how he/she feels about it;

E. *Evaluative:* A response which shows that the receiver has assessed the sender's problem as well as the relevance of his/her reactions. The receiver also indicates what the sender might or ought to do.

The following exercises [50] give you an opportunity to practice the five styles in order to help someone to adjust in a new cultural environment in the best possible way.

Please (1) read the description of the situation and write down what you would say assuming you wanted to use each of the five styles; (2) share your answers with the other participants; (3) select the best examples you have for each type and report to the group when the time comes up; and (4) discuss with the group the appropriateness of each response. response.

---

[50] The exercises have been developed for a workshop organized by the International Communication Agency, Washington, DC, for a group of twenty escort-interpreters (January 1979).

SITUATION 1.

A foreigner who has been in your country for a couple of days tells you that he cannot take it any more, it is too much for him, he is homesick and that he wants to go home at once.

Understanding response: _____

_____

_____

Probing response: _____

_____

_____

Supportive Response: _____

_____

_____

Interpretive response: _____

_____

_____

Evaluative response: _____

_____

_____

SITUATION 2.

Assume that you are an escort-interpreter and that you meet the foreigner you have been assigned to at the airport. His first reaction is to let you know that he did not expect a female escort-interpreter to assist him in his stay in the country. This has to be changed at once.

Understanding response: _____

_____

_____

Probing response: _____

_____

_____

Supportive response: _____

_____

_____

Interpretive response: _____

_____

_____

Evaluative response: _____

_____

_____

4. **Time:** Two to three hours.

5. **Conceptual Framework:**

INPUT 1.
Four Different Types of Verbal Communication[51]

TYPES	INTENTIONS	BEHAVIORS
1. SOCIABLE	Meet social expectations.	Respecting social conventions, chit-chatting, exchanging amenities, anecdotes, jokes, reports of events, factual information...
2. PERSUASIVE	Change the other person.	Directing, persuading, blaming, demanding, evaluating, advising, praising, concealing, defending, diagnosing, assuming, competing, imposing, provoking, controlling, pressing...
3. EXPLORATORY	Clarify and issue.	Exploring, searching, pondering, wondering, reflecting, questioning, speculating, elaborating, expanding...
4. AUTHENTIC AND SYNERGISTIC	Exchange meanings and reach mutal transformation.	Being aware, active, understanding, accepting, up-front, explicit, creative, clear, honest, caring, supportive, constructive, discreet, responsive, cooperative, congruent.

INPUT 2
The Five Listening and Responding Styles and Their Uses

It seems that Americans use the five listening and responding styles in the following frequency: (1) evaluative, (2) interpretive, (3) supportive, (4) probing, and (5) understanding.

No style is in itself good or bad. It depends upon the people involved as well as the situation they are in. However, it has been shown that:

---

[51] Adapted from S. Miller, E.W. Nunally and D.B. Wackman, *Alive and Aware, op. cit.* A Modification and Elaboration of W.F. Hill, Hill Interaction Matrix: Scoring Manual Use, Los Angeles Youth Studies Center, 1961.

(A) The overuse or underuse of any style can be a handicap when counselling other people;

(B) The failure to select the appropriate response explains quite a great number of miscommuications;

(C) The understanding response can be quite powerful, especially at the outset of the interaction;

(D) To avoid giving an evaluative response in the early stages of a relationship is indicated in most cases (a value judgment often leads to another value judgment);

(E) The usefulness of the five styles can be roughly described as follows:

Understanding: helps the sender expand upon his/her ideas, feelings, perceptions, etc., and increases the accuracy of communication between the sender and receiver.

Probing: helps to clarify the problem and assist the sender in exploring the full implications of his/her decision.

Supportive: useful when the sender needs to feel accepted and is looking for support and reassurance.

Interpretive: helps the sender realize the impact of what he/she just said upon the receiver. This can lead to a constructive confrontation.

Evaluative: useful when the receiver is specifically asked to make a value judgement, to disclose his/her own values, attitudes and feelings.

INPUT 3
Using Communication Skills Across Cultures

The facilitator introduces five communication skills which have been identified by social scientists as useful:

☐ Showing interest and understanding (attending)

☐ Using silence

☐ Paraphrasing

☐ Asking open-ended questions

☐ Reflecting feelings

The participants are asked to meet in small (4-5 person) groups and discuss the following:

1. Can all the five skills be used in any culture?

2. What are the shortcomings of the skills if used in foreign cultures?

3. How to adjust the use of the skills?

According to the group discussions I have attended, it seems that all five skills can be used in various cultural settings with the following provisions:

a. their expressions are congruent with the norms of the cultural environment, *i.e.*, silence is acceptable, you show your interest by nodding, you paraphrase from time to time (not all the time), etc.;

b. their impact on the people who belong to the other culture(s) is closely monitored.

6. Handouts and Readings:

(a) Handouts:

Communication Modes: An Experiential Lecture, *The 1972 Annual Handbook for Group Facilitators*, p. 173.

Stumbling Blocks to Intercultural Communication, LaRay M. Barna, *Readings in Intercultural Communication*, Vol. 1, SIETAR.

Openness, Collusion and Feedback, *The 1972 Annual Handbook for Group Facilitators*, p. 197.

Hill Interaction Matrix (HIM), Conceptual Framework for Understanding Groups, *The 1973 Annual Handbook for Group Facilitators*, p. 159.

A Question of Style, D.K. Berlo, *The Personnel Administrator*, July/August 1974.

The Circular Process of Social Interaction, *Reading Book for Laboratories in Human Relations Teaching*, NTL Publications.

Personal Counselling Across Cultural Boundaries, C.H. Clarke, paper presented at the International Communication Association Conference, Montreal, Canada, April 1973.

Helping Those "In the Middle:" The Interpreters in the Intercultural Communicating, Provo, UT: Language Research Center, Brigham Young University, 1979.

"How to Tell When Someone is Saying 'NO,'" in *Topics in Culture Borrowing, Vol. U*, by J. Rubin, Honolulu: East-West Center, 1976.

"On Relating," T.I. Rubin, *Mainliner*, February 1977, pp. 27-28.

(b) Readings:

Brammer, L., *The Helping Relationship: Process and Skills*, Englewood Cliffs, NJ: Prentice-Hall, 1973.

Byker, D. and L.J. Anderson, *Communication as Identification: An Introductory View*, New York: Harper & Row, 1975.

Carkhuff, R.R., *Helping and Human Relations,* New York: Holt, Rinehart & Winston, 2 vols., 1969.

Combs, A. and D. Syngg, *Individual Behavior: A Perceptual Approach to Behavior,* New York: Harper & Row, 1959.

Goffman, E., *The Presentation of Self in Everyday Life,* Woodstock, NY: The Overlook Press, 1973.

Mischel, T. (ed.), *Understanding Other Persons,* Oxford: Basil Blackwell, 1974.

Mok, P.P., *I Speak Your Language,* New York: Drake-Beam & Associates, 1973.

Rogers, C.R., *On Becoming a Person,* Boston: Houghton Mifflin, 1961.

Ruesch, J. and G. Bateson, *Communication: The Social Matrix of Psychiatry,* New York: The Norton Library, 1969.

Skinner, B.F., *Beyond Freedom and Dignity,* New York: Knopf, 1971.

Stephenson, W., *The Study of Behavior,* Chicago: University of Chicago, Midway reprint, 1953.

THE PRACTICE OF EMPATHY

If somebody 'sees' something that the rest of us do not see — seeing being a certain excitation of the central nervous system, to which the ego contributes — we say he is dreaming or crazy or out of touch with reality, because reality is the model, the consensus, the paradigm.

— A. Smith

Empathy is the ability to see and understand how other people construct reality, or more specifically how they perceive, discover and invent the inner and outer worlds. We all use empathy. All the time. We constantly guess what people think and feel. The problem is that in most cases we guess wrongly. We assume that what is going on in somebody else's mind is somewhat identical to our own psychic processes. We tend to forget that we are different. Sometimes, drastically different. To practice empathy is to recognize and take full advantage of those differences. It indeed gives us an opportunity to enrich ourselves and hundreds of original ways of shaping what *is*.

WORKSHOP 12

1. Aim: To understand empathy and improve our ability to see the world (or reality) as others do.

2. Objectives: Participants will:

(1) Define the meaning of *empathy* (exercises and all inputs under conceptual framework);

(2) Assess their ability to practice empathy (self-assessment exercise);

(3) Improve their empathic skills (group exercise and Gestalt exercise).

3. Process:

(a) The group reflects upon the two following statements:

"A human being is an organizer of reality with a wide variety of options. The more he exercises these options, the more human and the less animal he of she is."

— L. Leshan

"Human beings are constantly thinking about others and about what others are thinking about them, and what others think they are thinking about others, and so on. One may be wondering about what is going on inside the other. One desires or fears that other people will know what is going on inside oneself."

— R.D. Laing
— M. Phillipson
— A.R. Lee

(b) Participants are asked to write down on two special blank cards (1) what they think and feel, right now, of which other people in the room are not aware, and (2) what they see in others (*i.e.*, the group) about which others are not concerned. They do not sign the cards, which are collected and read to the group by the facilitators, who do not make any comments. A discussion on the meaning of empathy follows.

(c) Empathy can be defined as "the capability to put one's self into somebody else's shoes and in so doing understand how he or she constructs reality."

(d) *Measuring one's own ability to practice empathy (a self-assessment exercise).*

□ Participants are informed that they are going to have to listen to a taped critical incident [52]. It is a dialogue between Mr. Miller (an American project manager in Kenya), and Mr. Costa Maniatis (a Greek agronomist who works on the same project). The tape will be played twice so that participants can, first, get acquainted with the case and, second, identify as many cultural assumptions as possible, which are behind what the two characters say (*why do they say what they say?*). Participants are asked to use Mr. Miller's and Mr. Maniatis' culture frames or references to pinpoint their basic assumptions (not theirs). The exercise is called the "Attribution Exercise" [53].

□ Participants listen to the tape (Phase 1: the text which follows is *not* distributed) and try to record as many cultural assumptions as possible (*Figure 29*). The tape can be played twice to assist the participants in their recording.

THE MANIATIS CASE
Part One

Narrator: Mr. John Miller is American and leads a team of international ex-

---

[52] Adapted from H.C. Triandia and Vassilios (1972).

[53] "Attribution" because it has been shown that most people use their own frames of reference when they try to understand others.

perts in Kenya. Twelve experts are working on the project and Costa Maniatis (a Greek) is one of them. He is an agronomist.

The following dialogue took place between the boss, Mr. Miller, and Costa Maniatis:

C.M.: (knocking on door): Did you call me, Mr. Miller?

J.M. Ah, Costa, yes...come in. *(door shuts)* It is about the report required by the Ministry of Agriculture. How long will it take you to finish it?

C.M.: (surprised) I don't know, Mr. Miller...umm...Do you think...?

J.M.: No, Costa, no! *You* are in the best position to analyze time requirements. ments.

C.M.: Well, let's say ten days.

J.M.: Ten days...OK...let's say fifteen—allright? Then...it is agreed you will do it in fifteen days.

C.M.: Yes, Mr. Miller.

Narrator: In fact, the report needed 30 days of regular work. So the Greek worked day and night, but at the end of fifteen days he still needed one more day's work.

The following dialogue took place fifteen days later in Costa Maniatis' office:

J.M.: Well, Costa, where is the report?

C.M.: It will be ready tomorrow.

J.M.: But *we* agreed it would be ready *today*.

Narrator: From that day the relationship between Costa Maniatis and Miller became more and more difficult, and three months later, Costa asked for his transfer to another project.

Why did this happen?

Figure 29. Measuring one's own ability to practice empathy.

Who Said	What	Meaning What? (Cultural Assumptions)

□ After having given enough time to the participants to reflect upon what they have heard (between ten and fifteen minutes), part two of the tape is played. Participants check their list of assumptions without modifying them.

THE MANIATIS CASE
Part Two
A Systematic Cross-Cultural Analysis

Behavior	Attribution
American: How long will it take you to finish this report?	*American:* I'm asking him to participate.
	Greek: His behavior makes no sense. He is the boss; why doesn't he tell me. I'm going to ask for instructions.
Greek: I do not know. Do you think...	
American: You are in the best position to analyze time requirements.	*American:* He refuses to take responsibility.
	Greek: I asked him for an order.
Greek: Ten days.	*American:* I must press him to take responsibility for his actions.
American: Take fifteen. It is agreed you will do it in fifteen days.	
	Greek: What nonsense! I had better give him an answer.
	American: He lacks the ability to estimate time; this time estimate is totally inadequate. Better propose a longer period.
	American: I offer a contract.
	Greek: These are my orders. Fifteen days.

(*Narrator:* In fact, the report needed 30 days of regular work, so the Greek worked day and night, but at the end of the fifteenth day, he still needed one more day's work.)

American: Where is the report?	*American:* I am making sure he fulfills his contract.
Greek: It will be ready tomorrow.	*Greek:* He is asking for the report.
American: But we had agreed it would be ready today.	
The American is surprised.	*BOTH* attribute that it is not ready.
	American: I must teach him to fulfill a contract.
	Greek: The stupid, incompetent boss. Not only did he give me the wrong instructions, but he doesn't even appreciate that I did a 30-day job in sixteen days.
	Greek: I won't work for such a man.

□ Participants are now asked to *score* their ability to practice empathy.

Figure 30. Measuring one's own ability to practice empathy

Who said	What	Meaning What? (Cultural Assumptions)	Scoring (Check here when right)
American	How long will it take you to finish the report?	(1) Employees should be involved in the decision-making process.	□
		(2) Employees are accountable.	□
		(3) Planning is important.	□
Greek	I do not know.	(4) The question does not make any sense. The manager is accountable. To recognize that one does not know is OK.	□
		(5) It is the responsibility of the manager to **tell** the employee what to do and **how**.	□
Greek	Do you think..?	(6) The manager is the one who is supposed to know. He should provide some instructions to the employee.	□
American	No, Costa...	(7) The employee should take responsibility.	□
American	You are in the best position to analyze time requirements.	(8) Delegation of responsibility to those who know.	□
		(9) It is the role of the manager to press the team member to take responsibility for his/her own actions.	□
Greek	Well...ten days.	(10) Since the **boss** insists, an answer has to be given. After all, he is the "authority."	□
American	Ten days...OK. ...	(11) The **problem** has to be assessed. In this case, it is the team member's lack of ability to estimate time. (Problem orientation.)	□
American	Take 15. It is agreed you will do it in 15 days.	(12) A contract is offered.	□
Greek	Yes...	(13) Instructions are received.	□
American	Where is the report?	(14) Part of a manager's role is to make sure that the contract is fulfilled.	□

Who Said	What	Meaning What? (Cultural Assumptions)	Scoring (Check here when right)
Greek	It will be ready tomorrow.	(15) Today or tomorrow is all right. Besides, the report needed 30 days and it will be done in sixteen.	☐
American	But we had agreed that it would be ready today!	(16) Importance of deadlines. A manager should teach his employees to respect deadlines.	☐
Greek		(17) The wrong instructions were given, so the boss is incompetent.	☐
		(18) The boss is insensitive. (He does not appreciate that the job was done in sixteen days instead of 30.)	☐
		(19) One cannot work with someone who is incompetent and insensitive.	☐
		(20) No further discussion with the boss is possible. The only alternative left is to leave.	☐

Scoring

Please encircle the items for which you were right. Tabulate them according to the following procedure:

Empathy 1 = 1−2−3−7−8−9−11−12−14−16

Empathy 2 = 4−5−6−10−13−15−17−18−19−20

   Total (Empathy 1+2) = 20

Understanding Your Scores

Empathy 1:

☐ A score between 7 and 10 shows that you understand some of the key characteristics of the American culture (managerial) quite well.

☐ A score between 4 and 6 shows an average empathic ability regarding the American managerial culture.

☐ A score between 0 and 3 characterizes a lack of empathic ability regarding the American managerial culture.

Empathy 2:

☐ A score between 7 and 10 shows a good understanding of the Greek culture.

☐ A score between 4 and 6 shows an average empathic ability (could be improved).

□ A score between 0 and 3 shows a need for improving one's own empathic ability.

Overall Empathic Ability:

□ A score between 14 and 20 shows that one is quite able to put oneself into somebody else's shows.

□ A score between 9 and 13 means that the empathic ability could be improved.

□ A score between 0 and 8 characterizes a lack of empathic ability.

□ The group now receives the two tests of the dialogues between Messrs. Miller and Maniatis. They discuss a couple of issues:

a. Impressions regarding the results of the self-assessment exercise;

b. Obstacles to the practice of empathy across cultures; and

c. Basic guidelines to improve one's own empathic ability.

(e) *An exercise on cultural values and empathy.*

Teams of four to six people are set up and the same instructions are given to everybody:

THE SITUATION[54]

You are a group of East African experts from Kenya, Uganda and Tanzania and have been asked to rank in order of priority the six following suggestions to improve the technical assistance system as it now exists:

□ We need more advance planning for technical assistance, including a fairly detailed manpower-planning projection of the foreign personnel needed at the sectoral level.

□ Emphasis on training (new system because the counterpart method has generally proved unsatisfactory), and preference for the use of training institutions in the country or region.

□ Whenever possible it is best to avoid committing an entire development project to a team of complementary or competitive, foreign technical personnel who make the major policy and administrative decisions in regard to that project.

□ None of the East African countries has adequate evaluation machinery for critically reviewing programs of technical assistance. The proposal is to build adequate evaluation machinery for giving confidential reports on the performance of technical personnel (foreigners) and critically reviewing programs and projects of technical assistance.

□ If local capacity exists to do a piece of work, there should be no need whatever to engage foreign technical assistance — operational or advisory — for the job.

□ A local person has to be the head of the project (if such a person is availa-

---

[54] Extract from "Technical Assistance Administration in East Africa," edited by Uashpal Tandon, The Dag Hammarskjold Foundation, Uppsala, Sweden.

ble), who can fully understand the natural rhythm of the society's culture, history, value systems and vision of the future. Moreover, decisions at the highest level should be made only by those local heads and their committees and without the participation of foreign advisors.

The Process

Step 1: You have fifteen minutes to rank the six recommendations without speaking to anyone (using the matrix on the next page).

Step 2: Working in a team, reach a consensus on a common ranking. You have 30 minutes to accomplish your task.

Step 3. Compare your individual and team rankings with the ranking of the national experts (see ranking of East African experts on page 147).

Step 4: Back in your team, analyze the *values* which underlie:

    a. your individual ranking.

    b. your team ranking.

    c. the East African experts' ranking.

You have 30 minutes for this task.

Step 5: Sharing with the group (fifteen minutes).

    a. identifying key values.

    b. individual work versus teamwork.

    c. the practice of empathy.

Issues to be discussed:

☐ How is the East Africans' ranking different from the rankings of the group of Americans, Europeans, ...?

☐ How would their ranking be today?

East African Experts' Ranking:

1. Need for advance planning;

2. Use of local capacity;

3. Avoid committing entire development project to team of foreigners;

4. Recruitment of local project managers;

5. Training; and

6. Evaluation.

(f) *A Gestalt exercise to improve empathy.*

Two chairs facing each other are put in the middle of the room. The facilitator asks for a volunteer who sits on one chair and starts the process by saying something about the way people who belong to another culture behave. After a while, he (or she) stops and moves to the other chair and this time speaks about the same topics as if he were part of the other culture. The other participants observe and discuss the experience when the exercise is over.

A variation of this exercise consists of relating some clearcut cross-cultural confrontations and asking the participants to go through the same process for each chosen situation.

(g) One way to practice empathy is to make sure that during a conversation we do not just listen and respond or react to the words which

Six Propositions	Step 1 Individual Ranking	Step 2 Team Ranking	Step 3 East Africans' Ranking	Step 4 Difference Between steps 1 and 2	Step 5 Difference Between steps 2 and 3
Need for advance planning					
Training					
Avoid committing entire development project to team of foreigners.					
Evaluation					
Use of local capacity.					
Recruitment of local project managers.					
				Individual score:	Team score:

	Team 1	Team 2	Team 3	Team 4
Team scores				
Average individual score				
Gain score				

are used, but also to the meanings hidden behind the words. This process implies that we attempt non-verbal clues and check with the other person the accuracy of our guess regarding what he or she intended to say. It goes like this:

☐ **WORDS:** It is a terrible day today, isn't it?
☐ **MEANING:** I feel upset today.
☐ **RESPONSE TO WORDS:** Well, the forecast is not too bad for this afternoon.
☐ **RESPONSE TO MEANING:** Yes, anything I can do to help?

☐ **WORDS:** The situation is hopeless here.
☐ **MEANING:** I don't know how to cope....
☐ **RESPONSE TO WORDS:** I agree. Let's get out of this country.
☐ **RESPONSE TO MEANING:** Maybe we need some more time to understand the situation.

☐ **WORDS:** I do not like training.
☐ **MEANING:** I feel insecure when participating in training.
☐ **RESPONSE TO WORDS:** Come on, training can be useful!
☐ **RESPONSE TO MEANING:** What's bothering you?

Ask the participants to (1) come up with some examples of their own (*e.g.*, "the deadline is unrealistic," "teamwork is the answer to our problem," ...), and (2) practice in trios (cross-cultural interaction should be chosen) [55].

(h) *Matching our cultural assumptions with those of the cultural environment.*

Have participants come up with a clarification of their basic assumptions regarding the following items:

(1) Initiative:

(2) Self-Development:

(3) Conflicts:

(4) Teamwork:

(5) Making mistakes:

Participants meet in pairs and match their respective assumptions. They also discuss the impact of the differences in perceptions on their interaction.

(i) *The C. Rogers exercise.*

Participants meet in trios and discuss an issue (*e.g.*, the new international economic order) applying the following rules:

---

[55] Non-verbal clues are closely watched during this exercise.

☐ Listen with understanding. Do not make evaluations of what the other person says.

☐ Be empathic or "achieve his or her frame of reference in regard to the thing which is talked about."

☐ "Each person can speak up for himself only after he has first restated the ideas and feelings of the previous speaker accurately, and to that speaker's satisfaction."[56]

☐ The third person acts as an observer during the exercise. At the end, he or she has to summarize the key points made by the two other people to their full satisfaction.

4. Time: Two hours.

5. Conceptual Framework:

INPUT 1
The Empathic Matrix[57]

Assume that we have two individuals, A. and B., who try to understand each other. Here are some of the key interpersonal dimensions they have to take into account to reach a mimimum of empathy:

	A	B
1.	A	B
2.	PA(A)	PB(B)
3.	PA(B)	PB(A)
4.	PA[B(A)]	PB[A(B)]
5.	PA(AB)	PB(BA)

1. A. and B. are psychologically and culturally different. (Question: How different are we?);

2. A. has a certain perception of himself or herself as well as B. (Question: How do I perceive myself if I am A. and how does B. perceive himself or herself?);

3. A. has a certain perception of B. and vice versa. (Question: How do I perceive the other person and how am I perceived by him or her?);

4. A. believes that B. perceives him or her in a certain way and vice versa. (Question: What do I think of the other person's perception of

---

[56] Rogers, C.R., *On Becoming a Person: Dealing with Breakdowns in Communication—Interpersonal and Intergroup*, Boston: Houghton-Mifflin, 1961, p. 329.

[57] For more information about the empathic matrix, read P. Casse, "Interaction Sociale et Empathie," in *L'Information Psychologique*, No. 48, 4th Trimester 1972, pp. 65-76.

myself and what does the other individual believe I think of him or her?);

5. A. and B. have a certain perception of their relationship. (Question: A.B. = B.A.?).

INPUT 2
The Inference Theory of Empathy [58]

Empathy, according to the inference theory, is defined as the ability to infer what other people mean in behaving the way they do on the basis of the similarities between "them" and "us." ("If I had done/said the same thing, I would have meant the following. Therefore, that is what he or she meant!")

The key assumptions under the inference theory of empathy are:

(A) I can clearly understand the relationship between my action and its purpose;

(B) The same behavior performed by different people has the same purpose (maybe people mean the same thing when they behave the same way);

(C) To understand others, one has to experience their internal states first, *i.e.*, emotions, feelings, thoughts, ...

INPUT 3
The Social Theory of Empathy [59]

Empathy is learned through a step-by-step process:

Step 1: The child imitates other people's behavior without too much understanding.

Step 2: The child learns to "manipulate" symbols and look at himself as others do. He performs others' roles with some understanding this time. This happens through *playing*.

Step 3. The child learns how to *fantasize* about other roles without playing them. He is able to understand the network of roles he (or she) is part of, grasp the expectations which are typically related to the different roles, and behave accordingly (My teacher expects this from me, my father....).

Step 4. The clarification of others' roles and their expectations *vis-a-vis* one's self, leads to a constant re-definition of self ("I understand others, what they expect from me, how they perceive me, what I can expect from them").

According to this theory, roles are defined and taken so that indiv-

---

[58] Asch, S., *Social Psychology*, Prentice-Hall, 1972.

[59] Mead, G.H., *Mind, Self and Society*, Chicago: University of Chicago Press, 1934.

duals can understand each other and empathize. Moving from one culture to another implies (a) a new understanding of the roles as they are defined in the new setting, and (b) a re-definition of one's self.

6. Handouts and readings:

(a) Handouts:

"Are You Listening? (A Simple Technique for Really Hearing What Others Say)", *TMM&I*, Spring 1979.

Albert, R.D. and J. Adamopoulos, "An Attributional Approach to Cultural Learning: The Cultural Assimilator," in *Topics in Culture Learning*, Vol. 4, 1976, Honolulu: East-West Center.

Bochner, S., "The Mediating Man and Cultural Diversity," in *Topics in Culture Learning*, Vol. 1, 1973, Honolulu: East-West Center.

(b) Readings:

Buber, M., *I and Thou*, New York: Charles Scribner's Sons, 1970.

Harris, T.A., *I'm OK — You're OK*, New York: Avon Books, 1973.

Johnson, D., *Reaching Out: Interpersonal Effectiveness and Self-Actualization*, Englewood Cliffs, NJ: Prentice-Hall, 1972.

Laing, R.D., H. Phillipson and A.R. Lee, *Interpersonal Perception (A Theory and a Method of Research)*, New York: Perennial Library, Harper & Row, 1966.

Luft, J. and H. Ingham, *The Johari Window: A Graphic Model for Interpersonal Relations*, Los Angeles: University of California, 1955.

Pirandello, L., *Chacun Sa Verité*, Paris: Gallimard, 1950.

Triandis, H.C., *Interpersonal Behavior*, Monterrey, CA: Brooks/Cole Publishing Co., 1977.

NEGOTIATION ACROSS CULTURES

The golden rule should be revised to read: Do not do unto others as you would they should do unto you. Their tastes may not be the same.
— G.B. Shaw

If one agrees that negotiation is the process by which an individual tries to persuade another person to change, or not to change, his or her behavior, one has to recognize that *people negotiate all the time!* A more sophisticated definition is the "negotiation is the process by which at least two parties with different needs and viewpoints try to reach an agreement on a matter of mutual interest." One should notice that, according to this definition, arguing, persuading and convincing are only parts of the negotiating process.

International or intercultural negotiation implies that (a) the parties involved belong to different cultures and therefore do not share the same ways of thinking, feeling and behaving or, another way to put it, the same values, beliefs, and assumptions; (b) the negotiation takes place in a cross-cultural environment, *e.g.*, an international organization, a third-party culture, etc.; and (c) the matter at stake is of a cross-cultural nature.

Managing negotiation means that the partices involved both *understand* what is happening during the negotiation as well as are able to adjust accordingly so that the process is controlled and everybody is able to achieve his or her objective (at least up tp a point).

The intercultural dimension of managing negotiation is characterized by the fact that the partners in negotiation have to go beyond what they are used to in terms of adjusting and controlling the dynamics of the interaction. In other words, they have to innovate!

WORKSHOP 13. [60]

1. Aim: To help workshop participants understand international-

---

[60] I am grateful to Ms. N. Lenthe and Mr. M. Karmer of the World Bank who helped me design this program.

intercultural negotiation and improve their negotiating effectiveness.

2. **Objectives:** Participants will:

(1) Define international-intercultural negotiation (discussion with trainer).

(2) Analyze five intercultural negotiation skills (the "Intercultural Negotiation Skills" exercise).

(3) Identify four negotiating styles as well as four modes of negotiation (conceptual framework: input 1).

(4) Assess their primary negotiation style (self-assessment exercise);

(5) Learn how to switch from one style to another (track exercises);

(6) Learn how to cope with different styles (group discussion);

(7) Examine some tactical and strategic aspects of intercultural negotiation (conceptual framework: input 2);

(8) Experience the negotiation process between two cultures (exercise and conceptual framework: input 3).

3. **Process:**

(a) The trainer introduces the concept of international/intercultural negotiation (see introduction to this chapter). The emphasis should be placed upon the fact that *managing* intercultural negotiation requires *knowledge* of what is happening during the negotiating process, *understanding* of the dynamics involved, *prediction* of the outcome of any move made during the negotiation, and, last but not least, *control* of the process through effective decisions.

(b) *Contracting for outcome:* Participants are asked to (1) clarify what they want to get out of the workshop and (2) specify how they will know that they have got what they wanted to get (individuals work on their own first and then in subgroups of three).

(c) Have small groups of four or five participants reflecting upon O. Klineberg's statement:

"The major hope seems to lie in a new approach to negotiation, a new concept of what can be done around the international conference table. Such an approach, if it could be realized, would have the following characteristics. First, it would be more flexible; ...Second, it would be more understanding; it would take into account how the situation appears to both sides, how our actions (whoever we may be) look to them, how our suggestions will be interpreted by those who see the world from a different perspective. Third, it would be less suspicious of the motives of others, and more willing to take a chance on the possibility that a sincere desire for peace is not the monopoly of one side. Fourth, it would be less greedy; it must approach the conference table not with the insistence that "our" side has to win, but with the readiness to find a solution that is reasonably satisfactory to both sides."

> — O. Klineberg
> *The Human Dimension in International*
> *Relations*, New York: Holt, Rinehart
> and Winston, 1964, pp. 145-146.

(d) An exercise in "International negotiation skills" is proposed to the group.

Instructions: Assume that you have to select someone who is going to represent your group in an international (intercultural) negotiation and proceed as follows:

Step 1. Meet in pairs and rank (1 being the most important and 5 the least important) the five proposed intercultural negotiation skills (see attachment). You have fifteen minutes to accomplish your task.

Step 2. Now meet with another pair and *negotiate* a common ranking of the same five skills. You have 30 minutes to reach complete agreement. Any extension beyond the 30 minutes will be penalized. You will be *recorded*[61] during the entire negotiation.

Step 3. Meet for debriefing.

The Five International Negotiating Skills
Ranking

□ **Skill A:** to be able to practice empathy and to see the world as other people see it. To understand others' behavior from their perspective.

□ **Skill B:** to be able to demonstrate the advantages of what one's proposals offer so that the counterparts in the negotiation will be willing to change.

□ **Skill C:** to be able to manage stress and cope with ambiguous situations as well as unpredictable demands.

□ **Skill D:** to be able to express one's own ideas in such a way that the people one negotiates with will objectively and fully understand what one has in mind.

□ **Skill E:** to be sensitive to the cultural background of the others and adjust the suggestions one wants to make to the existing constraints and limitations.

During the debriefing, the various rankings are identified and discussed. A break follows this phase.

(e) A self-assessment exercise is completed by the participants. No explanation is given about the meanings of **IN, NR, AN** and **FA** at this time.

---

61 Each negotiation is taped. Ideally, at least one negotiation is videotaped for demonstration purposes later on in the workshop.

NEGOTIATION SKILLS
A SELF-ASSESSMENT EXERCISE[62]

Please respond to this list of questions in terms of what you believe you do *when interacting with others.* Base your answers on your typical day-to-day activities. Be as frank as you can.

For each statement, please enter on the *SCORE SHEET* the number corresponding to your choice of the five possible responses given below:

1. If you have never (or very rarely) observed yourself doing what is described in the statement.

2. If you have observed yourself doing what is described in the statement OCCASIONALLY, BUT INFREQUENTLY: that is, less often than most other people who are involved in similar situations.

3. If you have observed yourself doing what is described in the statement about AN AVERAGE AMOUNT: that is, about as often as most other people who are involved in similar situations.

4. If you have observed yourself doing what is described in the statement FAIRLY FREQUENLTY: that is, somewhat more often than most other people who are involved in similar situations.

5. If you have observed yourself doing what is described in the statement VERY FREQUENTLY: that is, considerably more than most other people who are involved in similar situations.

Please answer each question.

1. I focus on the entire situation or problem.
2. I evaluate the facts according to a set of personal values.
3. I am relatively unemotional.
4. I think that the facts speak for themselves in most situations.
5. I enjoy working on new problems.
6. I focus on what is going on between people when interacting.
7. I tend to analyze things very carefully.
8. I am neutral when arguing.
9. I work in bursts of energy with slack periods in between.
10. I am sensitive to other people's needs and feelings.
11. I hurt people's feelings without knowing it.
12. I am good at keeping track of what has been said in a discussion.
13. I put two and two together quickly.
14. I look for common ground and compromise.
15. I use logic to solve problems.
16. I know most of the details when discussing an issue.
17. I follow my inspirations of the moment.
18. I take strong stands on matters of principle.

---

[62] An adaptation of the Interactive Style Questionnaire developed by Situation Management Systems, Inc.

19. I am good at using a step-by-step approach.

20. I clarify information for others.

21. I get my facts a bit wrong.

22. I try to please people.

23. I am very systematic when making a point.

24. I relate facts to experience.

25. I am good at pinpointing essentials.

26. I enjoy harmony.

27. I weigh the pros and cons.

28. I am patient.

29. I project myself into the future.

30. I let my decisions be influenced by my personal likes and wishes.

31. I look for cause and effect.

32. I focus on what needs attention now.

33. When others become uncertain or discouraged, my enthusiasm carries them along.

34. I am sensitive to praise.

35. I make logical statements.

36. I rely on well tested ways to solve problems.

37. I keep switching from one idea to another.

38. I offer bargains.

39. I have my ideas very well thought out.

40. I am precise in my arguments.

41. I bring others to see the exciting possibilities in a situation.

42. I appeal to emotions and feelings to reach a "fair" deal.

43. I present well articulated arguments for the proposals I favor.

44. I do not trust inspiration.

45. I speak in a way which conveys a sense of excitement to others.

46. I communicate what I am willing to give in return for what I get.

47. I put forward proposals or suggestions which make sense even if they are unpopular.

48. I am pragmatic.

49. I am imaginative and creative in analyzing a situation.

50. I put together very well-reasoned arguments.

51. I actively solicit others' opinions and suggestions.

52. I document my statements.

53. My enthusiasm is contagious.

54. I build upon others' ideas.

55. My proposals command the attention of others.

56. I like to use the inductive method   (from facts to theories).

57. I can be emotional at times.

58. I use veiled or open threats to get others to comply.

59. When I disagree with someone, I skillfully point out the flaws in the others' arguments.

60. I am low-key in my reactions.

61. In trying to persuade others, I appeal to their need for sensations and novelty.

62. I make other people feel that they have something of value to contribute.

63. I put forth ideas which are incisive.

64. I face difficulties with realism.

65. I point out the positive potential in discouraging or difficult situations.

66. I show tolerance and understanding of others' feelings.

67. I use arguments relevant to the problem at hand.

68. I am perceived as a down-to-earth person.

69. I go beyond the facts.

70. I give people credit for their ideas and contributions.

71. I like to organize and plan.

72. I am skillful at bringing up pertinent facts.

73. I have a charismatic tone.

74. When disputes arise, I search for the areas of agreement.

75. I am consistent in my reactions.

76. I quickly notice what needs attention.

77. I withdraw when the excitement is over.

78. I appeal for harmony and cooperation.

79. I am cool when negotiating.

80. I work all the way through to reach a conclusion.

NEGOTIATION STYLES

Score Sheet

Enter the score you assign each question (1, 2, 3, 4, or 5) in the space provided. *Please note:* The item numbers progress across the page from left to right. When you have all your scores, add them up vertically to attain four totals. Insert a "3" in any number space left blank.

1. _____	2. _____	3. _____	4. _____
5. _____	6. _____	7. _____	8. _____
9. _____	10. _____	11. _____	12. _____
13. _____	14. _____	15. _____	16. _____
17. _____	18. _____	19. _____	20. _____
21. _____	22. _____	23. _____	24. _____
25. _____	26. _____	27. _____	28. _____
29. _____	30. _____	31. _____	32. _____
33. _____	34. _____	35. _____	36. _____
37. _____	38. _____	39. _____	40. _____
41. _____	42. _____	43. _____	44. _____
45. _____	46. _____	47. _____	48. _____
49. _____	50. _____	51. _____	52. _____
53. _____	54. _____	55. _____	56. _____

(continued on next page)

57. _____ 58. _____ 59. _____ 60._____
61. _____ 62. _____ 63. _____ 64. _____
65. _____ 66. _____ 67. _____ 68. _____
69. _____ 70. _____ 71. _____ 72. _____
73. _____ 74. _____ 75. _____ 76. _____
77. _____ 78. _____ 79. _____ 80._____
IN: _____ NR: _____ AN: _____ FA: _____

(f) The theory regarding the four negotiating styles and four modes of negotiation is provided to the group and the participants are asked to relate it to their *negotiation style profile*. The trainer can use (1) the tally sheet for negotiating patterns, and (2) the conceptual framework: input 1, to present the theory on negotiation styles.

(g) A tape or videotape which has been used for the "international negotiation skills" exercise can be used for demonstrating to the group the four styles and four modes of negotiation.

(h) The group is split into small subgroups and participants are asked to find out the "right" answer (according to each style) to the following statements:

STATEMENTS	TYPICAL ANSWERS ACCORDING TO FOUR STYLES
1. Your boss says, "Sorry, but you have to rewrite your report."	1. *Factual style.* You say: "What do you mean by rewriting? Which parts do I have to rewrite? Do you have guidelines that I can use?..."
2. The representative of the government says: "Frankly, I would like to go ahead with the project we are talking about but I believe that my country is already too much involved in too many projects."	2. *Intuitive style.* You say: "Don't you see that this project fits into your overall program... look at the advantages... It is a good investment!"
3. Your secretary says: "I am terribly upset about the fact that I am the only one in this unit who works overtime. Sorry, but I cannot type your tables. They will have to wait."	3. *Analytical style.* You say: "Let's see who is doing what right now. Well, if you do not type them we are going to be late and that will lead to..."
4. One of the team members says: "I do not want to work with Mr. X."	4. *Normative style.* You say: "What's wrong with X? I think you're making a mistake. Do it for the last time..."

NEGOTIATION STYLE PROFILE

Enter now your four scores on the bar chart below. Construct your profile by connecting the four data points.

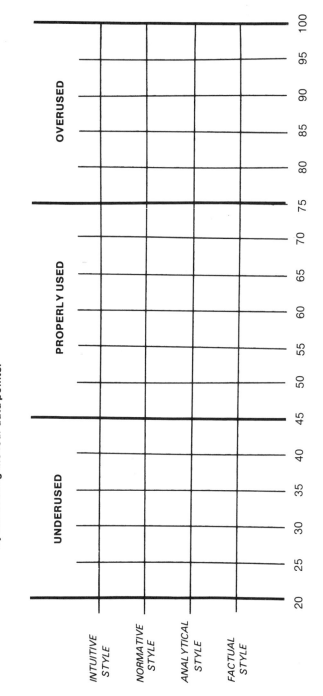

(i) Participants are instructed to reconvene in their negotiating teams, play back the tape and help each other identify the different styles they have used in negotiating (including the dominant one, if possible). They cross-check the results of their self-assessment exercise. A "tally sheet for negotiating partners" *(Figure 31)* is provided to the participants.

Figure 31. Tally sheet for negotiating patterns

Four Styles / Negotiating Partners				
1. FACTUAL **Basic Assumption:** "The facts speak for themselves." **Behavior:** Pointing out facts in a neutral way, keeping track of what has been said, reminding people of their statements, knowing most of the details of the discussed issue and sharing them with others, clarifying, relating facts to experience, being low-key in their reactions, looking for proof, documenting their statements. **Key Words:** Meaning, define, explain, clarify, facts.				
2. INTUITIVE **Basic Assumption:** "Imagination can solve any problem." **Behavior:** Making warm and enthusiastic statements, focusing on the entire situation or problem, pinpointing essentials, making projections into the future, being imaginative and creative in analyzing the situation, keeping switching from one subject to another, going beyond the facts, coming up with new ideas all the time, pushing and withdrawing from time to time, putting two and two together quickly, getting their facts a bit wrong sometimes, being deductive. **Key Words:** Principles, essential, tomorrow, creative, idea.				

3. NORMATIVE **Basic Assumption:** "Negotiating is bargaining." **Behavior:** Judging, assessing and evaluating the facts according to a set of personal values, approving and disapproving, agreeing and disagreeing, using loaded words, offering bargains, proposing rewards, incentives, appealing to feelings and emotions to reach a "fair" deal, demanding, requiring, threatening, involving power, using status, authority, correlating, looking for compromise, making effective statements, focusing on people, their reactions, judging, attention to communication and group processes. **Key words:** Wrong, right, good, bad, like.				
4. ANALYTICAL **Basic Assumption:** "Logic leads to the right conclusions." **Behavior:** Forming reasons, drawing conclusions and applying them to the case in negotioation, arguing in favor or against one's own or others' position, directing, breaking down, dividing, analyzing each situation for cause and effect, identifying relationships of the parts, putting things into logical order, organizing, weighing the pros and cons thoroughly, making identical statements, using linear reckoning. **Key Words:** Because, then, consequently, therefore, in order to.				

(j) Four teams are given the following assignment: Brainstorm and identify *when which style should be used* (a situational approach).

Team 1 works on the factual style which is quite often effective when the situation requires a clarification of the available information (what is it?).

Team 2 works on the intuitive style which is particularly indicated when a set of *objectives* (projections into the future) have to be identified.

Team 3 works on the analytical style which can be used to explore different *strategies* to achieve the agreed-upon objectives.

Team 4 works on the normative style which is helpful when a decision (evaluation) has to be made.

(k) The group is split into four subgroups which are requested to set up guidelines about how to cope with other negotiating styles. They compare their suggestions with the guidelines which have been produced by the other groups (see Figure 32).

Figure 32. Guidelines for Negotiating with People having Different Styles.

1. *Negotiating with Someone Having a Factual Style.*
□ Be *precise* in presenting your facts.
□ Refer to the *past* (what has already been tried out, what has worked, what has been shown from past experiences...).
□ Be *indicative* (go from the facts to the principles.
□ Know your dossier (including the details).
□ Document what you say.

2. *Negotiating with Someone Having an Intuitive Style.*
□ Focus on the situation as a whole.
□ Project yourself into the future (look for opportunities).
□ Tap the imagination and creativity of your partner.
□ Be quick in reacting (jump from one idea to another).
□ Build upon the reaction of the other person.

3. *Negotiating with Someone Having an Analytical Style.*
□ Use logic when arguing.
□ Look for causes and effects.
□ Analyze the relationships between the various elements of the situtation or problem at stake.
□ Be patient.
□ Analyze various options with their respective pros and cons.

4. *Negotiating with Someone Having a Normative Style.*
□ Establish a sound relationship right at the outset of the negotiation.
□ Show your interest in what the other person is saying.
□ Identify his or her values and adjust to them accordingly.
□ Be ready to compromise.
□ Appeal to your partner's feelings.

(l) *Track Exercises.* The purpose of this part of the workshop is to learn how to switch from one style to another.

Step 1. Participants meet in trios.

Step 2. Each participant identifies his or her *primary* style (*i.e.*, the style with which he or we feels most comfortable). The trainer announces that three exercises are going to be given and that each member of the trio will have an opportunity to practice (in an exaggerated way) his or her primary style with another member while the third member will play the role of an observer.

It should also be clarified that:

a. The primary style should be identified and presented to the other team members before knowing what the exercise is going to be.

b. Each round of the exercise will last five minutes.

c. The "performer" should overdo it in terms of using his or her primary style.

d. The member who responds to the "performer" does not have to use a particular style.

e. After each round, the observer will provide some feedback on what happened. Four minutes will be devoted to a discussion on the outcome of the interaction.

The trainer is now ready to present the exercises one by one:

First Round: "A friend and colleague of yours told you that your boss is not happy about your performance. You decide to go and see your boss to discuss this issue."

Second Round: "You have been invited by the boss of your boss to meet with him and discuss your request for a promotion. Present your case to him."

Third Round: "You have just learned that a colleague of yours is taking full advantage of a project you successfully initiated. You decide to have a conversation with that colleague."

Step 3. The participants select the styles with which they feel the least comfortable and practice the same way they did with their primary styles.

First Round: "You must inform one of your subordinates that his or her performance is very weak."

Second Round: "Express your views briefly on a controversial topic about which you feel strongly. Try to convince your counterpart of the validity of your position."

Third Round: "You feel very strongly that your talents are unrewarded. You meet with your boss to discuss the matter."

Step 4. This time the performer does not reveal which style(s) he or she is going to use during the exercise. It is up to the second member of the trio to (a) identify the style(s) used and (b) try to adjust accordingly.

First Round: "Por is a competent man who worked in a sugar refinery for some years. Because of this ability, his boss appointed him manager of a small branch to be constructed in his home town. Por is instructed to select the supervisory and production personnel from among the local people. A great many of the individuals whom he chooses are his relatives, both near and distant. This is against the policy of the organization and the boss is very upset. [63]   Assume that you are the boss and negotiate a solution to the problem with Por."

Second Round: "A large American tractor firm was planning to set up an assembly and service plant in Saudi Arabia. They had sent their representative, Mr. Alton, to Saudi Arabia to arrange some early production schedules. The main purpose of these schedules was to lay out a plan for the implementation of the plant over a three-year period. A Saudi firm was eager to be the local outlet. The executives of the local firm were eager and cooperative, but Mr. Alton still felt uneasy. He reported to his superiors that he was not sure of the sincerity of the Saudis' eagerness, since they were extremely reluctant to give him exact dates and plans for the implementation schedule. The Saudis seemed to want to adopt a "wait and see" attitude. [64]   Assume that you are Mr. Alton and negotiate an action plan with the Saudi representative.

Third Round: "Try to convince your counterpart that you are getting a lot out of this workshop."

(m) *Slow Motion Exercise.* Participants are requested to rank (individually) the five negotiating tactics which are provided hereunder according to their importance in relation to cross-cultrual negotiation.

Five Negotiation Tactics.

☐ Find common ground as rapidly as possible.

☐ Explore the differences.

☐ Get a "yes" as quickly as possible.

☐ Overwhelm the other party with facts and data.

☐ Be flexible.

Participants *plan* their negotiation and when they are ready go through a "slow motion" negotiating exercise *(Figure 33)* with another member of the group. The rules of the simulation are:

1. Each pair has 30 minutes to reach a consensus and a common understanding.

2. No verbal interaction is allowed. The sheet provided has to be used back and forth between the two negotiators.

3. The messages are decoded by the two negotiators according to the

---

[63]   From the Thai culture assimilator. Group Effectiveness Research Laboratory, Department of Psychology, University of Illinois, Urbana, IL 1967.

[64]   An adaptation from the Saudi-culture assimilator.

four negotiating styles and four modes when the exercise is over.

4. All participants share their findings.

Figure 33. Negotiation Across Cultures (A Slow-Motion Exercise)

SENDER	RECEIVER	MESSAGES	DECODING

(n) *The Red-Blue Culture Exercise* [65] The purpose of the exercise is to give an opportunity to the group to experience the negotiation process between two different micro-cultures (the Red and Blue cultures). More specifically, participants will check the impact of some basic assumptions regarding the objectives of the negotiation, trust, conflict, power, and decision-making on negotiating.

Process:

1. The facilitator splits the group into two negotiating teams which meet in two different rooms. Two observers for each team are also selected.

2. He or she explains that the exercise is about negotiation between two cultures. The tally sheet is given to each team *without* any explanation. The tally sheet *(Figure 34)* is reproduced on a flipchart so that everybody can focus upon the same information. The two teams have ten minutes to clarify the given information. The facilitator is ready to answer any question they may have. Checklist for observers is also distributed *(Figure 35)*. It is pointed out that observers cannot interfere during the exercise. They are free to move around.

---

[65] This is an adaptation from the "Prisoners' Dilemma" exercise, *A Handbook of Structured Experiences for Human Relations Training*, University Associates Press, Vol. III, pp. 60-62.

3. The facilitator clarifies the fact that Rounds 4, 7 and 10 are preceded by a five-minute negotiation. It means that each team will have to select a representative (not necessarily the same one for each round), and send him or her to the negotiation meeting which will take place in a third room. The negotiation between representatives will be taped or video-taped.

4. It is important to leave complete freedom to the two teams as far as the clarification of the purpose of the exercise is concerned. However, questions regarding who selects what and the meaning of the various possible combinations should be thoroughly answered.

5. Round 1 begins and after three minutes the decisions made by the two teams are written on flipcharts. Then the groups move to round 2 and so on.

6. Rounds 4, 7, and 10 consist of a five-minute negotiation between two representatives of the Red and Blue cultures and a three-minute decision-making session.

7. Round 10 is followed by the announcement of the final decision.

8. Since this exercise can be "heavy" at times and lead to sensitive reactions, the debriefing part is *critical*. At least *one hour* should be devoted to the processing of what has happened. Observers should report first, participants should feel free to say whatever they want and clarify all issues they have identified. The facilitator will memorize the key points from time to time and relate what is said to real life situations.

Figure 34. Negotiation Between Two Cultures
(Tally Sheet)

Blue Culture

	X	Y
A	+3 +3	+6 −6
B	−6 +6	−3 −3

Red Culture

AX: Both teams win 3 points
AY: Red loses 6 points,
     Blue wins 6 points
BX: Red wins 6 points,
     Blue loses 6 points
BY: Both teams lose 3 points

ROUND	MINUTES	CHOICE		CUMULATIVE POINTS	
		RED	BLUE	RED	BLUE
1	3				
2	3				
3	3				
4*	5= Negotiation 3= Decision				
5	3				
6	3				
7**	5= Negotiation 3= Decision				
8	3				
9	3				
10**	5= Negotiation 3= Decision				

A = De-briefing in sub-group using tapes
B = De-briefing in total group.

* Payoff points are doubled for this round
** Payoff points are squared for this round

Figure 35. Negotiation Exercise
Checklist for Observers

Questions	*Content*	*Process*
(1) Did the group clarify its objectives?	What did they *want* to achieve through negotiation?	How did they clarify their objectives? (Once and for all, or ...)
(2) What was the impact of trust (or mistrust) on the negotiation process?	Did the trust issue come up during the negotiation?	How did the group handle this issue?
(3) What about some basic assumptions regarding:		
— Conflict	Was there any conflict?	How was it handled by the group?
— Power	Was there any power confrontation ("power game") during the negotiation?	How was power used during the negotiation?
— Decision-making	What were the key decisions?	Who made the decisions? How?

Other issues to be discussed:

a. the meaning of winning and losing;

b. taking risks;

c. using a mediator or third party (advantages and disadvantages);

d. competition;

e. leadership;

f. role of representatives selected for the negotiations;

g. pre-conceptions (influence of past experiences on the negotiating process);

h. breaking negotiation;

i. short-term versus long-term.

4. Time: Between ten and twelve hours.

5. Conceptual Framework:

INPUT 1

Psychological types (C.G. Jung) and Negotiating Styles.

As we have seen before (Chapter 3, two different ways of perceiving according to C.G. Jung's psychological types), the psyche possesses two ways of collecting data or gathering information about the outer and inner worlds: *the senses* and *the intuition.* According to the same model, the mind also has two different approaches regarding the treatment or processing of information: the *thinking* and *feeling* functions.

The Psychic Compass: Two Processing Functions

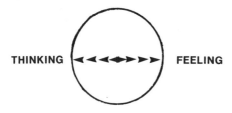

(a) *Thinking:* We process the information collected through our senses and intuition in a logical, neutral, objective, analytical, systematic and "scientific" way. One compares, differentiates, abstracts, specifies....

(b) *Feeling:* We process data using our values to assess their relevance and importance: we like or don't like, it is good or bad, right or wrong, important or not. The collected information is weighted according to one's own value system. It colours our evaluation of emotions and sensitivity. It makes us human.

All the issues pointed out on pages 42 and 43 are relevant.

The Complete Psychic Compass [66]

Senses

Thinking **Feeling**

Intuition

---

[66] For more information on the psychic compass as defined by C.G. Jung, consult Progoff, *Jung's Psychology and its Social Meaning,* New York: Anchor Books, 1973, pp. 86-99.

The four dominant psychic functions determine the nature of the *negotiation styles:*

PSYCHIC FUNCTIONS	NEGOTIATING STYLES
Sensing	Factual
Intuition	Intuitive
Thinking	Analytical
Feeling	Normative

1. *FA or Factual Style.* People using the factual style negotiating roles are cool, collected, patient, down-to-earth, present-oriented, precise, realistic, able to document their statements, sticking to the facts that speak for themselves.

2. *IN or Intuitive Style.* This style is characterized by a charismatic tone, a holistic approach (the entire situation is reviewed at the same time), a strong imagination, a tendency to jump from one subject to another, a lot of ups and downs, a fast pace, a deductive way to approach problems as well as a future orientation.

3. *NR or Normative Style.* For those people who use this style negotiating is basically *bargaining.* They judge, assess, and evaluate the facts according to a set of personal values. They appeal to feelings, offer bargains, propose rewards and incentives. They look for compromise.

4. *AN or Analytical Style.* The basic assumption which underlies this style is the "logic leads to the right conclusions." These people form reasons, analyze each situation in terms of cause and effect, put things into logical order, weigh the pros and cons, use a sort of linear reasoning. They are unemotional and focus upon the relationship of parts.

(d) *Four Modes of Negotiating.* Any individual can use his or her psychic energy in four different ways when negotiating:

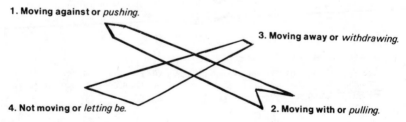

1. Moving against or *pushing.*

3. Moving away or *withdrawing.*

4. Not moving or *letting be.*

2. Moving with or *pulling.*

(1) *Moving against or pushing:* Explain, demonstrate, take the lead, repeat, clarify, confirm, define, express feelings, argue, appeal, judge, disagree, attach, pinpoint flows, challenge,...

(2) *Moving with or pulling.* Listen, build upon others; ideas, agree, summarize others' ideas, paraphrase, reveal motivations and interactions; solicit criticism, look for common ground, reflect back others' feelings...

(3) *Moving away or withdrawing:* Avoid confrontation, contact, conflict, change the subject, use silence, do not answer questions...

(4) *Not moving or letting be:* Observe, watch, focus on the here and now, flow with the forces around, be flexible, adjust, adapt, enjoy,...

INPUT 2

Some findings on negotiation (from C.L. Karrass, *The Negotiating Game*, New York: Thomas Y. Crowell Company):

(1) Persons with higher aspiration levels win higher awards.

(2) Skilled negotiators with high aspiration levels are big winners regardless of whether they have power or not (sometimes the lack of power decreases aspiration level).

(3) Large initial demands improve the probability of success.

(4) Losers make the largest concessions in a negotiation (people who make small concessions during negotiations fail less).

(5) Losers tend to make the *first* compromise.

(6) Skilled negotiators make smaller concessions as the deadline approaches.

(7) A very high unexpected initial demand tends to lead to success rather than failure or deadlock.

(8) Skilled negotiators are benevolent when they have power.

(9) Successful negotiators use concession in a dynamic way. They plan around each individual issue in a way which is independent of any sequence.

This list of findings should be presented and discussed, keeping in mind that they apply mainly to American situations. What about the intercultural dimension, or, in other words, are they applicable or valid in other cultural environments?

INPUT 3 [67]

The three basic assumptions toward intergroup disagreements and their management (*see following page*):

[67] Adapted from Blake, R.R., M.A. Shepard and J.S. Mouton, *Managing Intergroup Conflict in Industry*, Houston, TX: Gulf Publishing Co., 1964, p. 13.

INPUT NO. 1 [67]

The three basic assumptions toward intergroup disagreements and their management:

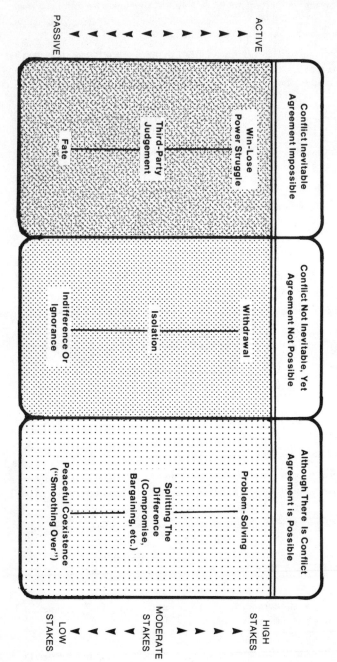

6. Handouts and Readings:

(a) Handouts:

The Behavior of Successful Negotiators, Huthwaite Research Group.

Berlew, D.E. and R. Harrison, "Strategies and Tactics of Negotiation," Situation Management Systems, Inc., 1977.

Glenn, E.S., D. Withmeyer and K.A. Stevenson, "Cultural Styles of Persuasion," in *International Journal of Intercultural Relations.*

Harrison, R., *Role Negotiations in Readings Organizational Psychology*, Second Edition, D.A. Kolb, I.M. Rubin, and J.M. McIntyre, Eds, Englewood Cliffs, NJ: Prentice Hall, 1974.

Harrison, R., *Role Negotiations in Readings Organizational Psychology*, second edition, D.A. Kolb, I.M. Rubin, and J.M. McIntye, eds., Englewood Cliffs, NJ: Prentice Hall, 1974.

Harrison, R., *Role Negotiation: A Tough Minded Approach to Team Development.*

Milburn, T.W., "Conflict in Cross-Cultural Interaction: An Updating on the State of the Art. SIETAR, 1977.

Nowotny, O.H., "American versus European Management Philosophy," *HBR*, March-April, 1964.

Sherwood, J.S. and J.E. Glidewell, "Planned Renegotiation and Norm Setting," *1973 Annual Handbook for Group Facilitators.*

Walton, R.E., "How to Choose Between Strategies of Conflict and Collaboration," in *Reading Book for Laboratories in Human Relations Trainings*, NTL, Washington, DC.

Wells, L.T , "Negotiating with Third World Governments," *HBR*, March-April 1964.

(b) Readings:

Deutsch, K.W., *The Analysis of International Relations*, Englewood Cliffs, NJ: Prentice Hall, 1978.

Deutsch, M., *The Resolution of Conflict (Constructive and Destructive Processes)*, New Haven: Yale University Press, 1973.

Fisher, H., *Public Diplomacy and the Behavioral Sciences*, Bloomington, IN: Indiana University Press, 1972.

Jung, C.G., *Psychological Types*, Princeton, NJ: Bollingen Series, Princeton University Press, 1976.

Karrass, C.L., *Give and Take: The Complete Guide to Negotiating Strategies and Tactics*, New York: Thomas Y. Crowell Co., 1974.

Klineberg, O., *The Human Dimension of International Relations*, New York: Holt, Rinehart & Winston, 1964.

Likert, R. and J.G. Likert, *New Ways of Managing Conflicts*, New York: McGraw-Hill, 1976.

Nierenberg, G.I., *Fundamentals of Negotiating*, New York: Hawthorn Books, 1973.

Patai, R., *The Arab Mind*, New York: Charles Scribner's Sons, 1973.

Prosser, M.H., *Intercommunication Among Nations and Peoples*, New York: Harper & Row, 1976.

Walton, R.E., *Interpersonal Peacemaking: Confrontations and Third-Party Consultation*, Reading, MA: Addison-Wesley, 1969.

Chapter

12

TRAINING IN OTHER CULTURES

The work in process becomes the poet's fate and determines his psychic development. It is not Goethe who creates Faust, but Faust which creates Goethe.

— C.G. Jung

In an effective learning, training process, a careful blend of three strategies—adapt, adopt and retain—on the part of both the trainer and trainee work synergistically. The result is the creation of a new set of cultural assumptions, values and beliefs on training and learning that neither the trainer nor the trainees possessed individually beforehand. Training in another culture is certainly a creative act. It seems obvious that beyond the adapt, adopt and retain modes, the trainer has to be *innovative* and able to identify possibilities beneath the surface of well-es-established social and cultural norms. A trainer is an entrepreneur! He or she is also an artist.

WORKSHOP 14. [68]

1. Aim. To examine a few key aspects of training in other cultures.

2. Objectives: Participants will:

(1) Observe some of the main implications of training in foreign cultures (conceptual framework: all inputs);

(2) analyze the trainer-trainee relationship within the framework of C. Jung's theory on the psychological types (self-assessment exercise and group discussions).

3. Process:

(a) Three case studies to illustrate the creative dimension of designing and conducting training programs in foreign cultures.

---

[68] This workshop has been designed in cooperation with Ms. T. Kolan of the World Bank, Washington, DC. The workshop was offered to participants at the Seventh International Training and Development Conference (14 June, 1978, Washington, DC).

Case No. 1. A training consultant from culture X is invited by culture Y (a foreign country) to conduct a training program. He organizes it in the following fashion:

☐ at the outset of the seminar, he asks the trainees to clarify/assess their *training needs* and *expectations;*

☐ based on the trainees' responses, he formulates come clearcut *training objectives* that would lead to behavioral change;

☐ using the *experiential learning* technique, he involves the trainees in the learning process as much as possible.

The entire experience results in a real disaster! Both the training consultant and the trainers are deeply frustrated. The trainees are convinced that the trainer is incompetent. The trainer believes that the trainees lack motivation.

Why the failure? (Have the group discuss this before proceeding.)

Because the trainer expercted the trainees to adopt his style without considering the postential clash between two different sets of assumptions, values and beliefs related to training and learning in culture X and culture Y. Folloiwng is a table which lists the hypothetical values and assumptions which may have impeded communication between the trainer and trainees. *(see Table 1)*

Case No. 2. Although highly unlikely, let us assume that the same training consultant is invited back by culture Y to conduct a second training program for the same group of trainees. Now, he knows. He *changes* his style and training strategy to fit the cultural patters of the host country...but...failure again!

Why? (Have the group answer.)

Because during the first training program the trainer had exposed the trainees to a new and different training style. While it was alien and unsuccessful, the trainees had nevertheless developed a broader perspective. For the second training program they therefore *expected* the trainer to use a "different" approach again. But instead the trainer *adopted* the style to which the trainees were accustomed. Nothing new was created. The trainees wondered why the trainer was brought in from another country when a local trainer could have given the training. The trainer, on the other hand, was utterly perplexed.

Case No. 3. The trainer is invited back by the same group for the third time. And it works. The trainer and trainees are able to interact and succeed in maximizing the learning process.

Why? (Proceed as before.)

Table 1

Two Sets of Cultural Values and Assumptions
Regarding Training and Learning

Culture X	Culture Y
Training needs: The trainees are responsible for their own learning. Since they know their needs better than the consultant, they should tell the trainer what to cover in the program.	**Training needs:** The trainees do not think in terms of assessing their own needs. To have needs means to have *shortcomings!* It is the responsibility of the trainer, as an expert, to provide a forum for new information and "tell them" what their needs are. He, and he alone, is responsible for the outcome of the training program.
Training objectives: Planning is crucial in organizing and controlling the learning process which leads to new knowledge, skills and attitudes. Effective learning and behavioral change stem from well-clarified training objectives. The desired outcome of a training program is the measurable level of learning and behavioral change.	**Training objectives:** Establishing training objectives is perceived as a *threat* by the trainees (if they do not reach them it will mean they have *failed*). Besides, clearcut training objectives prevent flexibility and adjustment in terms of the learning process. The only possible evaluation is that of the trainer's performance.
Experiential learning: "Learning by doing" is the best technique. Trainees learn by experimenting. They are encouraged to use all the resources which exist in the "learning community." Self-directed learning is preferable.	**Experiential learning:** Trainees observe and learn from the trainer. They perceive the "learning by doing" process as too risky and inefficient (it's a game). They do not like exercises and simulations which they perceive as making them look foolish. The trainer is *the* resource person.

Have the group discuss the above table. A complementary exercise is to reverse the roles, *i.e.*, the person from culture Y becomes the teacher and the member of culture X the learner.

Because they both have learned to *adapt, adopt* and *retain* their assumptions and values regarding training and learning. The outcome of this interactive process is intercultural synergy.

(b) Participants are asked to identify *their dominant psychic function* using the following self-assessment exercise: [69]

Psychic Function: A Self-Assessment Exercise.

For each question, select as spontaneously as possible the right answer for yourself. Do not be afraid of being subjective since the exercise is based on the assumption that people know themselves much better than one thinks. After all, if you don't like the outcome you can still question it.

	Marginally (1)	Average (3)	Very much (5)
1. Do you enjoy working on new problems?	□	□	□
2. Are you good at noticing what needs attention now in a given situation?	□	□	□
3. Are you rather an unemotional person?	□	□	□
4. Are you interested in other people?	□	□	□
5. Can you predict how other people will react to a proposal?	□	□	□
6. Are you good at analyzing the pros and cons of a proposal?	□	□	□
7. Do you dislike doing the same thing over and over again?	□	□	□
8. Do you rely on past experiences to solve new problems?	□	□	□
9. Are you good at pinpointing flaws in a proposal?	□	□	□
10. Do you let your likes and dislikes interfere in your decisions?	□	□	□
11. Do you perceive the unknown as challenging?	□	□	□
12. Do you usually resent being interrupted when working on a project?	□	□	□
13. Do you perceive yourself as a logical person?	□	□	□
14. Do you enjoy teamwork?	□	□	□
15. Do you have many ups and downs when working?	□	□	□
16. Are you able to keep track of essential details?	□	□	□
17. Do you perceive yourself as a realistic person?	□	□	□
18. Do you put two and two together very quickly?	□	□	□

---

[69] This part of the workshop is based on C.G. Jung's *Psychological Types* as well as on the *Briggs-Myer Type Indicator*, Center for Applications of Psychological Types, Inc., Gainesville, FL.

19. Are you good at organizing things? .... ☐ ☐ ☐

20. Do you enjoy public relations work? .... ☐ ☐ ☐

Add up your scores using the following combinations:

Remember: Marginally =1, Average = 3, Very Much = 5.

Sensing Function	Intuitive Function	Thinking Function	Feeling Function
2. _____	1. _____	3. _____	4. _____
8. _____	7. _____	6. _____	5. _____
12. _____	11. _____	9. _____	10. _____
16. _____	15. _____	13. _____	14. _____
17. _____	18. _____	19. _____	20. _____
Total: _____	Total: _____	Total: _____	Total: _____

Identify your highest score. This is your dominant psychic function for the time being.

(c) People who show the same dominant psychic function meet in subgroups and identify their training and learning styles using the following two tables (Figures 36 and 37).

Figure 36. Training Processes and Styles of Trainers with Different Jungian Psychological Types

Trainers' Psychological Types	Training Processes
SENSATION	—enjoy running the same training programs over and over (they are on top);
	—dislike to have to improvise;
	—prepare themselves very well in advance and time themselves well before the group;
	—focus on too many facts;
	—are good at documenting their presentations, using training materials which prove their points;
	—are good observers;
	—usually do not stimulate the imagination;
	—are patient with the administration of the training programs;
	—are accurate with content;
	—prefer lecture to workshop.

Trainers' Psychological Types	Training Processes
INTUITION	—are imaginative in designing and training;
	—are innovative (never repeat the same seminar twice);
	—content of teaching programs focusses on "what's new in the field;"
	—are emotional in training. Sometimes not very accurate;
	—have a tendency to try to cover too much material in too short a time (do not time themselves well);
	—are possibility oriented. Can be inspiring;
	—are impatient with routine details. Not good in administering training programs;
	—like to organize workshops and learn from participants.
THINKING	—are very well organized in terms of structuring the training program;
	—are logical in their presentations (move smoothly from one point to the next) and good in reasoning;
	—are process oriented;
	—like to lecture;
	—are not group oriented;
	—cannot take criticism from trainees unless it is content related;
	—sometimes have difficulty in adjusting to learners' needs and expectations;
	—are unemotional;
	—are good in documenting or supporting the points made.
FEELING	—are good at helping people clarify their training needs and expectations;
	—are people oriented;
	—do not like to lecture. Prefer group learning processes;
	—like to organize simulation exercises, games and work with small groups;
	—are good facilitators;
	—look for reinforcement and positive feedback;

| FEELING | —sometimes lack focus (groups go off track under their leadership);
—emphasize group interaction rather than outcome;
—are sensitive to interpersonal confrontatons;
—are sympathetic to personal values that influence decisions. |

Figure 37. Learning Processes and Styles of Learning with Different Jungian Psychological Types

Learners' Psychological Types	Learning Processes
SENSATION	—prefer to begin learning with the familiar; —like to refer to established or standard ways of tackling new fields, areas; —learn at a steady pace; —prefer to use existing skills rather than learn new ones; —are fact oriented. Look for well-documented, facutal information; —like precision and brevity. Are patient with details; —want to reach conclusions; —don't trust imagination. Look for practicality; —prefer passive learning; —react after learning all the facts.
INTUITION	—like new ideas, new ways of learning; —enjoy discovering, learning a new skill (more than using it); —learn with ups and downs (learn in bursts of energy); —are future oriented. Enjoy learning about possibilities; —dislike facts, lengthy explanations; —like to choose their way of learning (self-directed learning); —like to provoke and to be challenged (lateral thinking). Look for challenge, stimuli; —are patient with complicated problems; —react too quickly to ideas.

Learners' Psychological Types	Learning Processes
THINKING	—like new ideas;
	—like to organize their learning (plan in advance, clarify their learning needs, obejctives, develop learning strategies);
	—are process oriented;
	—learn in a systematic way (step-by-step);
	—always look for proofs (cause and effect), for alternatives;
	—like to be on their own. Do not need groups to learn;
	—are not people oriented. Unemotional and uninterested in people's feelings;
	—need time to think things through.
FEELING	—like to relate learning to past activities;
	—like to learn in groups (people oriented);
	—need occasional reinforcements;
	—learning is influenced by their values (likes and dislikes);
	—can be very emotional;
	—like informal learning.

(d) They analyze the interaction between trainers and learners who have similar as well as different styles *(Figure 38)*.

(e) *Training and Learning: A Psychic Approach.* Assuming that a trainer is *intuitive* and the trainees are basically *sensing*, identify:

1. The style of the trainer (how does he or she behave?).

2. The style of the trainees (how do they behave?).

3. The impact they have on each other.

Dominant Psychic Function	Styles	Interaction
Trainer: *INTUITIVE*		
Group of Trainees: *SENSING*		

The matrix on page 183 gives an answer to the three questions, above.

4. **Time:** Four hours.

Figure 38. Matrix for Trainer/Learner Interactions (Based on Jungian Psychological Types)

Trainers' Styles → / Learners' styles ↓	SENSATION	INTUITION	THINKING	FEELING
SENSATION	Get along too well. Share facts and lose perspective.	*Complementary:* Facts are linked with new ideas (realism and imagination). *Conflicting:* Learners find trainer superficial (a dreamer). Trainer finds learners "cold" and unimaginative.	*Complementary:* Get along very well. Facts are logically linked (cause and effect). Trainer takes care of the process. Learners bring out the facts.	*Complementary:* Very effective combination. The trainer acts as a facilitator. Group work leads to identification of facts. *Conflicting:* Trainer is perceived as "too soft" and not knowledgeable enough. Trainer sees learners as too task oriented.
INTUITION	*Complementary:* Trainer focuses on facts and learners come up with ideas; build upon facts. *Conflicting:* Learners are frustrated because they want to go beyond the facts. Trainer finds learners unrealistic.	Get along very well (too well!) Dream together. Risk losing themselves in "esoteric" ideas.	*Complementary:* Trainer provides structure and learners exchange ideas (peer learning). *Conflicting:* Trainer wants to organize the learning process in a systematic way. Learners want to brainstorm.	*Complementary:* Trainer takes care of group processes, stimulates the exchange of imaginative ideas. Learners learn through interactions. *Conflicting:* Learners think the trainer focuses too much on good conversation and not enough on ideas, content.
THINKING	*Complementary:* Get along very well. Factual. Facts are integrated into the structure. *Conflicting:* Trainer focusses on facts but in a "loose" way. Learners ask for more structure. Not very imaginative.	*Complementary:* Trainer is very imaginative and learners are able to analyze ideas systematically. *Conflicting:* Learners evaluate all ideas and trainer feels under attack.	Get along very well. Too much structure and not enough facts, ideas, interactions.	*Complementary:* Trainer helps learners to listen to each other, cooperate, work in a team. *Conflicting:* Trainer resents the heavy cause and effect orientation and learners are upset about the over-emphasis on group work.
FEELING	*Complementary:* Trainer raises pertinent facts and relates them to experiences. Learners interact well. *Conflicting:* Learners are more interested in establishing good relationships than in dealing with content or facts and experiences.	*Complementary:* Trainer is ingenious in focusing on essentials. Learners are motivated and work well together. *Conflicting:* Trainer loses the learners who want to learn from each other instead of listening to the trainer who comes up with bright ideas.	*Complementary:* Trainer organizes exchange among learners who like to be able to work together. *Conflicting:* Learners resent (and resist) the tendency of the trainer to over-organize and look for flaws in exchange of ideas.	Get along very well. Interactions are good but lack content and structure. It is a club atmosphere.

5. Conceptual Framework:

INPUT 1

The Adjustment Process in Training and Learning Across Cultures

The Trainer	The Trainees
He or she *retained* his assumptions and values which were relevant, useful and acceptable to the trainees.	They *retained* certain assumptions and values because of their relavance and importance.
He or she *adapted* his other assumptions and values to fit with culture Y.	They *adapted* other assumptions and values to fit the trainer's style.
He or she totally disposed of some assumptions and values and *adopted* replacements from the host culture.	They *adopted* certain of the trainer's assumptions and values out of a developed and broadened perspective.
He she creates new way to cope (synergy) and train.	They also create new ways to learn (synergy).

INPUT 2

A Few Basic Cultural Assumptions and Their Influence Upon the Transfer of Training Technologies

SET 1	SET 2
A. Training is *needed.* It is a must.	A. Training is not a must. Professional *experience* is much more effective.
B. Training is possible. "You can train people."	B. You cannot train peole. People teach themselves. The only thing you can do is help.
C. Training takes time. ("You do not change an individual in two weeks.")	C. Training is an ongoing process. It can change someone in two minutes.
TRANSFER APPROACH: Give them what you know...	**TRANSFER APPROACH:** Get acquainted and adjust your transfer.

INPUT NO. 3
Three Different Ways of Managing Training Across Cultures:

1. **The One-Way Process**

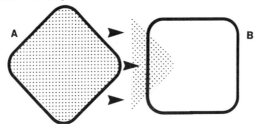

A knows something that B does not know. He will transfer his knowledge to B, who is responsible for adapting it to the constraints of his environment (if necessary).

2. **The Two-Way Process**

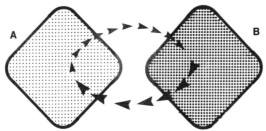

This is a cooperative process. A and B know different things. They start to exchange their knowledge and know-how and build upon this sharing. They learn from each other.

3. **The Synergistic Process**

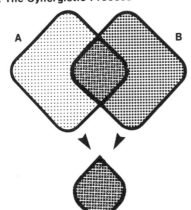

A and B are able to be innovative and *create* something which fits the situation they have to cope with in an original way.

6. Handouts and Readings:

(a) Handouts:

"Culture Simulation as a Training Tool," Mel Schnapper, *International Development Review*, SID, 1973/1.

"Enlarging Scientific Teak Team Creativity, R.D. Doering, *Personnel*, 3-4/1974.

Useem, R.H., Building New Cultures, paper presented at the 1977 SIETAR Annual Conference, Chicago.

Haines, D.B., *Training for Culture-Contact and Interaction Skills*, Aerospace Medical Research Laboratories, Wright-Patterson AFB, OH, 1964.

(b) Readings:

Briggs Myer, I., *Introduction to Type*, Center for Application of Psychological Type, Gainesville, FL, 1976.

Cox, D., *The Teachings of C.G. Jung*, New York: Barnes & Noble Books, Harper & Row, 1968.

Harding, E., *The I and the Not I*, Princeton: Princeton University Press, Bollingen Series, 1973.

Singer, J., *Boundaries of the Soul (The Practice of Jung's Psychology)*, New York: Anchor Books, 1973.

The Myers-Briggs Type Indicator (A Manual), Palo Alto, CA: Consulting Psychologists Press, 1962.

*Faced with the bewildering profusion of animated
objects, we create an abstraction, an abstract universal
image which conjures the welter of impressions into a
fixed form. This image has the magical significance of
a defence against the chaotic flux of experience. The
abstracting type becomes so lost and submerged in this
image that finally its abstract truth is set above the
reality of life.*

— C.G. Jung

*And if it is true that we acquired our knowledge before
our birth, and lost it at the moment of birth, but after-
ward, by the exercise of our senses upon sensible
objects, recover the knowledge which we had once
before, I suppose that what we call learning will be the
recovery of our own knowledge....*

— Plato

4   *CONCEPTUALIZING*

Chapter 13

MAKING CULTURE SHOCK WORK FOR YOU

To be related to one's individuality means to accept all that is encountered within as meaningful and significant aspects of the single whole.

— E.F. Edinger

The experience of culture shock or of the cross-cultural adjustment process, as I prefer to call it, can be destructive.it can also be a genuine opportunity for self-awareness and personal growth. I indeed contend that each time an individual encounters cultural differences, he or she learns something about others as well as himself or herself. Each step of the confrontation with other constructions of reality is an occasion for learning and growing. Again, in most cases, the problem lies in the fact that one is not aware of what is happening, that one does not understand the process and consequently that one is unable to control the situation so that it becomes a positive, rewarding experience.

WORKSHOP 15.

1. **Aim:** To analyze the cross-cultural adjustment process as an opportunity for personal growth.

2. **Objectives:** Participants will:

(1) Identify the various phases of the cross-cultural adjustment process looked at from a psychological viewpoint (prsentation of the model)

(2) Relate the teory to personal experiences (exercises).

(3) Look for ways to ease the process (conceptual framework: inputs 1 and 2).

3. **Process:** The "individuation process" as described by C.G. Jung[70] is used to illustrate the various phases of adjusting to a new cultural environment from a psychological viewpoint. The workshop is organized as follows:

---

[70] See E.F. Edinger, *Ego and Archetype (Individuation and the Religious Function of the Psyche)*, Baltimore: Penguin Books, 1974.

☐ The facilitator explains the model, covering one phase after another.

Phase 1. Inflation Phase.

In our day-to-day life it happens that at certain times we feel extrememly good, on top either because we experience from inside ("from within") a set of warm feelings and intuitive truths, or because of some intellectual discoveries which allow us to explain in a rational way what life is all about, what the world is...what to be means. C. Jung called this a *state of inflation*. It is mainly characterized by two situations:

☐ the ego plunges into the unconscious and experiences (not without some kind of overwhelming sensations) the depth of the self, the intensity of the essence of our being, the strangeness of what one is without knowing it.

☐ the ego reaches a high and concentrated level of consciouness which provides a clearcut answer to some of the key quesions we can have at the time. All the pieces fall together, the explanation *"va de soi"* it is rational, logical, factual, and...documented.

The two above situations create a sense of **exhilaration** and power. That **extremely** appreciated impression leads to an *inflated act*. The individual strongly believes that whatever he or she is going to do, it will be successful. It cannot fail. So, a risk is taken and...it fails or it does not lead to the expected results. Then the individual feels cheated, punished, rejected, frustrated and certainly disappointed.

Figure 39. Summary of phase 1 of the individuation process

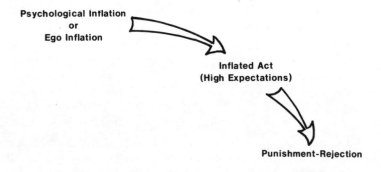

Psychological Inflation
or
Ego Inflation

Inflated Act
(High Expectations)

Punishment-Rejection

☐ Before analyzing the second phase of the individuation process, participants meet in trios and relate the theory presented so far to personal experiences. They try to cover the following questions:

(1) Describe a state of inflation that you have experienced in the past.

(2) What were your expectations at that time?

(3) What did you do (inflated act)?

(4) What was the result of your action?

(5) Relate phase 1 of the individuation process to the "cross-cultural adjustment experience."

Phase 2. Alienation Phase.

Phase 2 is determined by the reactions the individual has when he or she experiences punishment or rejection. In most cases, the person feels bad and lost. The negative feelings which surface at the moment are almost always connected with a strong impression of being *alienated.* It is why this phase is called the *alienation phase.* The state of alienation is characterized by two main psychic reactions:

(a) One feels miserable because powerless. One thinks that one has no power whatsoever over one's own fate.

(b) One feels manipulated by others..a The degree of alienation varies from one individual to another. Moreover, some people remain stuck there for quite a long time. Others move very quickly to another step which is the *recovery stage.* In order to cope with the situation, the individual can use a series of options which can be either emergency solutions to the problem at stake or more constructive in the sense that they lead to better self-awareness as well as a growing experience. Let's examine these two categories of potential solutions:

(a) *The Emergency Solutions:* The individual can use the options described below:

Scapegoating: "I am right, they are wrong. They are responsible for what happened to me. They should also be punished...."

Using Fixations: Doing over and over again what is thought to be the solution; whereas it is obvious that it is not working ("more" will do it!).

Fantasizing: Using fantasies to "reconstruct" the situation so that it fits the subject's expectations.

Using Compensations, such as food, drugs, drinks, buying, sleeping, sex.

It must be said that scapegoating, using fixations, fantasies and compensations are not bad in themselves. As a matter of fact, they can be very helpful. The problem is to avoid being stuck with them and miss the opportunity for self-actualization, as we shall see later.

(b) *The Constructive Solution:* Here the individual is able to sit back, take stock, put things into perspective, assess what happened in a more neutral objective way and learn from the entire experience. This is called *objective self-examination.*

Figure 40. Summary of phase 2 of the individuation process

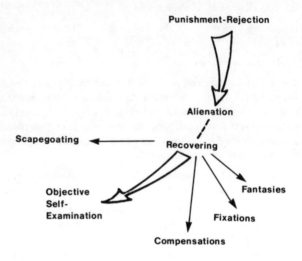

The group meets again in trios and works on the following issues:

☐ Identify one state of alienation that you have experienced before. Describe the situation as briefly as possible and focus on your feelings, saying: "At that time, I felt...."

☐ Come up with an example of "emergency solutions" that you personally know for being real and useful. Discuss it in your trio.

☐ Do you know other compensations? List them on a flipchart.

☐ What are the obstacles to the implementation of objective self-examination?

☐ Can intercultural communication trigger a state of alienation? Explain and illustrate.

Phase 3. Learning Phase.

The third phase in the process is *learning*, mainly learning about one's own "self." This involves:

☐ Learning about one's own *limitations* ("We are not as great as we thought we were, we are different from what we believed we were, we have shortcomings, weaknesses...").

☐ Learning to *accept* oneself as one is, accept others as they are, and be accepted by them as we are (humility).

□ Learning about the potential that one has ("I am also richer than I thought, I have strengths of which I was not aware, I have potentialities...").

□ Learning to actualize the potential that I possess.

Figure 42. Summary of the learning phase

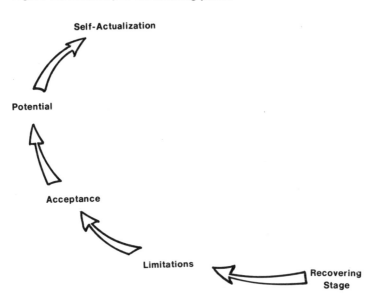

Issues to be discussed in trios:

□ Identify at least two limitations that you have and of which you have recently become aware.

□ What prevents people from accepting us as we are?

□ Describe in ten lines the kind of person you think you *could* become.

□ Relate the individual phase to the cross-cultural adjustment phase.

□ Comment on the following statement:

"Every life is the realization of a whole, that is, of a self, for which reason this realization can also be called "individuation." All life is bound to individual carriers who realize it, and it is simply inconceivable without them. But every carrier is charged with an individual destiny and destination, and the realization of these alone makes sense of life."

— C.G. Jung

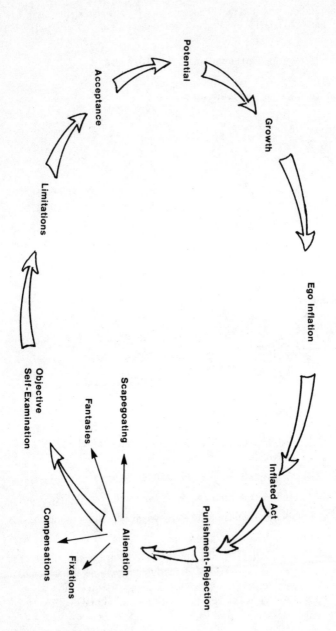

Figure 42. Summary of the individuation process [71]

The three key points in the process are:

☐ **Punishment and Rejection:** This part of the process is vital. If one is not punished, one misses the opportunity to go through the entire process, learn and grow.

☐ **Alienation:** Most people get stuck at the point of alienation. They feel miserable and remain so for a long time. It seems that it is a permanent state. They cannot see the end of their "bad luck." They question the meaning of what they are doing, the meaning of life.

☐ **Acceptance:** To accept one's self is not as easy as it seems. Many people have some difficulty giving up a certain view that they have of themselves.

4. **Time:** One hour.

5. **Conceptual framework:**

INPUT 1

Shifting between various basic priorities: the natural rhythm of life (The *I Ching* Model). [72]

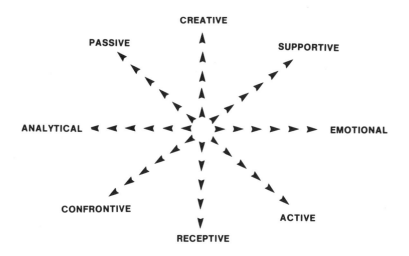

---

[71] "Multicultural man, embodying, as he does, sequential identities, is open to the continuous cycle of birth and death as it takes place within the framework of this own psyche. The lifestyle of multicultural man is a continuous process of dissolution and reformation of identity." in P.S. Adler, *op. cit.*

[72] Wilhelm, R., *The I Ching, or Book of Changes,* Princeton, NJ: Princeton University Press, Bollingen Series, 1950.

Check on the scale below how you value different priorities:

to be verbal........................	.... to be silent
productivity.......................	.... stand still
confluence	.... confrontation
to be happy.......................	.... to feel sad
socializing........................	.... being alone
being satisfied with oneself	..... being dissatisfied with oneself
to be in control	.... to be shy
to know...........................	.... to be confused
to be full of energy...............	.... to be tired
to have an aim....................	.... to be aimless

INPUT 2

The psychic energy cycle: a Gestalt model [73]

To learn to let it be can help or ease the individuation process. Below is a Gestalt model which can enhance the understanding of how to adjust to a new culture.

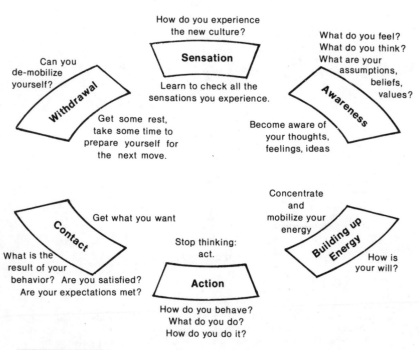

---

[73] Adapted from J. Zinker, *Creative Process in Gestalt Therapy*, New York: Vintage Books, 1977.

6. Handouts and Readings:

(a) Handouts

"Yin/Yang: A Perspective on Theories of Group Development," *The 1976 Annual Handbook for Group Facilitators*, p. 169.

Casse, P., "The Jungian Approach to Learning," (in press).

(b) Readings:

Campbell, J., *The Portable Jung*, New York: Penguin Books, 1976.

Harding, M.E., *Psychic Energy: Its Source and its Transformation*, Princeton, NJ: Princeton University Press Vollingen Series, 1973.

Jacobi, J. and R.F.C. Hull (eds.), *Psychological Reflections*, Princeton, NJ: Princeton University Press Bollingen Series, 1978.

Jacobi, J., *The Way of Individuation*, London: Hodder & Stoughton, 1965.

Jaffe, A., *The Myth of Meaning (Jung and the Expression of Consciousness)*, New York: Penguin Books, 1975.

Jung, C.G., *The Undiscovered Self*, Boston: Little, Brown & Co., 1958.

————, *Memories, Dreams, Reflection*, New York: Vintage Books, 1965. 1965.

————, *Man and His Symbols*, London: Aldus Books, 1964.

————, *Modern Man in Search of a Soul*, New York: A Harvest Book, Harcourt, Brace & Co., 1933.

————, *The Integration of the Personality*, London: Routledge & Kegan Paul, Ltd., 1952.

Neumann, E., *The Origins and History of Consciousness*, Princeton, NJ: Princeton University Press Bollingen Series, 1973.

Progoff, I., *The Death and Rebirth of Psychology*, New York: McGraw-Hill, 1956.

Chapter

14

THE PSYCHOLOGICAL DIMENSION OF INTERCULTURAL COMMUNICATION

Psychic processes therefore behave like a scale along which conscious-ness 'slides.' At one moment, it finds itself in the vicinity of instinct, and falls under its influence; at another, it slides along to the other end where spirit predominates and even assimilates the instinctual processes most opposed to it.

— C.G. Jung

Let's go back to the psyche or cross-cultural mind. After all, it is there that everything happens: perceptions, discoveries, and constructions of realities. A combination of different theories has enabled us to identify five key states of consciousness. Each state has its own characteristics and influence upon the way one lives, reacts, behaves, communicates, negotiates, and what have you. One cannot diassociate intercultural com-munication from psychic processes. As Goethe said, "All that is outside, is also inside."

WORKSHOP 16.

1. Aim: To understand the basic structure of the psyche and its in-fluence upon intercultural communication.

2. Objectives: Participants will:

(1) assess their current states of consciousness (self-awareness exer-cises);

(2) apply the model of the five states of consciousness to (a) the cross-cultural adjustment process, (b) intercultural communication, and (c) cross-cultural negotiation (exercises).

(3) determine ways of "managing" the psychic processes (conceptual framework: inputs 1 and 2).

Process:

(a) Participants fill out the "Psychic Self-Assessment Exercise" *(Figure 43).*

Figure 43. A Psychic Self-Assessment Exercise

Please check the appropriate answer for *each* question. Do not think too much. Make your choice spontaneously. There is no right or wrong answer. Take your overall present situation into account when choosing.

	Not at all	Somewhat	Above Average	Extremely so
1. Are you desireless?	☐	☐	☐	☐
2. Do you fully and exclusively deal with the situation you are in?	☐	☐	☐	☐
3. Are you in a non-judgmental spirit?	☐	☐	☐	☐
4. Would you describe your situation as painful?	☐	☐	☐	☐
5. Are you in a state of panic?	☐	☐	☐	☐
6. Do you feel that a day may pass as if it were a minute and a minute may feel like an eternity?	☐	☐	☐	☐
7. Do you behave effortlessly and just flow with the situation?	☐	☐	☐	☐
8. Do you try to understand what the situation is?	☐	☐	☐	☐
9. Are you bored and/or disappointed?	☐	☐	☐	☐
10. Do you feel lost and that your situation(s) is hopeless?	☐	☐	☐	☐
11. Do you have a sense of wholeness and completeness?	☐	☐	☐	☐
12. Do you perceive your situation as a growing experience?	☐	☐	☐	☐
13. Do you perceive yourself as rational?	☐	☐	☐	☐
14. Do you feel frustrated?	☐	☐	☐	☐
15. Do you experience some kind of depression?	☐	☐	☐	☐
16. Would you describe your situation as both simple and extraordinary?	☐	☐	☐	☐
17. Are you detached?	☐	☐	☐	☐
18. Are you trying to be objective in analyzing "all" the facts relevant to the situation?	☐	☐	☐	☐
19. Do you experience some kind of fear?	☐	☐	☐	☐
20. Do you feel alienated?	☐	☐	☐	☐
21. Do you experience some kind of "absolute" truth?	☐	☐	☐	☐
22. Do you experience simultaneous pleasant experiences?	☐	☐	☐	☐
23. Do you feel unemotional?	☐	☐	☐	☐
24. Do you worry about what you "should" do?	☐	☐	☐	☐
25. Do you question the meaning of your life?	☐	☐	☐	☐

SCORING SHEET

Enter the following scores for your selected answers in the space below: *Not at all* = 1; *Somewhoat* = 2; *Above Average* = 3; *Extremely so* = 4. Please note that the item numbers progress across the page from left to right. When you have all your scores, add them up vertically to attain the five totals.

1. _____   2. _____   3. _____   4. _____   5. _____
6. _____   7. _____   8. _____   9. _____ 10. _____
11. _____ 12. _____ 13. _____ 14. _____ 15. _____
16. _____ 17. _____ 18. _____ 19. _____ 20. _____
21. _____ 22. _____ 23. _____ 24. _____ 25. _____

Final Scores: ·

_____ _____ _____ _____ _____
  12   24   48   96   192

(b) A theoretical explanation is provided to the group using the model on the next page.

The ego slides along the psychic scale and stops from time to time determining basically five states of consciousness:

A. The middle level of consciousness with its *analytical state* (48) [74]. The individual does not feel good or bad. He or she just gets data from the inner and outer worlds and processes them in an objective, systematic, analytical and neutral way.

B. The lower level of consciousness with its two psychic states, *e.g.*, the *functional and neurotic states* (96 and 192). The ego can go "down" into the psyche and experience the darker side of human consciousness. The functional state is characterized by the fact that the individual is able to perform, to do what he or she is supposed to do (or wants to do) but the act is *painful* and *difficult*. The neurotic state is defined as an extremetly dangerous experience in the sense that the individual feels lost, alienated and miserable. He or she cannot function any longer. It is a block.

C. The higher level of consciousness with two psychic states, *e.g.*, the *satori and nirvana states* (24 and 12). The ego can (fortunately enough) also go up into the psyche and live some very rewarding, enriching and blessing experiences.

The satori state manifests itself by a series of enjoyable reations such as a feeling of peace, harmony, authenticity. The individual performs without any effort. He or she flows with the forces around them. Everything comes up naturally, spontaneously. It just happens!

Nirvana is an exceptional state of consciousness, mainly characterized by the abandonment of the individual into what is. It is a state ofintegra-

---

[74] The numbers used to characterize the various states of consciousness are borrowed from Gurdjieff's theory (see reading list).

The psyche and its five states of consciousness

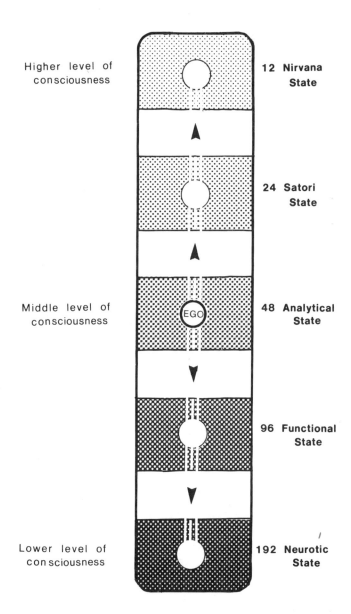

Higher level of consciousness — 12 Nirvana State

24 Satori State

Middle level of consciousness — EGO — 48 Analytical State

96 Functional State

Lower level of consciousness — 192 Neurotic State

tion, transcendence and bliss. Words cannot be used to describe the overwhelming experience of nirvana.

A few remarks about the model.

(1) Each individual has the psychic capability to experience the five states of consciousness.

(2) It seems that the higher level of consciousness cannot be fully appreciated if one has not previously experienced the lower level.

(3) Different states of consciousness can be experienced according to the various situations in which the individual is involved (24 because the individual is in love and 96 because he or she has a problem at work).

(4) According to the Italian psychologist R. Assagioli, the psychic processes can be controlled at least up to a point. [75]

(5) We believe that the five described stages of the psyche are universal but that their definitions are culturally biased.

Below is a more complete description of the five states' key characteristics *(Figure 44).*

(c) Participants are now asked to go back to their self-assessment and:

1. Identify their scores for the five states of consciousness (the highest, the lowest, others).

2. Try to understand the relationship between their existing states of consciousness and the *situations* to which they relate.

3. See what they can eventually do in order to change their psychic reality.

(d) The trainer explains what is behind each state of consciousness, using the model on page 206.

(e) Subgroups of four to six are set up and work on the cross-cultural implications of the psychic model (page 207).

1. Adjusting into a new culture.

2. Intercultural communications.

3. Negotiation across cultures.

---

[75] Assagioli, R., *The Act of Will*, New York: Penguin Books, 1976.

Figure 44. Identification of the Five States of Consciousness

Numbers	States	Identification
12	Nirvana	■ sense of truth, completeness, wholeness. ■ desireless, compassion, absoluteness, unity, one-ness. ■ bliss, ecstasies, selfless. ■ integration of polarities (to be and *not* to be). ■ sense of revelation, transcendence, creative imagination, intuition. ■ spiritual drive, religious feelings, metaphysical experiences, mysticism. ■ cosmic awareness.
24	Satori	■ simplicity, humility, autonomy, harmony. ■ laziness, effortless, strainless, smoothness, needless. ■ detailed, adapted, adjusted. ■ enjoying, flowing, being in touch, in tune, being grounded, feeling good, centering. ■ peaceful. ■ total attention, authenticity, genuineness. ■ natural effectiveness.
48	Analytical	■ suspension of judgment and valuation. ■ analytical, factual, logical, neutral, objective, systematic. ■ painless and feeling-less (no negative or positive emotions). ■ accepting ambiguity, probing, inquiring, observing, watching, learning, understanding. ■ open, exploratory. ■ focussing on "here and now." ■ willingness to see all aspects of an object (ideographic perception).
96	Functional	■ able to perform, but painfully. ■ judging, evaluating, classifying, attributing, comparing, naming, generalizing, categorizing, pushing. ■ disappointed, frustrated, afraid, dubious, inhibited, tense, nse, insecure, sad, dependent. ■ self-pity, egocentrism, headaches, migraines, lack of sleep. ■ feeling guilty, bored, out of touch, annoyed, strained, lonely, non-adjusted.
192	Neurotic	■ blocked, lost, isolated, alienated, sick. ■ feeling hopeless, aimless, miserable, insane. ■ self-destructive, aggressive, paranoid, maniacal, depressive. ■ panic, revenge, hate, cruelty, obsession. ■ being passive, submissive, psychotic, evil.

The states of consciousness in perspective

SOURCES   **BEHAVIOR**

the need to outgrow
one's own life and
reality, to belong to the
whole.

both passive and active,
receptive and creative,
thinking and feeling,
supporting and confront-
ing.

12

the need to be, to
experience the here and
now.

flowing with the forces
around, in tune with the
situation at hand, letting
be.

24

the need to be aware,
understand and control.

being a witness, watch-
ing and drawing conclu-
sions from factual obser-
vations.

48

the need for security,
sensation and power.

fleeing, fighting, with-
drawing, giving up, being
afraid, frustrated, bored,
hostile, intimidated.

96

the need for exploring
the deep shadow of
one's own personality
and actualizing the dark
side of human nature.

experiencing the "quin-
tessence of evil," behav-
ing in a way which does
not make sense for
others.

192

1. Adjusting into a new culture

States of Consciousness

Types of Reactions

Nirvana

12

creative interaction with the new cultural enviroment, personal expression and growth.
(TRANSCENDENCE)

Satori

24

one sees the differences and one is able to enjoy them.
(MULTICULTURAL APPROACH)

Analytical

48

controlled adjustment (one understands one's own reaction, their reactions, the interactions).

Functional

96

adjustment, but permanent criticisms are made about the new cultural environment.

Neurotic

192

rejection of the new cultural environment.

2. Intercultural communication.

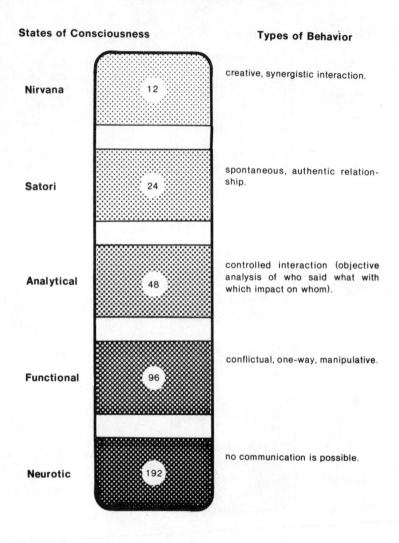

States of Consciousness		Types of Behavior
Nirvana	12	creative, synergistic interaction.
Satori	24	spontaneous, authentic relationship.
Analytical	48	controlled interaction (objective analysis of who said what with which impact on whom).
Functional	96	conflictual, one-way, manipulative.
Neurotic	192	no communication is possible.

3. Negotiation across cultures.

States of Consciousness   **Types of Behavior**

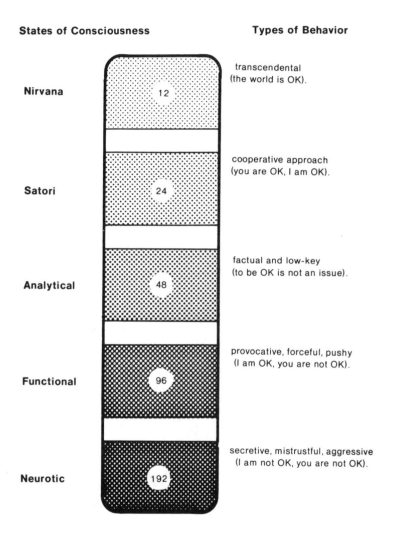

Nirvana — 12
transcendental
(the world is OK).

Satori — 24
cooperative approach
(you are OK, I am OK).

Analytical — 48
factual and low-key
(to be OK is not an issue).

Functional — 96
provocative, forceful, pushy
(I am OK, you are not OK).

Neurotic — 192
secretive, mistrustful, aggressive
(I am not OK, you are not OK).

(f) Participants come up with a list of key intercultural issues and apply the model to them.

The issues could be:

☐ conflict resolution;

☐ teamwork;

☐ helping others;

☐ the transfer process;

☐ making decisions;

☐ motivating;

☐ managing a project;

☐ training across cultures;

☐ problem solving;

☐ self-development.

4. Time: Between two and four hours.

5. Conceptual framework:

INPUT 1

Managing psychic processes   (Assagioli's approach). [76]

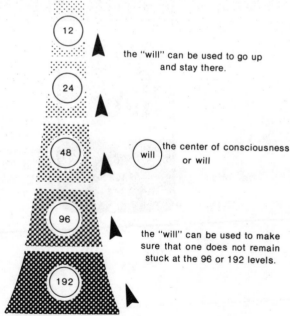

[76] Assagioli, R., *The Act of Will, op. cit.*

Assagioli suggests three steps in the reinforcement or development of the will:

(1) First, one has to realize that the will exists.

(2) Next, one must discover that one is his or her will.

(3) Finally, the development of the will can take place focussing on (a) making it stronger, (b) more effective (reinforcement of the "ability to obtain desired results with the least possible expenditure of energy"), and (c) controlling its direction or use ("the good will").

INPUT 2
How to Become Aware and be "In Charge"

The following model can be used in order to reinforce our self-awareness as well as our accountability to one's self and others. [77]

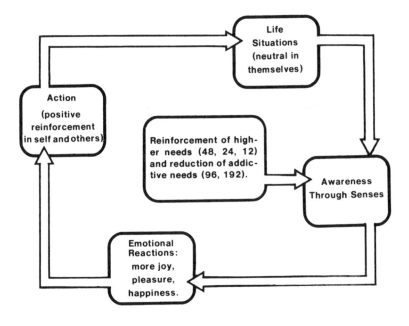

---

[77] The model is based on Ouspensky's and Skinner's theories (see readings).

6. Handouts and Readings:

(a) Handouts:

"Centering," *The 1977 Annual Handbook for Group Facilitators*, pp. 99-101.

Campbell, J., "Seven Levels of Consciousness," in *Psychology Today*, December, 1975.

Koestler, A "Cosmic Consciousness," in *Psychology Today*, April 1977.

"What is Psychoanalysis?," *The 1975 Annual Handbook for Group Facilitators*, pp. 246-248.

(b) Readings:

Assagioli, R., *Psychosynthesis*, London: Penguin Books, 1977.

Campbell, J., *Seven States of Consciousness*, New York: Harper & Row, 1974.

Castaneda, C., *A Separate Reality*, New York: Pocket Books, 1971.

Harding, M.E., *The I and the Not I*, Princeton: Princeton University Press, Bollingen Series, 1965.

Ichazo, O., *The Human Process for Enlightenment and Freedom*, New York: Arica Institute, 1976.

James, W., *The Varieties of Religious Experience*, New York: A Mentor Book, 1958.

Keyes, K., *Handbook to Higher Consciousness*, Kentucky: Cornucopia Institute, 1976.

Lilly, J.C., *The Center of the Cyclone*, New York: Bantam Books, 1972.

Maslow, A.H., *Toward a Psychology of Being*, New York: Van Nostrand, 1968.

Ouspensky, P.D., *The Fourth Way*, New York: Vintage Books, 1971.

Speeth, K.R., *The Gurdjeiff Works*, New York: Pocket Books, 1976.

Suzuki, D.T., *An Introduction to Zen Buddhism*, New York: Grove Press, 1978.

*In everyday life we are
continually evaluating
evidence, though we may
not be aware of making
judgement.*

— M.L.J. Abercrombie

EVALUATING

ASSESSING INTERCULTURAL TRAINING EFFECTIVENESS

The primary purpose of [evaluation] is to improve teaching and learning — not, as so often misunderstood, to justify what we are doing.

— M. Knowles

There are two main justifications for a systematic evaluation of cross-cultural training effectiveness. [78] First and foremost, the idea is to measure the nature and scope of the return on training investment. An attempt is made to match the cost involved in the design and implementation of intercultural training programs with the related benefits. Secondly and from a much more practical standpoint, the purpose is to compare the situations before and after training at pre-determined intervals to see which degree the training endeavour has achieved its objectives and adjust the program accordingly.

The difficulties in evaluating cross-cultural training effectiveness are numerous. Three of the major issues can be singled out:

(a) to set up *training objectives* aimed at changing behavior is a very delicate task.

(b) to review the *results of training* in terms of behavioral change is difficult and in most cases subjective.

(c) it is not easy to assess the *benefits of training* in quantifiable terms.

I strongly believe that evaluating for the sake of evaluating is a waste. Evaluation must be integrated into the entire learning process. Moreover, it has to address at least two key questions:

☐ what are the trainees going to do with what they have learned in the training program? (What is useful in the program?)

---

[78] Cross-cultural training can be defined as a systematic way of acquiring or modifying knowledge, skills, attitudes and behavior in relation to becoming aware of, understanding and relating to people who belong to different cultures or micro-cultures.

☐ How are the participants going to cope with the resistance (internal and external) they will meet when trying to apply what they have learned? (How effective is the program?)

WORKSHOP 17.

1. Aim: To assess the usefulness of a cross-cultural training program and to help participants prepare themselves for the implementation of what they have learned in real life situations.

2. Objectives: Participants will:

(1) prepare an action plan based on what they have learned during the training program (self-assessment);

(2) Learn how to assess the *effectiveness* of a cross-cultural workshop (questionnaire, Gestalt exercise, and conceptual framework: inputs 1 and 2).

(3) Plan the transfer of knowledge and skills from the workshop to real life situations (exercise).

3. Process:

(a) At the end of the seminar or workshop, participants make a diagnosis[79] of what they consider to be their strengths and weaknesses regarding their intercultural aptitudes: What they think they are good at and less good at from a cross-cultural viewpoint. They also identify as clearly as possible the key areas for improvement *(Figure 45)*.

(b) They identify *obstacles* which will prevent them from implementing their action plans in the most effective way and set up *strategies* to change. When ready, they meet in trios and each member presents to the two others, who play the role of devil's advocates,[79a] his or her diagnosis as well as action plan. The following model can be used by the participants:

Cross-cultural diagnosis: an integrated model

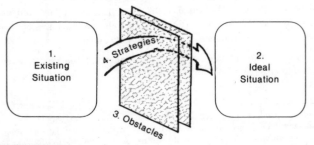

---

[79] See *Figure 5* on page xx.
[79a] They practice the five basic listening and responding styles (see pp. 134-136).

Figure 45. Diagnosing Cross-Cultural Aptitudes

Cross-Cultural aptitudes	Diagnosis			Action Plan		
	Not Good	Average	Very Good	Do More Do Better	Stop Doing Do Less	Start Doing Do Differently
1. Communication ■ expressing one's self ■ listening skills ■ empathy others:						
2. Adjustment Skills ■ toleration of ambiguity ■ non-judgmental attitude ■ probing skills others:						
3. Other Skills: ■ ■ ■						

Checklist:

1. Where am I right now?

2. Where do I want to be?

3. What prevents me from being what I want to be?

4. How can I achieve what I want in the best possible way?

(c) *A Gestalt Evaluation.* At the very end of the workshop, three chairs are placed in the middle of the room. They face each other and a sticker is placed on the back of each chair so that the participants can identify the three subgroups which are going to meet: the trainees, the trainers, and the people responsible for the program. Three volunteers are requested to initiate the process which goes as follows:

Step 1. Briefing of participants: "Three groups are going to meet in the middle of the room and speak about the workshop (or seminar) on behalf of either the trainees, the trainers, or the persons in charge of the program. They will say everything they want to."

Step 2. Three volunteers sit down on the chairs and one by one, start to make comments on the workshop, its objectives, content, methods,... (the facilitator controls the situation by giving the floor to each volunteer, one at a time) the volunteers speak up without conversing with one another at this stage.

Step 3. After a first round, the facilitator interrupts the process and asks participants who are ready to join one of the three subgroups.

Step 4. Subgroups of trainees, trainers, and "program manager" are set up. Members of the same team talk to each other when the floor is given to them by the facilitator. They listen to what the other teams say, talk about that they said but cannot (yet) talk *to* them.

Step 5. The facilitator stops the process from time to time so that participants can join in the subgroup in the middle of the room.

Step 6. When everybody is standing in the middle of the room (three teams organized around the volunteers), the facilitator gives permission to the teams to talk to each other (one at a time).

Step 7. The facilitator encourages a general discussion (participants talk to each other as they wish).

Step 8. The discussion becomes more and more spontaneous. It is now a free discussion between the participants. The facilitator stops the process when a certain fatigue surfaces in the group. Participants are asked to summarize the key points of this evaluation.

(d) *Resistance to Change: A Gestalt Perspective.* Two subgroups are set up facing each other: Team 1 speaks on behalf of those who have attended the seminar and meet *some resistance* when back in their environment (whatever it is). They talk about other people's reactions *vis-a-vis* their effort to implement what they have learned in the seminar.

Team 2 speaks on behalf of the people who have not attended the program and have to relate to the participants who try to implement what they have learned in the seminar. They talk about the participants' behaviour.

The exercise lasts between ten and fifteen minutes. When it is over, the group discusses the following issues:

1. Why do people resist?

2. Isn't there something positive in resistance? What is it (about the usefulness of resistance to change)?

3. What are the main forms or expressions of resistance? (List at least five: direct confrontation...).

4. What about thre trainers' resistance: do they also resist? In what way(s)?

5. What are some of the key guidelines (tactics) that one can use to take full advantage of the resistance phenomena?

(e) The following questionnaire is given to the participants who are asked to:

1. review and revise it so that it fits their purpose or need;

2. fill it out; and

3. comment on the evaluation.

CROSS-CULTURAL WORKSHOP
Evaluation

I. Overall Evaluation

1. Taken as a complete unit, I rate this workshop as:

1	2	3	4	5	6	7	8
(weak)			(average)				(excellent)

2. The subject matter was:

1	2	3	4	5	6	7	8
(ill treated)			(well treated)				(very well treated)

3. How do you assess the usefulness of this course?

1	2	3	4	5	6	7	8
(not useful at all)			(useful)				(very useful)

II. Specifics

Learning Process:

4. Training Objectives were:

    1   2   3   4   5   6   7   8

(not clarified)   (clarified)   (very well clarified)

5. Training objectives were achieved:

    1   2   3   4   5   6   7   8

(not achieved)   (achieved)   (very well achieved)

6. Session components are well integrated and in the most logical sequence:

    1   2   3   4   5   6   7   8

(not integrated)   (integrated)   (very well integrated)

7. Total time of seminar was distributed over different parts approriately:

    1   2   3   4   5   6   7   8

(not very well distributed)(well distributed)   (very well distributed)

Seminar content:

8. To what extent was the material presented to you new?

    1   2   3   4   5   6   7   8

(old)   (average)   (new)

9. What was your personal interest in the subject matter?

    1   2   3   4   5   6   7   8

(weak)   (average)   (excellent)

10. What is your personal understanding of the subject matter as a result of this seminar?

    1   2   3   4   5   6   7   8

(not improved)   (improved)   (very much improved)

Training Methods:

11. Did the training methods foster effective learning?

    1   2   3   4   5   6   7   8

(weak)   (average)   (Excellent)

Learning Climate:

12. Did the seminar leader encourage sufficient and equal participation?

    1   2   3   4   5   6   7   8

(weak)   (average)   (excellent)

13. Were the leader's directions clear?

    1   2   3   4   5   6   7   8

(not clear)   (clear)   (very clear)

14. Were the discussions kept on course?

    1   2   3   4   5   6   7   8

(rarely)   (average)   (most always)

III. Other Comments

15. The three strongest parts of the workshop were:

    1.

    2.

    3.

16. The three weakest parts of the workshop were:
    1.
    2.
    3.
17. The workshop could be improved by:

---

4. Time: Two hours.

5. Conceptual Framework:

INPUT 1

The training evaluation process: A participatory approach.

The training evaluation process can be described as a cycle:

A. *First Step: Assessment of cross-cultural training needs.*

The trainer and trainee initiate the process of identifying and analyzing the training needs. This can be done by matching what is mainly expected from an individual living and working in an intercultural setting with the actual situation of the people involved in the learning process.

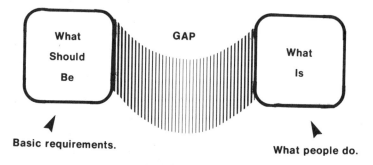

What
Should
Be

GAP

What
Is

Basic requirements.

What people do.

Any gap which can be pinpointed leads to a serious examination of the potential sources of discrepancy. Needs are assessed according to ten dimensions properly matched (see table below).

	Situational Requirements		Individual's Situation		Training Needs	
	Current	Potential	Current	Potential	Current	Potential
KNOWLEDGE						
SKILLS						
ATTITUDES						
BEHAVIOR						

B. *Second Step: Designing the training program.*

Once the needs have been identified, it is the responsbility of both partners, trainer and trainee, to make a decision regarding (1) is training the solution? and (2) what kind of trainng is required, *i.e.*, individual, group, on-the-job?

The design of the program includes the following steps:

1. Setting up objectives. [80]

2. Determining the content of the program (modules).

3. Deciding upon the sequences to be followed (structure).

4. Selecting the relevant training methods.

5. Preparing the evaluation phase.

C. *Third Step: First Evaluation—post training.*

It is by and large recognized in the training field that an immediate evaluation after training is useful but insufficient. To maximize the effectiveness of this first evaluation, a questionnarie can be constructed to extract information on the following items:

1. Were the objectives worthwhile?

2. Were they achieved?

3. How do participants intend to use what they have learned?

4. How do they assess the content of the program, its structure, the training techniques used, the style of the trainer(s), the training material(s) used, the timing, the training facilities...?

---

[80]   Mager, R.F., *Preparing Instructional Objectives*, Belmont, CA: Fearon Publishers, 1975.

5. What do the participants suggest to improve the program?

It is also suggested that once the questionnaire is completed, a free discussion be organized with the group of participants so that a maximum of ideas (synergy) can be collected by the trainer.

D. *Fourth Step: Second Evaluation—post training.*

Three to six months after completion of the training program, another evaluation should take place to measure the impact of training upon the "cross-cultural performance" of the trainees. Ideally a questionnaire or checklist would have been developed at the end of the training program by the trainees to assess their own effectiveness and progress. They will (1) fill out their own questionnaire from time to time, (2) ask some of their counterparts (from the other culture or micro-culture) to do the same, and (3) match their own perceptions with theirs. This cross-checking process should ideally be ongoing.

INPUT 2
The training evaluation process: The search for alternatives.

We strongly believe that two completely different approaches can be applied to training evaluation. In both cases, evaluation is so completely integrated into the training process that is loses its specificity as a special step in the training cycle.

The first one can be called the *team approach* and it consists of providing an opportunity to the entire group of people who are working together to go through the training process. This means that they assess their own needs, identify internal and/or external training consultants if needed, control the training program and actually organize or manage their own individual and team development. In other words, training becomes an integral part of the team work program. Training is put back where it belongs: in the work environment. An ongoing review of the results achieved (or not achieved) constitutes the evaluation process. Team members are asked to answer the following two questions:

(a) Does training work?

(b) Is training worthwhile?

Issue: Where is the incentive for managers to use this approach? Do they know how to do it?

The second option is the *small project approach.*

It aims at giving a group of representatives of a selected functional group (engineer, secretaries, loan officers,...) a special assignment, namely to assess the training needs and priorities of their peers.

The process can go as follows:

Phase 1: With a minimum of information and interaction with the selected target group, an internal or external training consultant designs a *workshop.*

Phase 2: Representatives (ten to twelve) of the target group participate in the workshop and in so doing, help the trainer assess the needs in depth, adjust the program accordingly and on the spot if possible. It is a real workshop.

Phase 3: Representatives go back to their respective working environments, try to apply what they have learned, and are invited back to participate in a follow-up seminar two or three months following the workshop. The purpose of the follow-up session is mainly to refine the objectives and the program so that they are more adjusted to actual needs.

Phase 4: More representatives are invited to new workshops. The process goes on and on and never stops. Improvements are made after each workshop and follow-up session.

6. Handouts and readings:

(a) Handouts:

"Conflict Resolution Strategies," *The 1974 Annual Handbook for Group Facilitators,* p. 139.

"Managing the Dynamics of Change and Stability," *The 1975 Annual Handbook for Group Facilitators,* p. 173.

Towards Cross-Cultural Research: A Variety of Perspectives in Topics in Culture Learning," Vol. 4, 1976, Honolulu: East-West Center.

(b) Readings:

Brislin, R. and J. Charles, *Research on Cross-Cultural Interaction,* Honolulu: East-West Center, January 1977.

Improving Cross-Cultural Training and Measurement of Cross-Cultural Learning (Vols. I and II), Denver: Center for Research and Education, 1973.

Segall, M.H. and R.W. Brislin, *Cross-Cultural Research: The Role of Culture in Understanding Human Behavior,* New York: Consortium for International Studies in Education, 1975.

Huse, E.F., *Organization Development and Change,* New York: West Publishing Co., 1975.

Knowles, M., *The Adult Learner: A Neglected Species,* Houston, TX: Gulf Publishing Co., 1973.

_____, *The Modern Practice of Adult Education: Andragogy versus Pedagogy,* New Yrok: Association Press, 1972.

Kirkpatrick, D.L., *A Practical Guide for Supervisory Training and Development*, Reading, MA: Addison-Wesley, 1971.

Lippitt, G.L. *Visualizing Change (Model Building and the Change Process)*, Fairfax, VA: NTL—Learning Resources Corp., 1973.

Chapter

16

MARKETING INTERCULTURAL TRAINING

Getting there isn't half the fun - it's all the fun

—*Robert Townsend*

It is now widely recognized that the success of international trade, diplomacy, tourism as well as the maintenance and improvement of relations between sectorial institutions such as industries, banking, health organizations, religious groups and the public depend on sound intercultural understanding. It is even accepted that the survival and growth of a society — and beyond of the human species — are also related to cultural empathy.

Cultural empathy is thus the key. Unfortunately, everybody does not automatically possess the ability to construct reality the same way as others do. A physician who works in a hospital does not look at things the same way that a patient or a nurse does. Their values are different. A public civil servant perceives his or her role in a way which sometimes broadly differs from the user's perceptions. Their assumptions regarding what should be done and how are not alike. A business man who tries to convince people from a foreign country to sign a contract with his company can get lost in the process of handling the negotiation by misreading the clues (verbal and non-verbal) that he gets from his counterpart. Meanings are expressed differently from one culture to another.

The actualization of new cultural patterns in the human psyche has to be learned. And it can be learned human beings have indeed the ability to become different and in so doing to understand others from their own perspective. To foster that kind of learning is the issue.

The need for qualified professional intercultural trainers and consultants is obvious. In other words, a *market* is out there. Unlimited. Almost untouched. But where are the good intercultural training and consulting programs?

Too many good trainers and consultants have not yet had an opportunity to perform and help institutions and people in need of intercultural skills.

Too many organizations and managers have been burned by amateurs selling ineffective (and sometimes dangerous) programs.

Too many ill trained (or ill advised) individuals have suffered from bad intercultural experiences.

Too many recipients of assitance programs have been disappointed, frustrated and shocked (if not destroyed) by the insensitive attitude and behavior of well intentioned helpers.

The match between providers of cultural services and users (clients) has to be improved. How to do it is the purpose of the following chapter. Have fun!

WORKSHOP 18

1. **Aim:** To analyze how intercultural training can be marketed in an effective and useful way.

2. **Objectives:** Participants will:
   (1) Identify the needs and expectations of the users of cultural services (group discussion and conceptual framework: input 1);

   (2) Clarify key criteria used in developing and assessing the quality of intercultural programs (four intercultural training programs are used as case studies and conceptual framework: input 2);

   (3) Set up a strategy for approaching prospective clients (case study, group discussions and conceptual framework: input 3);

   (4) Analyze issues commonly encountered in the intercultural consulting field (group discussions);

   (5) Examine the main resources of intercultural specialists (group discussions).

3. Process

(a) The workshop participants discuss the following definition of MARKETING:

"Marketing is the process by which an individual (or group of individuals) tries to sell his or her service-product to potential clients."

The marketing process involves:

☐ An identification of the client's needs and expectations;

☐ A good understanding of the service or product to be sold;

☐ The management of the approach (strategy) to be used to convince the client to buy the service or product;

☐ A certain professionalism and work ethic.

Three questions to be answered:

(1) How would you define marketing from a cross cultural perspective?

(2) How would you define the cultural *services* and *products* to be marketed? What are they?

(3) What is international marketing?

(b) The group is split into two subgroups which have thirty minutes to prepare themselves according to the two sets of instructions that they receive from the trainer:

Subgroup A: Find as many arguments as possible in favor of the assertion that marketing is manipulating and exploiting people.

Subroup B: Find as many arguments as possible in favor of the assertion that marketing is helping and serving people.

The two subgroups have ten minutes each to present their arguments. A discussion follows (fifteen minutes maximum) and then the trainer asks the participants to pinpoint the main values, beliefs and assumptions which underline their respective positions.

(c) Assuming that four major target groups or potential clients can be identified (namely the public sector, the private sector, universities and international organizations), the group is divided into four teams which are requested to define the needs for cultural services of each sector. A checklist is provided by the trainer.

CHECKLIST

(1) Define, first the sector in terms of its mission, objectives, program, activities, resources, limitations ... ;

(2) Identify in broad terms the interest of the sector in the intercultural field;

(3) Pinpoint some of the basic intercultural needs of your assigned sector;

(4) Clarify what your sector expects from an intercultural training program;

(5) What are your major complaints about cross-cultural consultants?

(6) How would you define a successful intercultural intervention?

(7) Describe the profile of an ideal cross-cultural consultant?

(8) How much are you ready to pay for the service of a cross-cultural consultant?

On the next page is an illustration of the kind of answers one can get from a team working in the international sector (in this case the *"World Bank"*).

THE WORLD BANK AND INTERCULTURAL TRAINING

Mission of the organization	Interest - needs expectations	Complaints - problems	Ideal consultant - successful intervention	Cost of cross-cultural services
Mission: promote economic and social development in third world countries through the financing of projects	*Interest:* Intercultural communication is critical in the Bank operations	*Major complaint:* Difficulty to find out genuine intercultural specialists able to adjust their programs to the organizational needs.	*Ideal consultant:* A professional, a practitioner, an achievement oriented person.	*The consultant's fee will depend on:*
Objectives: Identify, design, evaluate, supervise development projects placed under the responsibility of governments	*Needs:* Orientation programs for people coming from all over the world, going on mission to Asia, Latin America, Africa, interacting with foreigners inside and outside the organization.		*Successful intervention:* An intervention whose outcome can be measured in quantitative terms.	□ the felt need; □ his or her experience in the field; □ his/her reputation; □ the quality of the first proposal; □ the market; □ the standard fee paid by the organization to consultants.
Activities: Health, nutrition, industries, rural development, etc.	*Expectation:* Maximize organizational outputs through intercultural training.			

When each team is ready, a plenary session is held and answers to the eight above questions are presented.

(d) Four outlines of intercultural training programs are distributed to the participants who assess their respective qualities on an individual basis:

A. Outline of an intercultural orientation program on Belgium designed for a high level American manager (and his wife) who had been asked to move to Brussels and take over an important position in the Belgian office of the company (private corporation). It should be noticed that (i) it was the first time that the couple was going to leave the USA and live in a foreign country and (ii) only one day had been granted to the intercultural consultant to implement the briefing program.

A CROSS-CULTURAL BRIEFING ON BELGIUM

OBJECTIVES OF THE BRIEFING PROGRAM

1. To become more aware of how some of the values, assumptions and behaviors that Americans take to Belgium may affect their ability to communicate effectively with the Belgian people.

2. To gain knowledge of the Belgian culture and understand some of the key differences between the two cultures.

3. To develop some core cross-cultural communication skills to cope with the "problems" of living and working in Belgium.

4. To enhance interest and appreciation of an overseas living experience.

5. To analyze the cross-cultural adjustment process and focus attention on "family adaptation" to life in Belgium.

SCHEDULE

Morning: (The Intercultural Experience: Overall Aspects)

9: - 9:30   Introduction to the program (objectives, content, structure) and clarification of *expectations*

9:30 - 10:15   Intercultural communication

— definition
— five facts about intercultural communication
  (simulations and exercises)
— learning how to learn: a cross-cultural model

10:15 - 10:30   Coffee Break

10:30 - 12:00   The cross-cultural adjustment process

— understanding the process
— controlling the process

12:00 - 12:30   Learning about one's self (Briggs-Myers exercise)

12:30 - 2:00   Lunch

Afternoon: (The Intercultural Experience: Culture Specifics)

2:00 - 3:00   Four value orientations and their impact on intercultural communications (American versus
Belgian)

3:00 - 3:15   Coffee Break

3:15 - 4:00   The practice of empathy

— measuring one's ability to practice empathy
  (self-assessment exercise)
— practicing empathy with Belgians
  (role-playing)

4:00 - 5:00   Discovering Belgium: a situational approach

5:00 - 5:30   Summary and evaluation (a Gestalt exercise)

B. Proposal of a training program on cross-cultural communication for a
group of ICA escort-interpreters responsible for assisting foreigners
visiting the USA.

Description of the seminar

PURPOSE

The seminar will aim at reinforcing the awareness and sensitivity of a group of about fifteen escort-interpreters regarding the *intercultural dimensions* of their job.

Considering that it will be a pilot-seminar, it will also enable the people in charge of the program to assess (a) the need for a program (b) the participants' reactions vis-à-vis the objectives, content and methods used in the program and (c) the participants' expectations for any kind of follow-up or improvement.

OBJECTIVES

☐ To introduce the participants to the notion of cross-cultural communication focussing on the specific *tasks* they have to perform;

☐ to identify and analyze one of the key cross-cultural problems (or issues) that escort-interpreters have to cope with when working with foreigners visiting the USA;

☐ to experience and discuss some of the core skills that the participants can use in order to ease the cross-cutural adjustment process most visitors go through when arriving in the USA;

☐ to gather enough information from the participants (resource people) to design a simulation which will deal with "the practice of empathy."

CONTENTS AND METHOD

After a brief introduction, the participants will have an opportunity to experience the cross-cultural adjustment process and reflect upon some of the typical reactions people have when confronted with an ambiguous situation, i.e., a new cultural environment. Using their own experiences and acting as resource persons, they will work on real life cases and examine what has been done to ease culture shock and take full advantage of the adjusting process. A set of core cultural communications and counselling skills will be identified for this purpose. The seminar will end up with an attempt to integrate the cultural and psychological aspects of adjusting to another culture.

The seminar leader will present information through a variety of methods including lectures, group-discussions and simulations.

SCHEDULE AND PROGRAM

9:00 - 9:30	Introduction to the cross-cultural dimension of the Escort-Interpreter's job.
9:30 - 10:30	Analysis of the cross-cultural adjustment process: □ The meaning of "adjusting" to another culture □ Behavioral patterns typical of (a) people experiencing culture shock and (b) people having to work with them
10:30 - 10:45	Coffee Break
10:45 - 12:30	Intercultural communication and counselling skills (core skills which can be used by Escort-Interpreters who have to perform a set of specific tasks).
12:30 - 1:00	The cultural and psychological aspects of "experiencing" another culture

SUGGESTED READINGS

Condon, J.C. and Yousef, F. *An Introduction to Intercultural Communication.* The Bobb-Merill Company, Inc., New York, 1975.

Leshan, L. *Alternate Realties.* M. Evans, New York, 1977.

Hall, E.T. *Beyond Culture.* Doubleday & Co., New York, 1976.

Postman, N. *Crazy Talk, Stupid Talk.* Delta Books, New York, 1976.

Evan, G. *The Skilled Helper.* Brooks/Cole Publishing Company. Monterey, California, 1975.

HANDOUTS TO BE DISTRIBUTED DURING THE SEMINAR

Oberg, K. Culture Shock and the problem of adjusting to new cultural environments. (FSI Publication)

Hall, E.T. "The Silent Language in Overseas Business." HBR, May-June, 1960.

Rhinesmith, S.H. and Hoopes, D.S. The Learning Process in an Intercultural Setting. (Regional Council for International Education. June 1972).

Hanson, P.G. Giving Feedback: an interpersonal skill. The 1975 Annual Handbook for group facilitators. Jones and Pfeiffer (p. 147)

A short bibliography.

EXERCISES TO BE USED DURING THE SEMINAR

☐ Simulation on culture shock.

☐ The Cross-cultural Adjustment Process: A Model/Exercises in sub-groups.

☐ Listening and Responding Styles: Assessment and Group Exercises.

C. Proposal for a credit course on "US-Latin American intercultural communication" to be taught as part of the summer school program of Georgetown University

COURSE DESCRIPTION

Purpose of Course

The course is designed for people who wish to analyze some of the intercultural aspects of US-Latin American relations including Americans' perceptions of themselves, their views of Latin Americans, and interaction between them.

Objectives of the Course

Participants will have the opportunity to:

(a) define culture as a paradigm for human survival;

(b) analyze intercultural relations, communication, negotiation and conflict resolution in a US-Latin American perspective;

(c) participate in seminars conducted by three Latin American guest speakers who will discuss:

Politics, Education and *Development* from a US-Latin American Viewpoint;

(d) prepare a paper and participate in a symposium on "Management in North American and Latin American Cultures."

Method of the Course ·

The class will constitute a "learning community" and participate in such activities as self-assessment exercises, workshops, group discussions and seminars. Short lectures will be made by the instructor. Participants will work in teams on selected issues. Reading assignments will be given and handouts distributed during the course.

Course Requirements

Participants in the course will be requested to read two books as well as several articles. They will have to prepare a short paper on a topic to be selected among a list of *managerial activities* to be provided by the instructor at the end of the first session. The paper will constitute an input for the symposium on "Management in the US and Latin American Cultures." The exam will consist of selecting four questions out of a list of ten and answering them as thoroughly as possible.

Requested Readings

Stewart E.C., *American Cultural Patterns: A Cross-Cultural Perspective*, Washington, D.C.: SIETAR, 1972.

Latin America. Published by the Brigham Young University (Language and Intercultural Research Center — Communication Learning Aid.) 1979.

Optional Readings

Casse P., *Training for the Cross-Cultural Mind*, Washington, D.C.: SIETAR, 1980.

Condon, J.C. and Yousef F., *An Introduction to Intercultural Communication*, New York: Russel R. Windes (ed.), 1975.

Harris, P. and Moran R., *Managing Cultural Differences*, Houston: Gulf Publishing Co., 1979.

LeShan L., *Alternate Realities*, New York: Ballantine Books, 1976.

Knowles M., *Self-Directed Learning*, New York: Association Press, 1975.

Course Description

> *Session 1.*

> > *Objective:* To define the meaning of cultures as paradigms for human survival.

> > *Content:* Introduction to the course — clarification of course objectives and students' expectations — definition of cultures —the origins of cultures (Three Theories: Kluckhohn's, Harris' and Wilson's) — Presentation of a "Psycho-Cultural" model to analyze and understand cultures - US cultural patterns.

Optional Readings

Harris, M., *Cows, Pigs, Wars and Witches (The Riddles of Culture)*, New York: Vintage Books, 1975.

Wilson, E.D., *On Human Nature*, New York: Bantam Books, 1978.

Kluckhohn, C., *Mirror for Man*, New York: McGraw-Hill, 1943.

Handout

The Kluckhohn Model (Kluckhohn F. and Strodtbeck, F., *Variations in Value Orientations*, Evanston, Illinois: Row, Peterson and Co., 1961.)

> *Session 2.*

> > *Objective:* To examine the process of cross-cultural relations.

> > *Content:* Latin American cultural patterns — coping with another culture — the illustration of US-Latin American intercultural relations — the practice of empathy.

Optional Readings

Hall, E.T., *The Silent Language*, New York: Anchor Books, 1959.

Hall, E.T., *The Hidden Dimension*, New York: Anchor Books, 1959.

LeShan, L., *Alternate Realities*, New York: Ballantine Books, 1976.

Handout

Adler, P.S., *Beyond Cultural Identity: Reflections on Cultural and Multicultural Man*, Honolulu: East-West Center, August, 1974.

Session 3.

Objective: To learn how to communicate more effectively across cultures.

Content: The definition of intercultural communication —four value orientations and their impact on communication —communication styles — the US-Latin American example —the application of a set of basic intercultural communication skills in US-Latin American context — the gestalt approach to intercultural communication.

Optional Readings

Hall, E.T., *Beyond Culture*, New York: Anchor Press, Doubleday, 1976.

Postman, N., *Crazy Talk, Stupid Talk*, New York: A Delta book, 1976.

Triandis, M.C., *Interpersonal Behavior*, Monterey, Ca.: Brooks/Cole Publishing Co., 1977.

Handout

Hall, E.T., "Learning the Arabs' Silent Language," in *Psychology Today*, August, 1973.

Session 4.

Objective: To study the intercultural negotiating process between the US and Latin American countries.

Content: Defining intercultural negotiation — intercultural negotiation skills — a comparative analysis of negotiation styles —negotiation strategies and tactics: the US versus the Latin American approach.

Optional Reading

Klineberg, O., *The Human Dimension of International Relations*, New York: Holt, Rinehart and Winston, 1964.

Karras, C.L., *The Negotiating Game*, New York: Thomas Y. Crowell Co., 1970.

Bellenger, L., *Les techniques d'argumentation et de négociation*, Paris: EME, 1978.

Handouts

Glenn, E.S., Withmeyer, D., and Stevenson, K.A., "Cultural Styles of Persuasion", in *International Journal of Intercultural Relations*, Vol. I, Number 3, Fall 1977.

Radway, R.J., "New Dimensions of Negotiating in Latin America", in *Reference Manual on Doing Business in Latin America* (Center for Latin America — University of Wisconsin, Milwaukee), 1978.

Session 5.

Objective: To analyze the conflict resolution approaches typical of US-Latin American countries.

Content: The cross-cultural dimension of conflicts —handling conflicts in the US and Latin American cultures —conflict management between the US and Latin American countries.

Optional Reading

Blake, R.R., Shepard, M., and Mouton, J., *Managing Intergroup Conflict in Industry*, Houston: Gulf Publishing Co., 1964.

Deutsch, M., *The Resolution of Conflict (Constructive and Destructive Processes)*, New Haven: Yale University Press, 1973.

Likert, R., and Likert, J.G., *New Ways of Managing Conflicts*, New York: McGraw-Hill Book Co., 1976.

Handout

Conflict in Cross-Cultural Interaction: An Updating on the State of the Art, T.W. Milburn, Ohio State University, Mershon Center, (SIETAR, 1977).

Session 6.

Seminar on "Politics in the US and Latin American Countries" conducted by a guest speaker.

Session 7.

Seminar on "Education in the US and Latin American Countries" conducted by a guest speaker.

Session 8.

Seminar on "Development in the US and Latin American Countries" conducted by a guest speaker.

Session 9.

Symposium on "Management in the US and Latin American Cultures."
Presentations will be made by the students on topics selected among the
following list of managerial activities:

Planning	Innovating
Interviewing	Training
Delegating	Promoting
Decision-Making	Coaching
Appraising Performance	Managing Stress
Problem-Solving	Managing Change
Motivating	Organizing
Working in Teams	Defining Job Requirements
Managing Time	Using Power
Leading	Others . . . . . .

Session 10.

Exam.

D. Proposal for a "training of trainers" program on cross-cultural communication requested by the German Foundation for International
   Development[81].

Topic: Introduction to the five types of cross-cultural training which
         will be covered in the 3 day program

Objectives: To present a model in which the advantage and disadvan-
              tages of the five types of training are presented. A basic
              assumption is that any choice to be made by a trainer has
              potential positive and negative aspects, and that both should be
              considered carefully. The five types of programs are presented
              here in some detail so that this material may be useful for
              review as the week progresses:

Various formal orientation programs have been designed to prepare
people from one culture to interact effectively, and with a minimum of
stress, in other cultures. Such programs are usually designated by these
characteristics: short term; staffed and budgeted for the explicit purpose
of training for intellectual encounters; concerned with an audience about
to interact in cultures other than their own; and centers around techniques designed to change attitudes and behavior. These programs are

---

[81] Designed by Brislin R.W. and Pedersen P.B. from the Culture Learning Institute of the
     East-West Center, Honolulu, Hawaii 96848, USA.

thought to be more efficient substitutes for other means of learning about inter-cultural contact. For example, extensive travel and residence abroad are often cited as the best preparation for effective cross-cultural interaction; yet these methods are too time-consuming, too inefficient, and too expensive for widespread use.

Most programs use one or more of these five approaches:

(1) *Cognitive training*, in which people are presented various facts about other cultures. Program content may include information on topics as diverse as food, climate, male-female relations, economy, and decision-making styles. Programs of this type are currently the most common, and they are the easiest to prepare since information about various cultures is efficiently catalogued in libraries (e.g., through the Human Relations Area Files system). The disadvantage is often reported by people who participate in the program. They complain that the facts presented add up to no meaningful whole and that nothing is said about what to *do* with the facts.

(2) *Self-awareness*, in which people learn about the cultural bases of their own behavior. For example, we have observed programs during which Americans discussed their own concern with individuality while Japanese discussed their concern with the individual as an integral part of a group. This approach would seem efficient since people in an orientation program could pursue self-awareness no matter what other country is to be the focus of their interaction in the future. Expenses might be greater if people are grouped according to country-of-assignment rather than country-of-background. A shortcoming of the approach is that there has been no clear demonstration that self awareness leads to effective intercultural interaction.

(3) *Attribution training*, in which people learn the explanation of behavior from the point of view of people in other cultures. This approach eschews imposed explanations of behavior from people outside a culture. For example, a student at the East-West Center from Laos once verbalized an imposed explanation, and his own explanation, for a certain behavior.

I agree that Western observers complain about our indirect response to things. We consider it polite. Westerners consider it not frank but you have to bear in mind that among Laotians these are not problems. Being in that kind of society with these values, we have learned to understand the message that other people are sending without it being stated in words. It is not so much what you say but the way you say it that counts.

The attribution method demands the preparation of materials for each culture in which people in a program are to interact. People from the other cultures must participate in the development of the materials. Such preparation is expensive and time-consuming but ideally the product will be first-rate materials that can be circulated and used in many different programs.

(4) *Behavior modification,* in which people analyze the aspects of their own culture that they find rewarding and punishing. The people then study other cultures to determine which of these rewards and punishers are present and how they can be obtained or avoided. For instance, people who enjoy long periods of privacy would analyze how to obtain this reward in cultures where norms of interpersonal interaction make deviates of people who isolate themselves for even short periods of time. The advantage of this approach is that a person's probable reaction to life in another culture is explicitly analyzed. The disadvantage is that the concepts of learning theory (many of the terms are those of Skinner) connote "control" and "loss of freedom" to many people and so the entire approach is distasteful to them.

(5) *Experiential learning,* in which people actively participate in realistic simulations of other cultures. Sometimes called "total immersion," this approach involves all the senses of the participants and their total cooperation in satisfying their needs. For instance, contract teachers about to work in Micronesia have been trained in rural parts of Hawaii. There, they provided their own food, dug their own latrines, rationed the available water, made their own entertainment, and so forth. The point, of course, is that such activities are performed on a day-to-day basis by Micronesians and that outsiders must understand the behaviors to interact effectively in Micronesia. The advantage of the technique is that the relation to reality is greater than any of the other approaches. The disadvantages are the expense of preparations and the danger that some people will not be able to cope with such an intense experience.

First day (morning)

Topic: *Cognitive training;* case study of "critical incidents in cross-cultural communications."

Objectives: (1) To present a brief videotaped case study of a critical incident illustrating aspects of cross-cultural communication with a discussion guide; (2) to focus on one particular videotaped incident such as the first incident on the Japanese videotape (Manual A, incident # 1) and relate that incident to problems participants might be facing and (3) to demonstrate a training technique for using brief case studies as learning resources.

Methods: To briefly introduce the critical incident technique, distribute the manual to participants, watch the videotape and discuss the incident using the prepared discussion guide.

First Day (afternoon)

Topic: *Self Awareness* through using a listening exercise followed by the "Cross-cultural trade off" or "Interpersonal game."

Objectives: The listening exercise would increase the participant's skill in communicating clearly to their partner in a dyad and in listening carefully. The cross-cultural trade off would allow participants to give and receive confidential information about how they perceive and are being perceived with a minimum of threat by limiting disclosure to the dyad itself. The exercises are both tightly structured and would demonstrate the value of structure in training persons to give and receive feedback appropriately. Both exercises should contribute to the participant's own self awareness while also providing them with a strategy for increasing other's self awareness.

Methods: In the listening dyad each person is required to repeat back to their partner (1) what the other person *said*, (2) what the other person *meant* and (3) what the other person was *feeling* when he said it. When the partner has agreed to all three levels of interpretation then the partner can respond to the original statement, but *not* before. The discussion topic should be an issue of some importance to both partners. In the Cross-cultural trade-off, dyads are organized (probably keeping the same dyads as in the listening exercise) and follow the procedure noted in the exercise, giving and receiving feedback according to the directions.

Second day (morning)

Topic: *Attribution training*

Objectives: To use critical incidents of reported bases for cross-cultural misunderstanding, and to analyze incidents based on the point of view of people in the host culture; to become familiar with the concept of attribution.

Methods: Study incidents from the "culture assimilator," review materials for people of American or Northern European background who have assignments in Thailand. Study each incident, which reports on a situation that could lead to misunderstanding based on the likely reactions of visitors and hosts; examine each of four alternative explanations for the incident; choose the best explanation based on the point of view of host nationals; note the feedback mechanism within the culture assimilator format when incorrect choices are made.

If time, prepare one critical incident in the culture assimilator format based on an interaction between people from different cultural and/or national backgrounds. Design four alternative explanations, all of which at first glance may seem reasonable, but only one of which is an accurate explanation based on the point of view of the person in the culture that *receives* the visit from a sojourner.

Second day (afternoon)

Topic: *Behavioral* training designs

Objectives: To view and discuss selected 30-second filmed stimuli from Kagan's Affective Sensitivity Scale of individuals in various roles. To study discrete behaviors out of context applying the principles of behaviorism analysis of complex behavior in an intercultural setting.

Methods: To show brief 16mm film clip from the Affective Sensitivity film to the group followed by discussion either with the Affective Sensitivity scale or some abbreviated form for debriefing.

Third day (morning)

Topic: *Experiential training*

Objectives: To investigate the technique of role playing in cross-cultural training by actually engaging in the technique; to learn about reorientation cross-cultural problems faced by sojourners as they return to their home countries after spending time in another culture.

Methods: View skits prepared and presented (on video tape) by participants at the East-West Center in Honolulu, Hawaii, who were about to return to their home country. Discuss the problems likely to be faced by such returning sojourners. Actually prepare and present short skits depicting a problem in cross-cultural communication or miscommunication through assignment of roles that will be played by various participants. Discuss advantages and disadvantages of using this technique, which presuppose active involvement of program participants.

Third day (afternoon)

Topic: Combination of *cognitive, self-awareness,* and *experiential training;* cross-cultural counseling.

Objectives: To use videotape self confrontation in several modes to teach the benefits of videotaped feedback from actual or simulated counseling interviews helping trainees (1) anticipate resistance, (2) articulate the problem, (3) diminish defensiveness and (4) learn recovery skills when working with clients from other cultures.

Methods: Four different modes would be presented including (1) a cross-cultural dyad in a five minute interview to be debriefed by the group at large using the Interpersonal Process Recall technique, (2) a cross-cultural triad using three real persons, two of which are in conflict (client/anti-client) with one another, (3) a cross-cultural triad using a counselor, client and anti-counselor and showing the demonstration videotape and (4) with a cross-cultural triad using a pro-counselor, client and counselor. We would solicit volunteers to videotape interviews using each of the four alternative models.

Participants meet in small groups and share their evaluations of the four presented proposals.

They are then asked to determine the *criteria* which can be used to assess the quality of an intercultural training program.

The following grid has been used in several workshops:

	CONTENT	PROCESS
OBJECTIVES	Are the objectives adjusted to real needs?	Are the objectives stated in terms of results to be achieved?
PROGRAM	Is the program relevant to the issues at hand?	Is the program structured in a logical way?
METHODS	Are the methods adequate for the target group?	Are the methods used in a rational way? Do they maximize the learning process?
MATERIALS	Are the training materials appropriately selected?	Are the materials presented in an effective way?

A critical step in the marketing process is to establish a good and effective rapport with the potential client.

The group is split into teams made up of participants who have *and* have not had experience in the intercultural consulting field. They work on the following problem:

CASE STUDY: HOW WOULD YOU APPROACH THIS CLIENT?

The Situation

1. An international organization has been conducting intercultural training seminars for its new employees for five years. The employees

come from all over the world and most of them travel to many countries to identify, prepare, appraise and supervise development projects.

2. The participants in the seminar (between 60 and 80) have different professional backgrounds and almost no awareness whatsoever regarding the existence and importance of intercultural activities. Some of them strongly believe that to be a "good" professional is quite enough to succeed in one's own job.

3. The seminar lasts one afternoon (3 hours) and focuses upon a) an introduction to intercultural communication; b) a definition of culture shock and c) an analysis of the cross-cultural adjustment process. Short lectures, subgroup discussions and simulations are used during the seminar.

4. The management of the organization is not quite interested in this program which had been initiated by the training manager. Many managers perceive the seminar as a waste of time, money and energy.

5. At the time of each seminar, many participants are excited and ask for more information on the subject.

The Problem

The training manager is looking for a training specialist in intercultural communication (a consultant) who could help him in assessing the impact of the one-afternoon seminar on the employees and in seeing how the program could be improved. Some of the key issues the training manager would like to clarify are:

a)   What are the typical reactions of the employees who join the organization? Do they follow the classical pattern of fleeing, fighting, and becoming dependent?

b)   What do fleeing, fighting and becoming dependent mean (illustrations) for the employees?

c)   Are there ways used by employees *and* managers to ease the adjustment process?

How could the answers to the three above questions help in improving the existing program?

According to several reactions to the problem commented by the management of the organization, it would seem that:

The following approaches are considered as inadequate:

(i)   tell the managers that you know the answer to the problem (this reinforces their skepticism);

(ii) propose a big survey (this is costly);

(iii) ask to have access to top management to guarantee its commitment as well as the success of the intervention (this creates insecurity).

The following approaches are considered as adequate:

(i)   propose a pilot program (the risk is perceived as limited);

(ii) involve the training manager in the process (It is thus an internal operation);

Participants prepare training proposals related to the topics hereunder:

☐ A seminar on "Inflation Across Cultures" for a governmental agency;

☐ A symposium on "Productivity Across Cultures" for a group of private corporations;

☐ A workshop on "Reducing International Tensions and Conflicts Through Better Intercultural Understanding" for an international foundation;

☐ A course on "The Intercultural Dimension of Human Rights" for a university;

☐ An action-plan to improve relations between industries (mainly chemical) and communities.

Participants are organized in small teams and asked to come up with a training device (slides, film, video-tape-recorder, booklet, etc. . . .) to illustrate the importance of culture shock for a group of skeptical business people involved in international operations.

Four typical reactions of the potential users of intercultural training program are introduced to the group which is asked to discuss them:

☐ They do not understand what intercultural training, education, and consulting means;

☐ They do not see how useful intercultural services could be for their own institution;

☐ They perceive intercultural activities as "soft" (interesting to talk about but not that important);

☐ They have been "burned" in the past with programs and projects which failed and put them into awkward positions;

☐ They do not know how to identify and select the "right" consultants, services and products.

Issues to be discussed:

   (i) Are the above reactions real? Document them with illustrations.

  (ii) Which reaction is the most common among the four identified potential users?

 (iii) How can one respond to those concerns?

(i) The group is divided into four subgroups (i.e. research, training, education, consulting) and answer the five questions given to them by the trainers:
Assuming that you are intercultural resource people:
☐ What do you have to offer?
☐ What are your strengths and weaknesses?
☐ How do you define an "ideal" contract with a client?
☐ How much will you charge for one-day consulting activity?
☐ How could you improve your "business" operations?

4. **Time:** Between one and two days.

5. **Conceptual Framework:**

INPUT I

THE NEEDS FOR INTERCULTURAL TRAINING

The needs for intercultural training:

I am convinced that much of our difficulty with people in other countries stems from the fact that so little is known about cross-cultural
communications.

> E.T. Hall
> *The Silent Language,*
> A Doubleday Anchor book,
> New York, 1973.

It has been shown, again and again, that in order to succeed in an
international mission it is not enough to be a good specialist or expert.
That it is even not enough to be able to handle basic communications. It is
indeed also necessary to be good at establishing and maintaining good
interactions and relationships with people who do not belong to the same
culture. Some *cultural sensitivity* seems to be required. The practice of
cultural empathy (or the capacity to see things as others do) should be
common behavior. Unfortunately, it is not. It is not mainly because our
educational systems have not taught us to understand our own culture
(ourselves as product of a culture), control our cultural biases, apprehend
others' cultural assumptions and values and handle cross-cultural situations. As summarized by Dr. E. Hall it seems that "Culture hides much
more than it reveals, and strangely enough what it hides, it hides most
effectively from its own participants." Most peoples have not been prepared to interact with foreigners or individuals who do not share the same
ways of thinking (cognition), feeling (emotion) and behaving (action).
They do not realize that their patterns of thinking and behaving, their
assumptions and values, are not universal. Most cultures do not have yet
the in-built capacity to assist their members in an analysis of *what they are
and why they are who they are* from a cultural point of view. So beyond the
necessary expertise, specialists working in international organizations
(private or public) should be able to:

(1) *understand the cultural meaning of their behavior.* The assumption
here is that *no* behavior is culture free. Any technical proposal, in
its substance and presentation, is culturally loaded. Anything we
think, feel, say or do is related to the *deep structures* of the culture
(or cultures) we belong to.

(2) *empathize with others* and understand their behavior using their
own cultural frame of reference. Any ethnocentric reaction should

be avoided. This emplies a constant "holding back" of any value judgment.

(3) *recognize the impact of their behavior on others* (in terms of positive and negative reactions) and vice versa.

(4) *adjust to the specific cross-cultural situations* they are involved in and participate in an ongoing *creative* process, namely *managing change.*

To reinforce what has already been said, we can also state that the needs for intercultural training are due to both an increase in interntaional communications and a lack of preparation for intercultural relations in most societies.

INPUT 2

AN ILLUSTRATION OF INTERCULTURAL TRAINING OBJECTIVES
(A Tentative List)

At the end of the program, the participants will be able:

AWARENESS	SKILLS
(1) To understand their behavior from a cultural perspective.	(1) To assess their basic assumptions and values using a set of appropriate techniques and instruments (I. Kluckhohn, E. Stewart, S. Rhinesmith)
(2) To understand others behavior from their cultural frame of reference.	(2) To practice empathy and predict accurately others' behavior
(3) To understand the cross-cultural dimensions of the person-to-person interactions they are part of.	(3) To diagnose potential conflicts and opportunities inherent to any intercultural relationship.
(4) To understand the intercultural adjustment process (unfreezing-moving-refreezing.)	(4) To take appropriate action in order to maximize opportunities and minimize conflicts.

INPUT 3

ON INDEPENDENT CONSULTING IN
INTERCULTURAL COMMUNICATION [82]

A career as an independent consultant offers challenges and hazards unlike any found in more traditional employment situations. The specific nature of the intercultural communication fields—the fact that they are essentially humanistic in application—heightens both the opportunities for reward and the potential for pitfalls.

An important element of this type of career pursuit that *cannot* be overlooked is that one has to be at least as good a businessman as he or she is an interculturalist. As an independent consultant, your livelihood will depend on how well you can sell yourself and your services to potential clients; your success will depend on your ability to anticipate and forecast your clients' needs and obligations; your peace of mind will come largely from your bookkeeping and contracting know-how.

The balance—for you as an interculturalist—will lie in the freedom to pursue the type of work you enjoy and feel the most confortable with. Within the limits of client need, you will be able to develop programs and approaches along your own innovative lines without the internal constraints of "the systems."

Before presenting a side-by-side comparison of the "pros and cons" of independent consulting, there is one more caution to be made. Unless you are extremely *lucky*, it will take about three years to develop the kind of practice that could support you comfortably. Unless you have enough money in the bank to live during that time, it would be a mistake to begin independent consulting without the "pad" of at least a part-time "money" job.

This kind of approach to consulting will afford you the opportunity to make a few contacts, perhaps take a few contracts to "get your feet wet" and to provide some on-the-job training in the intricacies of working with organizations from the outside.

Here, then, are some of the positive and negative elements of independent consulting. Although everyone's experience is different in this sort of loose occupation, these seem to be generally applicable to most consultants:

---

[82] Developed by S.J. Anspacher

Pros	Cons
1. Independent lifestyle.	1. lack of security and benefits of regular employment.
2. Freedom to develop in many directions, specializing in only what you choose and at what you are best.	2. necessity to "hustle" constantly, frequently giving precedence to the selling function over the practice of your profession.
3. direct responsibility for your own development and income level.	3. vulnerable to "soft" funding and/or purges involving your contacts or organizational priorities among your clients.
4. a lot of travel.	4. a lot of travel.
5. freedom from "duties" of working within the daily "grind" of an office atmosphere.	5. necessity to provide for your own clerical and research support; need versatility to fit into many different organizational structures.

The picture, as you see, is far from clear or one-sided. And of course, once the decision is made to pursue an independent career, for whatever reasons you have, the complications have just begun. Following is just a thumbnail sketch of the myriad elements involved in getting and performing on a contact, and, hopefully, keeping the client for future use.

1. *Getting leads.* This is the all-important making of contacts, building and maintaining your "network," and seeing to it that you and your services are known to an ever-increasing number of potential clients.

2. *Making the "pitch".* This is the heart of selling. If you can sell, you can make it. If you can't you might be able to muddle through at the expense of your gastrointestinal health. In the intercultural field, selling is particularly hard because you frequently have to begin with clients who don't understand exactly what it is you're talking about and are—to say the least—skeptical.

3. *Closing the deal.* Assuming you've sold them (congratulations!), you have to draw up the agreement/contract. Things to consider:

a) do you charge a flat fee or a per-day fee?
b) do you charge for preliminary consultations (presentations, etc.)?
c) to whom do you report (and who is going to be the final evaluator of your performance)?

Most organizations have guidelines that address these and the thousands of other elements of the contract. You will have to negotiate around those guidelines to get what you want and/or need. There are circumstances, of course, in which financial trade-off can be made for professional development, particularly at the beginning of your consulting career. You must be careful, however, that you never under-sell yourself, because losses in this area are very hard to recoup.

4. *Performance.* The fun part. In setting up your work plan, however, you'll have to take many elements into consideration:
a) can you do it alone? do you need other professionals? do you need substantial clerical or research support?
b) What is the time framework? how does that balance against the agreed-upon schedule for payments (are you going to have to work for six months in Tanzania on *per diem*)?
c) what process or system is going to be set up to evaluate your work (both on an on-going and post-projects basis)?

5. *On-going relationships.* As you are performing on a particular project, it might be prudent to devote a little of your time (your own time) to an on-going needs analysis, so that after the specific job is done, you'll have firm footing for offering new or additional services to the same client or another organization in a similar situation. This can sometimes lead to the establishment of a retainer-type relationship with a few clients: they pay you a set sum per year to guarantee your availability to work on their projects. This alleviates some of the hustling problems and may keep you from spreading yourself too thin.

A final point to bear in mind is that the intercultural business does not lend itself to the making of guarantees. You may be tempted in a selling situation to make promises about issues that are ultimately outside your direct control. You can point out trends and prove probabilities by dragging out statistics (if you can find them), but in the final analysis, every situation is different and what worked in one place may not work in another. Although this concept should be second-nature common sense to interculturalists, businessmen and organization executives frequently press for assurances. Resist.

Perhaps the most exciting part of being an independent consultant in this field is that you are constantly *in* intercultural situations. Perhaps the most challenging cross-cultural field of conflict is between intercultural practitioner culture and the business/organizational culture. At the least, it will be a constant source of stimulations to the independent consultant in intercultural communication fields.

6. Handouts and Readings

(a) Handouts:

Adler N.J., *Cross-Cultural Organization Development.* American Graduate School of International Management. July, 1978.

Adler N.J., *Cultural Synergy: The Management of Cross-Cultural Organizations.* McGill University, Montreal, Canada. 1980.

Brislin R.W., *A Case Study in Cross-Cultural Research.* SIETAR 1978.

Brislin, R.W. and Van Buren M., *Can They Go Home Again?* International Education and Cultural Exchange, a publication of the U.S. Advisory Commission on International Educational and Cultural Affairs, Washington D.C.

Culturgrams on Belgium (BYU, 1979).

Distefano J. A, *"Case Study in Multinational Corporations.* SIETAR 1978.

Distefano J.J., "Managing in other cultures: some do's and don'ts". *The Business Quarterly.* Autumn 1972.

Elmendorf J., *Helping Americans Learn About the World... (A study of Private Sector Activities).* Academy for Educational Development, Washington, D.C., 1978.

Feldman M.J., Coping with problems in meeting training needs for cross-cultural international training. ASTD, International Division (monograph).

Handbook for Intercultural Trainers (compiled by D.R. Barker with the assistance of D.L. Zeller and J. Murray) SIETAR, 1980.

Kohls R., "Issues in cross-cultural training". Paper presented at the second summer conference on intercultural communication. University of South Florida, 1978.

Lee J.A., "Developing Manager in Developing Countries". *Harvard Business Review.* November-December 1968.

Kvin P., "The Magic of Multinational Management". *Harvard Business Review.* November-December, 1972.

Lanier A.R., Packaged programs for the use of training divisions in preparing personnel for overseas assignments, ASTD, International Division (monograph).

Martinsson J.P., "Cross-Cultural Training". Paper presented at the second summer conference on intercultural communication. University of South Florida, 1978.

Nadler L., "The organization as a micro—culture". *Personnel Journal,* December 1969.

Pederson P., *A Case Study in Mental Health Cross-Cultural Counseling.* SIETAR 1978

Pedersen P.B. *A Cross-Cultural Training Model for Counselors.* International Student Advisor's Office. University of Minnesota.

Pedersen, P.B. *Counseling Clients from Other Cultures: Two Training Designs.* University of Minnesota.

Prosser M. *A Case Study in Communication.* SIETAR 1978.

Schnapper M. *Multinational Training for Multinational Corporations and International Organizations.* ASTD, International Division (monograph).

Smith E. *A Case Study in Transfer of Technology.* SIETAR 1978.

Tucker M.F. *A Case Study Evaluation of Cross-Cultural Programs.* SIETAR 1978.

(b) Readings:

Dible D.M. "Up Your Own Organization. *The Entrepreneur.* Santa Clara, Cal.

Drucker P. *Management (Tasks, Responsibilities, Practices)* New York: Mayer and Row. 1974.

Drucker P. *Managing for Results.* New York. Mayer and Row. 1964.

Drucker P. *The Effective Executive.* New York. Mayer and Row. 1967.

Lanier A.R. *Handbook for International Transfer (Your City).* New York. Overseas Briefing Associates. 1975.

Mailick S. (Ed) *The Making of the Manager: A World Study.* New York: Anelor Press - Doubleday, 1974.

Noer, D.M. *Multinational People Management: A Guide for Organizations and Employees.* Washington D.C. Bureau of National Affairs, Inc. 1975.

NTL (ed) *Three Forces in Learning.* Washington D.C. 1968.

Schein E.H. and Weschler I.R. (eds). *Five Issues in Training.* Washington D.C. NTL 1962.

Townsend R. *Up the Organization.* Greenwich, Conn. Fawcett Publication, Inc. 1971.

Vansina, L.S. *Improving International Relations and Effectiveness within Multinational Organizations in New Technologies in Organization Development,* vol. 2 (ed. John D. Adams) La Jolla, CA. University Associates, Inc. 1975.

Warren M.W. *Training for Results (A System Approach to the Development of Human Resources in Industry).* Reading, Mass. Addison-Wesley, 1969.

Reading List.

A list of twenty books to read:

Argyris, C., *Increasing Leadership Effectiveness*, New York: John Wiley & Sons, 1976.

Bateson, G., *Steps to an Ecology of Mind (A Revolutionary Approach to Man's Understanding of Himself)*, New York: Ballantine Books, 1972.

Berger, P.L. and T. Luckmann, *The Social Construction of Reality*, New York: Doubleday, 1967.

deBono, E., *The Use of Lateral Thinking*, London: Penguin Books, 1967.

Edinger, E.G., *Ego and Archetype*, Baltimore: Penguin Books, 1973.

Hall, E.T., *The Silent Language*, New York: Anchor Books, 1959.

Herman, S.M. and M. Korenich, *Authentic Management: A Gestalt Orientation to Organizations and Their Development*, Reading, MA: Addison-Wesley, 1977.

Ingalls, J.D., *Human Energy*, Reading, MA: Addison-Wesley, 1976.

Jung, C.G., *Man and His Symbols*, New York: Doubleday, 1964.

————, *On the Nature of the Psyche*, Princeton, NJ: Princeton University Press Bollingen Series, 1969.

Kluckhohn, C., *Mirror for Man*, New York: McGraw-Hill, 1943.

Knowles, M., *Self-Directed Learning*, New York: Association Press, 1975.

Leshan, L., *Alternate Realities*, New York: Ballantine Books, 1976.

Ornstein, R.E., *The Psychology of Consciousness*, New York: Penguin Books, 1972.

Perls, F.S., *Gestalt Therapy Verbatim*, New York: Bantam, 1969.

Progoff, I., *Jung's Psychology and its Social Meaning*, New York: Anchor Books, 1973.

Rogers, C.R., *Freedom to Learn*, Columbus, OH: Charles E. Merrill Publishers, 1969.

Schumacher, E.F., *A Guide for the Perplexed*, New York: Harper & Row, 1977.

Skinner, B.F., *Beyond Freedom and Dignity*, New York: Knopf, 1971.

Zinker, J., *Creative Process in Gestalt Therapy*, New York: Vintage Books, 1977.